"Finally! An insightful and frank discussion about the perspectives, expectations, and behaviors that impair marital relationships. With Shannon's expertise on sexual and emotional integrity and Greg's male perspective, *Every Woman's Marriage* offers practical guidance for reigniting the intimacy and passion every woman longs for."

—GINGER KOLBABA, managing editor of *Marriage Partnership*
magazine and author of *Surprised by Remarriage*

Praise for
Every Woman's Battle
by Shannon Ethridge

"This book sheds light on the often unspoken sensitivities and issues that women wrestle with. Not only is it well written, but it is liberating and refreshing with sound principles for overcoming the things that threaten to keep us from experiencing the fullness of joy that is part of God's big-picture plan for our lives."

—MICHELLE McKINNEY HAMMOND, author of *In Search of the Proverbs 31 Man* and *The Unspoken Rules of Love*

"In today's permissive culture, it's dangerously easy for even the most principled of women to reason away unhealthy thoughts, attitudes, and flirtations with men who aren't our husbands. In *Every Woman's Battle,* Shannon Ethridge bravely and respectfully draws a line in the sand for all of us. This is a must-read for every woman who desires true intimacy and sexual integrity."

—CONSTANCE RHODES, author of *Life Inside the "Thin" Cage*

"There's a common, almost Victorian, myth that women don't really struggle with sexual sin. That myth causes many women to feel a double shame. The shame of struggling sexually is compounded by the assumption that few, if any, women share the same battle. Shannon Ethridge artfully and boldly unveils the war and offers women a way to enter the battle with courage, hope, and grace. *Every*

Woman's Battle will help both men and women comprehend the glorious beauty and sensuality of holiness. This is a desperately needed book."

—DR. DAN B. ALLENDER, president of Mars Hill Graduate
School and author of *The Healing Path* and *To Be Told*

"If you're like me, you want the deepest connection possible with your husband, you want a soul-to-soul connection not encumbered by anything that could damage it—and you're going to find Shannon's book immeasurably helpful in doing just that. *Every Woman's Battle* is the best resource I know for embracing God's plan for sexual and emotional integrity as a woman."

—LESLIE PARROTT, author of *When Bad Things
Happen to Good Marriages*

"Many of my *Bad Girls of the Bible* readers have tearfully confessed to me their struggles with sexual sins—promiscuity, adultery, and self-gratification among them. Since we cannot pretend Christian women don't face these temptations, it's a relief to have a sound resource like this one to recommend. Shannon Ethridge's straightforward, nonjudgmental, step-by-step approach can help women come clean in the best way possible—through an intimate relationship with the Lover of their souls."

—LIZ CURTIS HIGGS, best-selling author of *Bad Girls of the Bible,
Really Bad Girls of the Bible,* and *Unveiling Mary Magdalene*

Readers Rave About
Every Woman's Marriage

"Thank you so much for writing this book. It was given to me by a dear friend at a very good time in my life. My husband has been in Iraq for a year, and I only get to see him every four months. There were so many things in the book that I realize I was guilty of, such as disrespect, wanting to be in control, and belittling him, not to mention my sexual hang-ups that affected our marriage. Now I have a much better understanding, and I told my husband over the phone recently, 'I get it now. I'm sorry.' He jokingly replied, 'It's about time. It's only been seventeen years!' He was right. This breakthrough has been a long time in coming, so *thank you*!" —Becky

"I can't thank you enough for *Every Woman's Marriage* and *The Sexually Confident Wife*! There aren't words to describe how these books have changed our marriage for the better. We actually turn off the TV and read them together, talking about the things we're learning as we go along. I can honestly say I'm more in love with my husband than when we married. We have recommended these books to family, friends, and coworkers and will continue to do so!" —Patti

"Shannon, I would like to thank you so much for your book. I've been married for seven months, and your book has been a blessing. I bought it right after my husband and I had a big fight. I wanted to blame him for everything, but I believe the Holy Spirit led me to your book! I was fighting the voice inside me saying how entitled I was to a pity party, but I'm so glad I didn't go down that road. It was exactly what I needed to read. I shared a lot of it with my husband too. Thank you for being so open and so real in your writing. You have inspired me to be the same way. God bless you!" —Marcy

"I just read the last page of *Every Woman's Marriage* after having devoured *Every Woman's Battle* last week. I cannot even eat my lunch without stopping and thanking you for writing this, for your honesty and your openness about an area that so few women admit or talk about. I read thoughts that I've had and didn't know anyone else had! I'm experiencing great healing—healing I didn't know was possible. I praise the Lord for the words He has given you to share!" —Tricia

"Thank you so much for this series of books you have written so candidly. I can't tell you how much reading *Every Woman's Battle* and *Every Woman's Marriage* has changed my life. Though I'm not 'fixed' yet, I have learned so much and applied so much of what I've learned to make a much happier place for my husband to come home to. I'm so glad they're titled *Every Woman's...* because it makes me feel better to know I'm not the only one. As I read of other women's struggles, I'd think, *This woman knows me inside and out!* I believe your books have played a huge part in saving my marriage. Know that you are doing God's work to change people's lives, and it's working!" —Linnea

"I just finished reading *Every Woman's Marriage,* and I want to say *thank you*! I was so amazed that there was another woman on this planet who felt and acted as I did but was able to find a way out! As I read the book, my own words would sometimes jump right out at me. It was such a blessing to my marriage to know that *yes,* other women do feel and react this way, and *no,* it's not the right way. Your book was filled with all the tools I need to effectively show love and respect to my husband. Thank you for allowing God to use you in the lives and marriages of millions of women. I am blessed to be one of them." —Carolyn

"I have been an avid reader of the Every Man/Woman series and have all of them, including the ones that my wife and I are reading with our children. I just completed *Every Woman's Marriage,* and from a husband's perspective, this was one of the best books on marriage I've ever read. I enjoyed the transparency you show in this book, and I could not agree more with all of your premises. It's always nice to read books from people who have been through the fires of marriage and overcome them. What an insight God gives us then! This book is exactly what a man needs and desires from his wife. If more wives understood this, the more astounded they would be at how their husbands would meet their emotional needs. Great job, and we are so glad to have this wonderful book in our library to share." —Michael

"Shannon, I heard you speak at the Thrive Conference in November and have been reading *Every Woman's Marriage.* Wow! I have been married two years (second marriage) and thought things were great except for a little bickering about kids and stuff. But this book opened my eyes, and I could see myself doing all this stuff to my poor husband. This awareness has already started changing our relationship as I am trying to follow through with all of your great recommendations. I feel confident that our marriage and family life will be much stronger from now on, so *thank you* for your wonderful book!" —Michelle

"I think *Every Woman's Marriage* is the best book I've ever read on marriage. At some parts, I felt that I could've written the book because it was so much like my own experiences. My husband and I have been married for seventeen years, and he's a pastor at a large church. I've been telling every one of my girlfriends and family members about your book. Thank you for writing it, sharing your experiences, and being so real and relatable." —Trudy

SHANNON and GREG ETHRIDGE

with Introduction by
STEPHEN ARTERBURN
and FRED STOEKER

WORKBOOK INCLUDED

Every Woman's Marriage

Igniting the Joy and Passion
You Both Desire

WATERBROOK
PRESS

EVERY WOMAN'S MARRIAGE
PUBLISHED BY WATERBROOK PRESS
12265 Oracle Boulevard, Suite 200
Colorado Springs, Colorado 80921

Details in some anecdotes and stories have been changed to protect the identities of the persons
involved.

ISBN 978-0-307-45857-5
ISBN 978-0-307-49972-1 (electronic)

Published in the United States by WaterBrook Multnomah, an imprint of the Crown Publishing
Group, a division of Random House Inc., New York.

WATERBROOK and its deer colophon are registered trademarks of Random House Inc.

Library of Congress Cataloging-in-Publication Data
Ethridge, Shannon.
    Every woman's marriage : igniting the joy and passion you both desire / Shannon and Greg
Ethridge ; introduction by Stephen Arterburn and Fred Stoeker.—1st ed.
        p. cm.
Includes bibliographical references.
    1. Wives—Religious life. 2. Christian women—Religious life. 3. Marriage—Religious aspects—
Christianity. 4. Man-woman relationships—Religious aspects—Christianity. I. Ethridge, Greg. II.
Title.
    BV4528.15.E84 2006
    248.8'435—dc22

                                                    2006001026

Printed in the United States of America
2011

10 9 8 7 6 5 4 3

SPECIAL SALES
Most WaterBrook Multnomah books are available at special quantity discounts when
purchased in bulk by corporations, organizations, and special-interest groups. Custom
imprinting or excerpting can also be done to fit special needs. For information, please
e-mail SpecialMarkets@WaterBrookMultnomah.com or call 1-800-603-7051.

This book is dedicated to our parents,
James and Joan Phillips
and
Jay and Wanda Ethridge,
who combined have been married almost one hundred years.
How fortunate we've been to have your examples
of unconditional love and commitment to live by.

contents

acknowledgments

Lisa and Randy Cooper, Charles and Martha Squibb, Bob and Kathleen Gray, and Linda and Jarratt Major—you've been the friends and mentors who have modeled biblical marriage and encouraged us most along the way. Thank you for being such inspiring examples of genuine love for God and for one another.

Dr. Tom Haygood—thank you for sharing our passion for healthy marriages and for helping us make our marriage much healthier than ever before. May your ministry and counseling practice continue to bear much fruit for God.

Julianne Davis—we appreciate how you've come alongside Shannon at many pivotal times in our lives. You are a godsend.

Karen Schulze, Betsy Smith, Dr. James McDaniel, and Pastor Bob Smith—thank you for your early review of parts or all of this manuscript. Your constructive criticism and encouraging affirmation gave us great confidence to press on.

Husbands and wives from Garden Valley Bible Church, Mercy Ships International, and Teen Mania Ministries, as well as visitors to the Shannon Ethridge Ministries Web site (www.shannonethridge.com)—thank you for sharing your testimonies that so vividly illustrate the issues most married couples face. This is as much your book as it is ours.

Becky and Dan DeGroat, Jill and Kerry Peterson, and Shelly and Mickey Lewis—thank you for going all out to make the "Taking Your Marriage Over the Top" conference possible. It was a real learning experience for all of us and provided much fodder for this manuscript.

Our friends and co-laborers at WaterBrook Press, Muntsinger and McClure Public Relations, and Pure Publicity—we couldn't reach nearly as many couples without your partnerships. Thank you for the amazing things you do to get the Every Man and Every Woman books into the hands of people worldwide. Your commitment to excellence truly glorifies God.

Liz Heaney—we can't imagine writing a book without your amazingly insightful editorial assistance. Thank you for speaking the truth with so much love. You and Casey are the best!

All of our friends who kept us lifted up in prayer as we wrote this book—we appreciate your storming the gates of heaven on our behalf and interceding for married couples everywhere.

And finally, but most of all, we want to acknowledge that You, Jesus, are the glue that holds us together. Thank You for teaching us by example how to love one another without limits.

From Fred Stoeker

Much rides on a marriage, doesn't it? It's incredible when you stop to think about it. Perhaps that's the truth that kept you from tossing your marriage into the trash bin labeled "Wasted Time" and getting on with yet another search for an improved relationship. Sometimes a spouse's heart can seem hard.

But I wonder how many times some couples rush out of marriage without realizing how hard their *own* hearts were in the marriage? Speaking from personal experience, I find it difficult to spot a hard heart in the mirror. When Brenda told me mine was there years ago, I couldn't see it until the day she sat me down at the kitchen table, looked me straight in the eye, and flattened my world with these words: "I don't know how to tell you this, so I'm going to tell it to you straight. My feelings for you are dead."

Her declaration took me by surprise. She was the sweet girl God Himself chose for me. She was my wife—and all my hopes and dreams were tied up in her. I'd have done anything for her. How could that be happening?

I asked Brenda a few questions after her stunning declaration. "Honey, what about it? Do you still love me?"

"Yes," she said. "I still love you."

"If the love is still there, then how come your feelings for me are dead?"

Brenda's inability to put it into words left me confused. For the next week, waves of panic washed over me, buckling me in unguarded moments. Finally one day, as I stepped into the kitchen for a glass of milk, tears pooled in my eyes once again. After I poured myself a glass, I stood for a long time, just staring at the refrigerator through tear-filled eyes. Then I pointed to heaven, declaring, "God, I don't care how much gravel I have to eat, but I am not getting a divorce."

That was the day I softened my heart, the day I knew it was time to pay a real price, a much deeper price than I'd ever considered paying before. God said in Ephesians 5 that I must lay down my life for my marriage, just as He laid down His life for His bride, the church. I hadn't even begun to approach such sacrifice.

I lifted up that desperate statement to God twenty years ago. Recently, a deacon said to me, "Fred, I know only two couples who enjoy a level of intimacy that allows them to talk to each other about absolutely anything—even their sins— without fear and with total love. You and Brenda are one of them."

How did we get here from there? *Every Man's Marriage* tells the story about how I once thought that marital leadership meant I was the one who never had to change, but I came to learn that leadership requires embracing more change in me than I ever dreamed possible. It's about carrying the honor of being the one who sets the example, the one who is the quickest in the household to search his heart for flaws and change them before he disrespects his wife to the core of her soul.

I've seen men read *Every Man's Marriage* and turn their marriages around when they put the principles in place. But I've also heard from men who said, "Fred, I agree with your book, and I believe I have to change some things in the way I treat people around here, especially my wife. I'll admit that she pointed out some of these things to me even before you did, but I haven't been listening.

"I'm ready to listen, and I'm hoping my wife is too. I've been telling her some things that she's not hearing, either. Is there a book out there that you can recommend that talks about the other side of the issue?"

Yes, there is, and it's the one you're holding in your hands. If there is anything I've learned along the way with Brenda, it's that marriage is about change. It's about becoming the spouses God intends us to be. This book gives us the opportunity to listen to the Lord's direction one more time and to change.

I have been looking forward to the day *Every Woman's Marriage* would be published for a long time, and I couldn't be happier that Shannon Ethridge is the author. From the first day I met her, I was impressed with her passion for sexual purity and her passion for oneness in marriage. She has a level of clarity of God's personal vision for her life that few people ever know.

But it wasn't until I met her husband, Greg, and shared breakfast with the two of them that I really understood what God had done when He chose her to write the Every Woman's book series. After seeing them together and hearing her speak publicly and privately about her love for Greg and for all that marriage means, I knew *Every Woman's Marriage* would be in good hands. I can't wait to read the e-mails from men and women whose lives have been changed as a result of Shannon's fine work here.

From Stephen Arterburn

If you were to spend time with Fred and Brenda, you would see that their love for each other is the real deal. Their closeness is rare and beautiful, and it inspires many of us to take a second look at marriage, how it works well and how it does not.

I have seen in my own life how things don't work out well, and it hasn't been pretty. Many of you may share that sad and painful experience. It could be because you are married to a man unwilling to see marriage from any other view than the one he crafted for himself, or a man whose marriage philosophy was handed down to him by unknowing family or clergy.

Fred and Brenda's story of their tough marital journey (as written in *Every Man's Marriage*) was a masterpiece on what God intended marriage to be. It was radical and went against what numerous biblical educators were teaching. Fred pointed out what husbands often do to cause harm to a marriage, and then he talked about what men can do to reverse the damage.

After the book was released, the letters and e-mails came in, stating that this against-the-grain book opened the eyes of the blind and the ears of the deaf. Miracles happened, and we were thrilled to hear of lives changed and marriages healed. Women sang our praises for introducing the concepts of mutual submission and rich, loving intimacy to their marriages. It's amazing what can happen when two people willingly look at themselves and go to work on the defects. We men needed to do that.

Now it is time for women to have a tool to examine themselves and their role in marriage. *Every Woman's Marriage* is that tool. Shannon Ethridge almost destroyed her marriage, but she found great hope and healing by taking care of her own issues rather than pointing the finger at her husband, Greg. I admire her for her strength and her biblical wisdom. The marriage she and Greg have today is a testament to the truths found in this great book.

My prayer for you is that you will open this book with an open mind, not looking for parts that verify you're doing the right thing, but looking for areas that need work in your own heart and home. If you do, your marriage can be much different and much better, the beginning of a new way of living for both of you.

Allow me to leave you with two cautions, however. First, not every troubled marriage enjoys a happy ending like the marriages of the Stoekers and the Ethridges. Even if you do everything within the pages of this book, you have no guarantee that your marriage will be healed. Why? Because it takes two to heal a marriage, and without the two of you working together, you cannot find healing, growth, and deeper intimacy.

But you can count on a couple of things happening. You will change the dynamics of your marriage, and you will change your relationship with God. You can't implement these principles and stay the same. The difference can lead your marriage to heal.

My second caution is this: do not think that divorce fixes very much. From personal experience, I can state that it does not. So I leave you with a challenge. Read this book with great anticipation. Then be patient and see what God can do.

Finally, thanks for allowing Shannon and Greg to lead you to a new look at yourself and your marriage. I hope you like what you see.

when hearts
grow cold

desperate housewives, desperate husbands

"You just don't meet my emotional needs!" After seven years of marriage, I was actually thinking of leaving Greg and my two young children in pursuit of the "love" I felt entitled to but didn't feel I was getting in our relationship. I had no idea where I would go or how I would make it on my own, but I wasn't sure I could survive a lifeless marriage. I felt like I was nothing more than a maid, cook, nanny, and occasional outlet for sexual tension, positions for which I was sadly underpaid.

I couldn't imagine how my heart had grown so cold toward my husband. We met on April 21, 1989, when I visited a local church's singles group for a game night. Although I don't believe in love at first sight, Greg definitely caught my attention that evening as he stood head and shoulders above all the other single guys (literally, since he's six foot seven). Every time we had to pair off with a partner for another game, I hoped Greg and I would wind up together, but no such luck. However, things did begin to warm up between us as we got to know each other over the next several weeks, and we began dating exclusively that summer. Every morning I walked through the neighborhood praying, *Lord, I want to marry whomever You want me to, but if You are looking for my input, I'd like it to be Greg!*

I soon felt 110 percent sure that Greg was the man I wanted to spend the rest of my life with. By Thanksgiving I was desperate for him to pop the question, and he finally did just before Christmas. He said, "You plan the wedding, and I'll plan the honeymoon." That sounded great to me.

We married on April 21, 1990, exactly one year after we had met. Even my dad knew Greg was definitely the one for me. He said to me on the way down the aisle, "Don't you even think about changing your mind, or I may have to put a shotgun to your back!" The thought of backing out never even entered my mind. This was too good to be true, and I wasn't about to mess it up.

However, before the honeymoon was over, feelings of discontent reared their ugly heads. Greg had planned a trip to Walt Disney World for five days, followed by a two-day weekend in Clearwater Beach, Florida. The first morning we woke up in Orlando, I was completely wiped out from all the wedding festivities and traveling. I just wanted to leave the shades down, the covers up, and enjoy a few extra hours of sleep. However, I was awakened when Greg sat down on the edge of the bed, showered, shaved, dressed, and ready to go by 7:00 a.m. "Come on! Get up! Let's go have breakfast with Mickey!" he coaxed.

I gave in and dragged myself into the shower at that ungodly time of the morning. But after two hours of following Greg all over Epcot Center, his long legs trotting from ride to ride and my squattier legs galloping to keep up, I threatened to go back to the hotel room without him. He tried to slow down, fighting back his enthusiasm, and I tried to calm down, fighting my urge to complain about his choice of honeymoon spots. Although it was fun and we made some great memories, sprinting all over Walt Disney World was not my idea of a relaxing, romantic honeymoon. All that week I looked forward to lying on the beaches of Clearwater and just vegetating in the sun together as husband and wife.

But there would be no basking in the sun that weekend. We arrived at Clearwater Beach in the midst of a windstorm and a cold front that brought temperatures in the low fifties. Thinking that we'd not be spending much time indoors, Greg had booked a dumpy little hotel room, but we couldn't get out much since we only brought warm-weather clothes. We mostly watched movies and ate leftover pizza. The ambiance (or lack thereof), exhaustion, and disappointment eventually got the best of me. I don't remember what was said, only how we said it. Greg and I had our first major fight before we even returned from our honeymoon. I couldn't believe that he had failed to check the weather before we came and that he hadn't even consulted with me about how I envisioned spending our honeymoon. He, on the other hand, couldn't believe that I was insensitive enough to get so angry with him when all he had wanted was to surprise and delight me.

Of course, I wasn't going to let one little argument ruin the marriage. Greg was a committed Christian and a leader in the youth group, which inspired me to begin working with youth as well. He was fun and adventurous, and he took me on several group trips to go skiing, backpacking, and scuba diving. He was intelligent and <u>financially stable</u>, a graduate of Southern Methodist University and a certified public accountant. He was <u>extremely laid back</u> and had such a reputation of being a nice guy that no one ever got mad at him. No one, that is, except me.

Seven years and two children later I was constantly badgering Greg for not initiating romance anymore, for being too laid back. I had a long list of complaints: He never called me up for a date or offered to take me out to dinner. He didn't send cards or bring me flowers. <u>I was weary of having to hint around for my emotional needs to be met</u>, and I felt it didn't count if he didn't come up with the idea of how to do so himself. I was sick and tired of always picking up LEGOs and Tinkertoys, wiping children's noses and behinds, cleaning Goldfish and Cheerios out of the minivan seats, and feeling as if there had to be more to life.

With each passing day, I slipped deeper into depression. In hindsight, I realize that my unhappiness wasn't about what my husband was or wasn't doing; rather, it was about how I felt about myself. I needed Greg to affirm me, to make me feel beautiful, and to convince me that I was desirable, because I didn't know how to feel any of these things on my own. But at the time, I felt sure that he was to blame. I am not the first or only wife to feel this way. In fact, I've heard from many women who feel deep dissatisfaction with their husbands and their marriages.

STORIES OF DISCONTENT

Married fourteen years, Ramona thought she had wed Mr. Right, but feelings of <u>fear, bitterness, and rejection surfaced as she and her husband struggled to understand each other</u>. <u>He is rarely home</u>, leaving her to raise four young children on her own much of the time. There's been little romance or time for one another. He's consumed with his job and their financial status, and she is consumed with the kids and her work, which she admits is really just an outlet to get her emotional needs met by others. Their church obligations and kids' sports and extracurricular activities also take up an enormous amount of time and energy. Feeling overwhelmed by the lack of joy and passion in their relationship, Ramona says:

> My husband seems unable to express how much I mean to him and says
> it's because of the way he was raised and that men aren't good at that

stuff. I have felt lonely, cheated, and empty, and when other men begin to compliment me, I feel I am falling for them hook, line, and sinker. I've been guilty of emotional affairs but feel that God wants me to be strong and stay in this marriage. I've tried to romance my husband and captivate him, but it always seems we are worlds apart. I am tired of trying to be supermom, wife, and spiritual leader in this family. When is he going to step up to the plate and take over?

Of course, disillusionment can set in even before you become overwhelmed with raising children. After only one year of marriage, it's clear that Claire's reality isn't measuring up to her expectations. She laments:

We're usually either fighting or not talking much at all. The word *divorce* isn't in our vocabularies, but I frequently have thoughts about what my life could be like after my husband dies. I have a mental list of men I'd date. It's pretty long. They have all met different needs at different times. Then I think of how wonderful it would be to be single again. I'd be better off without his college debt and dirty socks. But I married him for a reason. What was it?

Ironically, Claire also recalls that she was miserable as a single woman and thought that getting married would solve all her problems. As her situation illustrates, getting rid of your single status only exchanges one set of problems for another, more complex set of problems.

Some women hold on to the hope that their unhappiness will eventually disappear and that life will somehow "get better." As Helen testifies, such hopes for a more fulfilling relationship down the road are often dashed:

It seems that every season of our marriage brings a new hope that things will surely get better right around the corner. We'll be happier when we can afford a house…when we have children of our own…when our children are out of diapers…when my husband finally gets that promotion that will allow me to be a stay-at-home wife and mother… when our children leave for college…when we don't have to pay for college anymore…when my husband and I retire. I've been waiting for a brighter tomorrow almost every day of the past twenty-seven years, and frankly, I wonder if we'll ever have the marriage I've always longed for.

Some women are so unhappy, they consider pushing the Eject button and leaving to find another man. That was the case with this woman, who signed her letter to an advice column "In Relationship Hell":

> Three years [into our marriage], I'm horribly unhappy. I am no longer in love with my husband, although I do care about him. My son is deliriously happy here in the suburbs with his two-parent family, and, at 13, would be very vulnerable to emotional problems should we get divorced.…
>
> Should I stick it out with my husband, who is my friend but not my soul mate, until my son is in college (five more years!)—even if this involves fantasizing about another man during sex? Or, should I get out and hope I find an available man to love?[1]

I have to wonder what part this woman has played in undermining her own happiness during the three years she's been married. If she finds yet another "available man to love," she'll more than likely discover that there's one common denominator in all her relationships—*her*. As long as that common denominator is <u>unhappiness with herself</u>, she'll be unhappy with any relational equation.

THE MISTAKE WE MAKE

Let's face it. Nothing magical happens once we put those rings on our fingers. If we were unhappy before marriage, chances are we'll go back to being unhappy shortly after the honeymoon. Marriage doesn't make us feel better about ourselves or solve our problems in the long run. No husband can be the White Knight who rescues us from all our issues and insecurities. <u>At some point</u> we have to put on our "big-girl panties" and <u>go through the work of resolving our own issues, remedying our own insecurities, and becoming happy with ourselves before we can truly be happy in marriage</u>.

But if we fail to acknowledge the need to work on our own issues, we believe that our relational problems must be *our husbands'* fault. We may mistakenly assume that our lives would be so much better if we just had a different man to love, and we may not stop to consider that *we* might play a part in our own dance of discontentment.

The truth is, no marriage is exempt from disillusionment. Even the brightest relationship has dark days clouding a couple's history together, raining on their "we have the perfect marriage" parade. On the exterior, a wife may appear to have the ideal marriage, but the interior landscape of her heart often reveals deep disappointment, anger, bitterness, and regret.

The same is true for many husbands. Don't think that that could possibly be the case with your husband? You may be in for a surprise. I certainly was. If anyone had asked me during the first seven years of our marriage whether Greg felt fulfilled, I wouldn't have batted an eyelash. "Absolutely!" would have been the response coming out of my mouth and the one I truly believed in my heart. But one day I got a wake-up call.

My Own Rude Awakening

It was probably the umpteenth time we were having the same argument. I didn't feel that Greg was making any attempt to meet my emotional needs—again. It had been days since we'd had any real conversation, weeks since we'd had sex, and months since he'd taken me out for any quality time together. Rather than lovingly asking him, "Am I doing something wrong that's causing your heart to grow cold toward me?" I am ashamed to say I went back to that lame old "You're too *passive*!" accusation and angrily blamed him for the lack of passion in our relationship. "Why don't you pursue me anymore? Does it ever occur to you to just pick up the phone and ask me if I want to go to dinner? Or to bring me flowers? Or ask me to go on a walk? Anything to show me that you still care?"

As I lay in bed for what seemed like half an hour, awaiting a response to my barrage of demanding questions, I grew more and more furious over what I felt was a major character flaw. Finally, I threw back the covers and dramatically exclaimed, "I'm so fed up with your passivity, I just can't sleep in the same bed with you tonight!"

Our kids were staying the night at their grandparents', so I stumbled into my daughter's room with my pillows in tow, only to turn on the light and discover that there were no sheets on her bed. As I went downstairs to the cold basement to fish her sheets out of the dryer, I was determined to send Greg the message loud and clear that his lack of attention to my emotional needs was not going to cut it with me any longer. When I got to the basement, the wet sheets were still in the washing machine. I had asked Greg to switch the laundry earlier, which he had forgotten to do. Now I was really mad.

Fishing my sleeping bag out of a downstairs closet, I returned to find Greg waiting for me in Erin's room. He asked, "Could you please not do this, Shannon? Just come to bed and let's talk this through. Sleeping apart isn't going to solve anything!"

At that moment, I had to make a choice. I could either soften my heart, swallow my pride, and return to our bedroom like a big girl, or I could die on this hill in a desperate attempt to prove how strongly I felt about this issue. I chose to stand firm atop the hill. I stuck my finger in the face of a man who stands fourteen inches taller than I and weighs almost one hundred pounds more and declared, "I will not stay in a lifeless marriage! Every time there's been a problem in our relationship, I've always gone to counseling by myself, but this time the problem is *yours,* so I suggest *you* go deal with it!" I crawled into my sleeping bag sobbing, and Greg retreated to our bedroom in defeat.

Twice during the night I heard Greg get up and walk into the room. I awoke hoping he was going to crawl into bed with me, apologize for his inattentiveness, and hold me for the rest of the night, but no such luck. Both times I drifted back to sleep by myself.

The next morning I couldn't believe what a wicked witch I had been—as if *yelling at him* was going to cause him to want to do a better job of showing me how much he loves me! I finally swallowed my pride and slithered back into our bedroom, surprised to find Greg lying on a wet pillow with a flushed face and a look of fear in his bloodshot eyes. Here's what Greg says about his night:

> Shannon went to bed around midnight, and I continued to think about all I wish I had said or done over the past few months to show her just how much I love her. Though I felt drained of energy, I couldn't sleep. I kept thinking, *I know what she likes and how to make her feel special, so why can't I remember to do those things? Why am I so motivated to*

work hard to please other people but can't seem to recognize when my own wife needs my attention? I felt like a complete failure as a husband.

Around 3:00 a.m., I began thinking about how much happier Shannon would probably be if I were just out of the picture altogether. I told myself that if anything ever happened to me, she'd be better off with the insurance money and a chance at a happier marriage with someone else than to be stuck in this "lifeless marriage," as she so often put it.

By 4:00 a.m., I had myself worked up into such a tizzy that I began wondering if she felt the same way—that she'd be better off without me. Though it sounds foolish to me now, because she has never been a physically violent person, I even had thoughts that Shannon might try to get rid of me. I envisioned her taking a butcher knife from the kitchen counter and coming into the room while I was sleeping. The thought scared me so badly that I got up twice in the middle of the night to see if she was out of bed, perhaps heading toward the kitchen.

By 5:00 a.m., I realized that such thoughts were ridiculous, and my fear turned to depression. Not only was I not living up to Shannon's expectations, but I felt like I was letting everyone else down too. I was working long hours and accomplishing little at the office. The more time I spent at work, the less time I had for my kids. We were under a load of debt, and bills kept piling up. Life just seemed to be knocking me down in so many ways, and I didn't feel I had the strength to get back up too many more times. *Perhaps I should just put the butcher knife into my own belly,* I thought. Fortunately, Shannon crawled into bed with me soon afterward, and I worked up the courage to tell her about what I'd been thinking.

When Greg told me about his night, I couldn't believe what I was hearing. A small part of me wanted to get angry again over the absurdity of the idea that I would ever bring physical harm to him. However, a larger part felt convicted as I realized, *Shannon, this is the effect your anger and disillusionment has on Greg. You are killing him with your own misery. This is not his problem; it's yours. If you ever want him to meet your emotional needs, you have to learn to* inspire *his affections rather than to* require *them. And how about recognizing that he has emotional needs too?*

Up until that unforgettable night, I had been blaming Greg for my unhappiness. But I could no longer deny that *I was the one who had been poking holes in the bucket of our marital bliss!* Within days we were in a counseling office together, where Greg made a vow not to harm himself, I made a vow to try to control my anger, and we made vows to each other to try to understand each other's emotional needs.

Lest you think that in this area Greg is unique among men, think again. Some women assume that all a husband needs to be happy is sex and a sandwich, and as long as he gets that on occasion, his wife can treat him however she wants. But a man has deep-seated emotional needs too—needs he may be unwilling or unable to communicate. If his wife ignores or denies those needs, he feels devastated and will take steps to protect himself with a fight or flight pattern. He may fight for his rights in the relationship by demanding that his wife submit to meeting certain expectations. Or, like Greg, he may prefer the flight response and withdraw emotionally from the relationship or even look for a more satisfying love somewhere else.

The reality is that men aren't all that different from women when it comes to their basic needs. Men have emotional needs too, and they can feel a sense of desperation when those needs aren't being met.

MEN HAVE EMOTIONAL NEEDS?

September 11, 2001, was a day of countless tragedies. Thousands lost loved ones in the blazes and subsequent collapses of New York City's Twin Towers. However, the tragic loss of loved ones didn't stop after the fires were extinguished. For eight wives married to New York City firefighters, each would later experience her biggest personal loss in an equally startling manner. Most claim they never saw the loss coming.

What loss am I referring to? The loss of their husbands, who left their marriages because they had fallen into extramarital affairs with women they had rescued from the burning buildings or with widows who had lost their husbands in the terrorist attacks. On the August 30, 2004, episode of *Oprah,* a representative from the New York City Fire Department explained that this is a relatively common phenomenon following a massive tragedy. Firefighters are encouraged to play "surrogate protector" to a widow's family, helping them to adjust to life without their loved one. However, the temptation to go from surrogate to substitute is obviously difficult for some to resist.

What struck me about the report was that the eight wives who had been left by their firefighter husbands claimed that they never saw the affair or the divorce coming. According to their perspectives, everything seemed fine in the relationship. However, the husbands told very different stories. <u>They claimed to have felt ignored, belittled, disrespected, and taken for granted</u>. Many reported wanting out of their relationships long before the affairs began.

Even though nothing can justify unfaithfulness in marriage, I believe there's a lesson we can learn from this disheartening story. It is this: *men need to feel like heroes to their wives*. They not only want their wives to meet their sexual needs, but they also want them to meet their emotional needs for <u>love, respect, appreciation, and admiration</u>. When these needs don't get met, a husband's heart will grow cold toward his wife. But it doesn't have to be this way.

GIVING WHAT WE LONG TO RECEIVE

As much as we long to have our husbands understand and meet our innermost needs, <u>we have to learn to give that which we desire to receive.</u>

So how can a woman understand a man's emotional needs? Better yet, how can you meet those needs in your husband, igniting the joy and passion you both desire and inspiring him to treat you the way you long to be treated? Read on, as we consider how desperate times call for desperate measures.

Refuel That Lovin' Feeling

In his book *The Truth About Cheating*, marriage counselor M. Gary Neuman surveyed two hundred husbands to discover the real reasons why they cheat on their wives. Not surprising, 48 percent of men rated <u>emotional dissatisfaction</u> as the primary reason they were unfaithful.

desperate times call for desperate measures

I'll never forget the day one of my best childhood friends got a new swing set for her birthday. Why? Because the scar on my forehead won't let me forget.

The contraption had the typical swings, a slide, and a U-shaped bar for twirling around, but it also had something cool I'd never seen on a swing set before. It was the shape of a cage and had two benches facing each other, allowing two people to "pendulum swing" at the same time. Two of the birthday party attendees climbed onto the benches, and I offered to push them, hoping I could have the next turn inside the cage. As I pushed, the girls squealed, "Higher!" so I decided to push the way I often pushed someone on a typical one-person swing—putting my hands on their back and plowing forward until I had run all the way under the swing to the other side. I braced myself to give it the old heave-ho, then pushed as high up in the air as I possibly could.

Suddenly I realized that the weight of the second person prevented me from pushing the swing high enough to go under the cage, but it was too late. My body movements were already committed to the task. Rather than running all the way underneath and through to the other side, I was caught up in the backlash of the pendulum swing. The footrest caught my forehead, knocked me down, and dragged me along the ground flat on my back.

As foolish as this maneuver sounds, many women today are caught up in a similar pendulum swing—feminism. When God created men and women, He designed us to be coheirs of His kingdom with a delicate balance of both power and submission to one another (we'll discuss mutual submission in chapter 10). In the centuries that followed, however, the balance of power swayed too far toward the male side, and women felt cheated of their basic human rights, particularly the

(continued on page 20)

For Starters...

Here's a sneak preview of some of the measures you can take to guard against desperate times.

1. Thank God daily for your husband, mentioning specific attributes that you admire and appreciate. Ask God to show you some specific ways that you can be a blessing to your husband that day, then be still and listen. Ask God to help you hold your tongue when needed and to speak the truth in love when needed. Express your desire to keep your heart soft toward your husband and for his heart to be drawn lovingly toward you as well.

2. Chase away each negative thought about your husband with three positive thoughts. It's okay to pray for God to change him or sharpen him in some way, but avoid complaining to God as if you don't appreciate the gift He's given you in your husband. Acknowledge that you don't have the insight to know what your husband truly needs, then trust that God knows (and will deliver) all that your spouse needs to become more Christlike. Also, each time you pray for God to change something in your husband, ask Him to change three things in you.

3. Thank God for the opportunities you have to create a happy home environment for your husband and children. If you don't enjoy housecleaning, laundry, cooking, decorating, and running errands, or if your work outside the home doesn't allow you the luxury to focus on such tasks very often, ask God for the grace to do what you can to make your house a place your family wants to come home to. Frequently remind yourself that your family and home life are your priorities and that what you do for your husband and family counts for all eternity.

4. If you are feeling crabby, give your husband fair warning that you just don't feel like yourself and perhaps need some time alone to relax, take a bubble bath, read, pray, or do whatever

else will help to calm you. If he can't give you that time, call a friend and ask her to take care of the kids for a little while, offering to do the same for her when the need arises. Our emotional and mental health can be fragile at times, so we have to handle ourselves with care when we're feeling out of sorts, being careful not to damage our relationships.

5. Because our disappointments are most often fueled by unmet expectations, avoid filling your mind with contrived ideas of what your husband "should" be like. Don't compare him to other men or harp on the ways he just doesn't measure up. Especially avoid comparing him to characters on television, in movies, or in romance novels, as these forms of entertainment paint very unrealistic portraits of how men typically conduct themselves in relationships.

6. Don't put on your husband's shoulders the burden of responsibility to meet all your emotional needs. Rather than blame him, remind yourself that getting your needs met is your responsibility, not someone else's. Look to God first, then other family members and female friends to satisfy some of your cravings for connection. Also keep in mind that he's not a mind reader. If you feel there is something you need that he can provide, don't hesitate to simply ask for it.

7. Take care of yourself—get plenty of rest, balanced nutrition, and consistent moderate exercise, and avoid unnecessary stress caused by overcommitment. Often the discontentment and disillusionment that a woman feels in marriage aren't as much about her unhappiness with her husband as about her feeling too tired, too fat, too sedentary, or too busy. All these issues can easily spill over into the marriage relationship, allowing the wife's misery to negatively affect both her and her husband, not to mention their children and other loved ones.

rights to protect themselves from physically abusive husbands, to own property, and to vote.

Today, however, some women are pushing in the opposite direction, resulting in women wanting power *over* men. I've heard some men refer to this bold breed of women as "feminazis." These women promote reproductive freedoms (abortion without the father's consent), alternative lifestyles (lesbianism), and a general hatred for the male gender.[1] Now many men are feeling the way women did long ago—somewhat cheated of their basic human rights to be respected in their homes and to be treated with dignity. Some even feel as if they are being emotionally abused by their wives and that they have no right to speak out about it.

Although I would have never considered myself a feminist, I've come to realize that many of us who grew up in the seventies and eighties have naively embraced some feminist philosophies without recognizing them as such. Unless we were raised underneath a rock and were completely sheltered from the many feminist messages in the media, we could not escape feminism's influence.

Dr. Laura Schlessinger commented on this pendulum swing in her book *The Proper Care and Feeding of Husbands* when she said:

> Commitment to marriage and child rearing was once viewed as the pinnacle of adulthood identity, so that women looked carefully for the "right" man for the job.… [Now] fewer women look upon marriage and child rearing as stable or even normal.…
>
> [Also,] grandiose self-centeredness about the value of women, paired with a virtual disdain for men, leads women to treat men badly. Too many women look at men with a sense of entitlement versus an opportunity for selflessness.[2]

This self-centeredness can't be denied if we look closely at our society. In some circles, women are applauded for their courage to leave their husbands and children to discover "who they really are" and to pursue their own dreams (as if a successful marriage and strong family life aren't sufficient goals). When it comes to marital discord, society insinuates that it's primarily the fault of men.

Hollywood has repeatedly taught us that men know nothing except how to use power tools, vegetate in front of a television, yell for another brewski, belch louder than the next numbskull, and complain that their wives don't give them enough sex. The decline of the masculine image in television and movies has created an undercurrent of disrespect and discord in many homes. Even worse, some families cultivate sheer animosity toward one another. Some spouses are even desperate to fast-forward to the "until death do us part" part of marriage. In 2003, of murder victims who knew their murderers (either as family members or through some other type of acquaintanceship, such as employment), 21 percent were killed by their own spouses or intimate partners. Seventy-nine percent of those victims were women; the other 21 percent were men.[3] While the circumstances surrounding each domestic murder in this country vary from case to case, there must certainly be an overwhelming sense of disillusionment, anger, resentment, and bitterness to cause such rage and violence. Let's face it. Men and masculinity are under attack. Even in Christian homes.

WHAT HUSBANDS HAVE TO SAY

When I asked husbands for examples of what goes on behind closed doors that makes a man's heart grow cold toward his wife, many jumped at the chance to unload their grief. Here are a few of the their responses:

- "If my wife gave me a monthly report card, every month I would get an F. No matter what I do, it's not good enough for her. Ninety-nine percent of the time I make the effort to do everything she asks me to do, or else I know there will be hell to pay that night. But other times I just think, *What's the use? She's not going to appreciate it anyway!*"

- "By all appearances, my wife is a wonderful person and well-thought-of by others as a good wife and mother. But if you were a fly on the wall at our house, you'd hear that she's often a completely different person in private. Her sharp tone and disrespectful attitude would cause your jaw to drop, and yet I'm supposed to keep a stiff upper lip and take it like a man."

- "My wife frequently says she understands that men have sexual needs, but she rarely ever delivers the goods! All I get most of the time is compassionate talk and a pat on the knee, accompanied by an excuse—she's too tired, too distracted, too busy to come to bed at a reasonable time."

- "It hurts when my wife accuses me of being disinterested in her and the kids if I need to rest for a few minutes when I get home from work. Once I'm accused of being a lazy person and lousy husband and father, the last thing I want to do is connect with my wife. The rest of the evening is pretty much downhill from there."

Clearly, none of these men feels like a hero to his wife. I doubt that any of these wives wanted to make their husbands feel this way. But too often we wives seem to assume that our husbands' hearts are made of steel. Perhaps the rings we wear on our fingers give us the impression that regardless of how we treat them, they'll always be by our sides.

I don't know about you, but I don't want a husband who is physically alive but emotionally dead toward me. I want Greg to be excited about our relationship and to look forward to coming home every day. I don't want him going through the motions to jump through my hoops just to keep me off his back. I want his heart to remain soft and warm toward me. However, I've come to realize that I can't have these things while taking him for granted and treating him disrespectfully, both of which I have done many times in the past.

Maybe you are thinking that your husband would never fall into the "desperate" category. Perhaps you've never heard him say anything remotely like these comments. Don't assume that if he's not talking about feeling dissatisfied it means he is happy. Men don't talk about their feelings openly like women do. Most say nothing and then harbor the pain deep in their hearts. This isn't a character flaw; it's just the way men are. They let their emotions drive them toward taking action to "fix" things, but if they suspect a problem can't be fixed or have no idea how to fix it, they often bury their frustration. However, whenever a person buries an emotion, it takes root in the heart's soil and often blossoms as other, more intense emotions. Most of the men who responded to our survey admitted that their frustration had blossomed into either fear or loathing of their wives, neither of which is something any woman would desire.

Perhaps you are wondering if these husbands told their wives how they felt. Most husbands claimed that yes, they had tried to communicate their feelings but were shut down by defensive comments. They said that they are tired of trying to convince their wives they have legitimate complaints and that if they insist on change, their wives will accuse them of being tyrants. Other men said that fear of making matters even worse prevented them from openly discussing these issues with their wives.

WHAT PART DO YOU PLAY?

If you are not happy in your marriage, don't make the mistake of putting on your husband all the responsibility to turn your marriage relationship around. It's *not* completely up to him. Problems are usually the result of *both* spouses' actions and attitudes.

Of course, when there does seem to be a problem, the wife is usually the first to suggest marriage counseling. But what are her expectations when she drags her husband through the door of the therapist's office? Her goal is usually for *him* to change so that *she* can be happy. Consider another passage from *The Proper Care and Feeding of Husbands:*

> [An unhappy husband and wife] go to a therapist, but sadly, [receive] an agenda: Traditional values are out, men are the bad guys, and women are oppressed. Their cure is either to feminize the husband or suggest divorce. Ken, a listener, confirmed that position when he wrote:
> "...Today's society insists that it is COMPLETELY THE MALE'S RESPONSIBILITY to [change].... Positive improvements to a relationship can ONLY occur if the husband is willing to alter his very nature, to tune in to his 'feminine' side, and learn how to think, respond, and 'emotionally perceive' the same way as his wife does.[4]

It's true that many women aren't happy; it's equally true that many men aren't happy. These *are* desperate times, and perhaps this desperation is an indication that it's time for us women to take desperate measures and ask ourselves, *Am I contributing to the demise of the masculine image by how I treat my husband?* Love takes two to tango, and as much as we want to throw stones at our clumsy partners, we all need to stop and ask ourselves, *What part do I play in my marriage's dance of discontentment?*

The bottom line is this: *Even if you firmly believe that 95 percent of the issues in your marriage are your husband's fault, are you willing to focus on the 5 percent that you do have control over?*

If so, the chances are very good that you could experience the joy and passion you've always dreamed of in marriage, and you could grow to become the ultimate fulfillment of your husband's greatest needs and desires as well.

PUTTING PRINCIPLES INTO PRACTICE

Writing a book with a subtitle like *Igniting the Joy and Passion You Both Desire* creates a lot of internal pressure. There have certainly been times since submitting this idea to my publisher that I wondered if I had any business writing such a book. Although Greg and I have had moments when we felt incredible emotional closeness and sexual passion, we've also had moments when our hearts felt chilled toward each other. The day I got my biggest boost of confidence for following through with this idea was actually the day that Greg and I were going away to a bed-and-breakfast to begin working on this manuscript together. I was put to the test in a big way. Greg will explain that test:

> Shannon and I had a writing retreat scheduled for several weeks, and we were both looking forward to it. However, I had an important board meeting scheduled for the following week and needed to get several financial reports completed and e-mailed out to the board members that Friday afternoon before leaving for our retreat. I was feeling incredibly stressed about it.
>
> My plan was to get those reports done and be home by 3:00 p.m. so we could drive the kids to her parents' house before going to the bed-and-breakfast. However, around 2:00, I realized my plan wasn't going

to work. I did the only thing I knew to do. I called Shannon (with fear and trembling) and asked if she would be willing to drive the kids to her parents' by herself, then come back and get me around 5:00 so I could have a couple of extra hours before leaving the office.

When Greg asked me to take the children by myself and come back to pick him up later, I hated the idea. I had envisioned us talking and brainstorming together in the car after dropping off the kids, and I shuddered at the thought of making that drive all by myself while he was still at the office. On the other hand, I knew there was no way he'd even ask such a thing unless it was really important. I felt as if the choice were up to me. I could start the weekend off on a sour note by responding the way I would have in the past ("We've had this planned for weeks, Greg! Why didn't you budget your time better? Why can't it wait? Why does work always have to come first? What about me? Why can't you put me first for once?"). Or, I could start the weekend off by putting his needs first and setting the tone for a wonderfully intimate experience. Fortunately, I was able to choose the latter.

I suggested, "Why don't I make a different deal with you? I'd prefer not to take the kids to my parents' without you because I'm really looking forward to the drive time together. Why don't I call the bed-and-breakfast and tell them we'll be later than expected, then wait until you are finished at the office so that we can head to Greenville together?"

Relieved, Greg responded, "I promise I won't be past 4:30!"

"Take until 5:00 if needed," I said, hoping he'd feel the extra slack I was intentionally giving him.

When Greg walked in at 4:58 p.m., he was relieved to have that project completed and appreciative that I wasn't upset. But the best thing was how it set the tone for our weekend together, as well as the week that followed. Greg says:

I couldn't believe that Shannon was cutting me that much slack and wasn't ticked off about doing it, either. Her decision to be so amiable made me feel respected and affirmed. She's always been attractive to me, but this particular weekend I was struck by how beautiful she appeared. She probably looked the same as she always does, but I saw her through fresh, new eyes—I felt like she really loved me, and that made it really easy to love her back.

When we returned home, Shannon knew I was under the gun to finish getting ready for the board meeting. I wound up working from 8:00 a.m. until midnight three nights in a row, which was something I'd never done before. It was stressful enough to have to work those kinds of hours, and I didn't need the stress of feeling like I was in the dog-house at home for having to work late. But Shannon's sympathy and commitment to oneness continued throughout that week. She never pestered me to come home but simply left a light on for me each night and called a couple of times each day to say she was thinking about me. She surprised me with dinner one night and brought enough groceries to last me a couple of days. By the time the board meeting was over later that week, I couldn't wait to get home.

While I wouldn't want Greg to regularly work such long hours, I have to under-stand that his position comes with an enormous amount of responsibility, which a few times each year requires an extraordinary investment of time and energy. I know that he'd much rather be home with us if he could, and keeping this thought fresh in my mind makes it much easier to sympathize with him during stressful work situations.

I share this illustration with you not to toot my own horn but to paint a vivid picture of what it looks like for a wife to take desperate measures in desperate times—in a constructive, affirming way rather than in a destructive way. Every mar-riage will go through some desperate times—that's just part of the terrain. It's what we choose to do in those desperate times that can make all the difference in the world to our husbands and to the joy and passion we experience in the relationship.

What's Coming Up

In the next part of this book, we'll stand back and take a look at the big picture of marriage, including how we hold the potential to minister to our spouses in ways that no one else can. Then in part 3 we'll examine some of the most common things that we (often subconsciously) do that cause our husbands' hearts to grow cold toward us. In part 4 we'll focus on how you can understand and meet your husband's most basic emotional needs. Finally, we'll discuss how you can throw fuel on the flame of your husband's passion toward you. When his passion is burning brighter and you are inspiring him to engage with you on an intimate level, you will both experience the joy and ultimate fulfillment you hope to have in your marriage.

Remember, you are not the only one who desires for your marriage to grow stronger, happier, and more fulfilling. It's also God's desire for you and your husband to have a relationship that doesn't just survive, but *thrives*!

PART II

looking at the
big picture

burning out
or just warming up?

I recently took a road trip with a friend (I'll call her Andrea) who had been swept off her feet just two weeks earlier by a single guy named James. Andrea talked at length during the four-hour drive about how great James appeared to be—incredibly good-looking, godly, and witty. As we walked past the cosmetics counter in Dillard's department store, Andrea stopped to get a sample card of Polo, James's favorite cologne, so she could be reminded of what he smells like. She couldn't say enough about him, but I had run out of things to say about Greg before we had even passed the county line.

James seemed attentive and sounded ideal. Andrea raved about how he called several times each day just to see what she was doing, how he said the sweetest things to her, and how he continued to assure her that he (and their relationship) was truly the real deal. When Greg would call me on my cell phone, it was to talk about where each kid had to be that day or to ask what he could make for supper. He said "I love you" before we hung up, but it wasn't magical. It didn't inspire any change in my tone of voice. No sweaty palms. No butterflies in my stomach. Just a routine conversation. Our relationship hasn't always been this way. There was a time when I did backflips whenever he called.

After I hung up, I made a mental note: *Guard your heart, Shannon!* I had to be careful not to be jealous of the intensity of Andrea's new relationship. I couldn't compare my marriage of fifteen years to this fifteen-day-old relationship. Maybe Greg and I didn't have the flame of intensity anymore, but we had something far more brilliant—the glowing embers of intimacy. Perhaps an analogy will help explain what I mean.

When Greg and I moved several years ago from the concrete jungles of Dallas to the piney woods of east Texas, we discovered a new simple pleasure—sitting around the campfire. Greg carved a perfect campfire spot out of the side of a hill just a few yards from our log cabin. Using railroad ties, he built a retaining wall and created plenty of seating for family and friends. As fun as it is to start the fire, roast wieners, toast marshmallows, tell campfire stories, sing songs, and just enjoy one another's company around the fire, my favorite time comes when all those activities are done and everyone has gone except Greg and me. That's when I'm able to reflect on just how much our marriage and that campfire have in common—it's really only after the raging flames die down that the glowing embers burn their brightest and create the most intense heat.

The same can be said for a marriage relationship, but I haven't always understood this.

WHAT HAPPENED TO OUR FLAME OF PASSION?

When Greg and I met, began dating, and were first married, I couldn't imagine ever wanting to be with anyone else. He made me feel special, cherished, and desirable. The flame of our passion for each other burned brightly. However, seven years and two children later, I didn't feel very special anymore. Our life together seemed to have lost its magic spark. Not understanding what was really going on, I thought our flame was dying. I didn't know it at the time, but some scientists believe there is actually a biological explanation for this common phenomenon in marriage relationships:

> The high of passionate love doesn't last forever. The body builds up a tolerance to the natural chemicals in the brain associated with being in love; more and more are needed to feel the same level of euphoria. Some people interpret the corresponding decrease in sexual energy to mean they are no longer in love, and indeed for some it does mark the end of a relationship. However, rather than an end to love, it may be a transition into the longer-lasting companionate love.
>
> It appears that the brain cannot tolerate the continually revved-up state of passionate love. As the newness of passion fades, the brain kicks in new chemicals, the endorphins, natural morphine-like substances that

calm the mind. The excitement may diminish, but the security of companionate love can provide a different, not necessarily lesser, pleasure.[1]

Because I had sought to remain in that "revved-up state of passionate love" with my husband, I failed to recognize the pleasure of our slowly developing "companionate love." Rather than beginning the hard work of stirring the embers of our relationship to renew a sense of excitement, I almost threw enough dirt on the fire to extinguish it altogether. Because I craved the euphoric happiness and intensity that are characteristic of a new relationship, I found myself gravitating toward new men—men who made me feel special, cherished, and desirable again because of the attention they gave me.

Almost everywhere I went, I would meet a man who seemed to create in me that spark of excitement that Greg didn't seem to ignite anymore. My aerobics instructor made me feel sexy again as he complimented me on how great I was looking as I lost my extra pregnancy pounds. After years of staying at home and watching too many reruns of *Sesame Street* and *Barney*, my college professor reminded me of my intelligence when he praised my research papers or class participation. A friend at church made me feel like a special confidante when he frequently called me at home during the day to complain about his marriage and to comment on how he wished his wife were more like me. I was getting lots of ego strokes, but they were all from superficial relationships—from men who only knew me from a distance. Greg, on the other hand, saw me close up. He knew the *real* me.

Fortunately, I got into counseling before my emotional affairs turned sexual, and my counselor helped me better understand myself and the sources of my discontent.

INTENSITY IS NOT GENUINE INTIMACY

I struggled during those years of my marriage because, like many women, I had failed to understand the difference between *intensity* and *intimacy*. *Intensity* is a feeling of extreme excitement or euphoria. It is a natural by-product of a brand-spanking-new relationship. Intensity often masquerades as intimacy. When we are getting to know new things about a person, we often think we are experiencing intimacy, but discovering new things about a stranger isn't intimate—it's just new. It may be exciting. It may feel intense. But it's often superficial and temporary. At best it's incomplete. For the most part, I only got to know the sides of these men that they wanted me to see. Those relationships often *felt* intimate, but the intimacy I was feeling was a false intimacy.

Genuine intimacy could only be found at home, where Greg and I both saw not just the good but also the bad and the ugly in each other. You see, *intimacy* can best be understood by breaking the word down into syllables: in-to-me-see. It's the ability to see into the heart, mind, and spirit of another person, which is impossible until after you've gotten to know that individual over a long period of time. It comes only after the intensity has worn off and you get to know things that most people can't possibly know unless they live with that person.

For example, I never really understood why sexual, emotional, and relational issues were such a struggle for me. Until Greg, no guy had taken the time to really get to know me, understand me, and recognize the root cause of my tendency to look for love in all the wrong places. Most men simply ran the other direction or took advantage of my vulnerability, but not Greg. He isn't a "love her and leave her" kind of guy; he was—and is—committed to our marriage for the long haul. So even though it hurt him deeply when he learned of my emotional infidelity, Greg was determined to help me overcome these dysfunctional patterns. While some men would take offense to that kind of information, he felt that as long as I was talking to him about it rather than hiding it, there was hope for us. Rather than run, he wanted to help me see beyond my weaknesses to my genuine needs so I could get those needs met in healthy ways and become the woman God created me to be.

So when Greg looked into my heart, what did he see that no one else could? He saw a hurting little girl who didn't understand who she was in Christ or that Jesus wanted to be the lover of her soul. He also saw a woman who failed to understand what high and holy callings marriage and motherhood are. Not long before this season of our lives, I had given up a challenging career in an office where I had received a lot of kudos on a regular basis, so staying at home with two kids was a hard adjustment for me. No one clapped when I scrubbed baby food off the highchair. No one cheered as I carted kids to ballet lessons and playgrounds. Greg recognized that I had looked to outside relationships for a sense of affirmation and as a remedy to the monotony of being a full-time, stay-at-home mom.

He also understood that I used these relationships as a form of medication to ease my pain from having a father who had never seemed interested in spending time with me. Greg realized that my need for so much attention and affection wasn't as much about *our* relationship as it was about my dysfunctional relationship with my dad. My father and I had a stormy relationship when I was growing up, and most of the men I felt attracted to were older and in some form of authority over me. That told Greg that I was craving a father figure. He knew he shouldn't try to fill that role, so he prayed to our heavenly Father that He would heal the hole in my heart. God proved Himself to be faithful during that time. Not only did He restore my relationship with my earthly father, but He also restored my self-esteem and my ability to remain faithful to Greg.

Because Greg didn't run when I was honest with him about my struggles, I recognized what a trustworthy man I had married, and I felt safe and secure in a relationship for the first time in my life. I learned to appreciate his patience, his wisdom, and his spiritual maturity in not blaming himself for my emotional infidelity. Because of his help, I was able to establish my footing upon a firmer foundation.

Discovering Greg's deep level of commitment to me has been far more satisfying than any "intense" moment I've experienced with him or any other guy. I have his unconditional love—in spite of my flaws. This is what genuine intimacy is all about. And that intimacy is far better than butterflies, sweaty palms, fireworks, or any other form of intensity.

Ironically, when intensity (or excitement) is at its highest, intimacy is usually at its lowest. The reverse is also true—when intimacy is at its highest, intensity can feel as if it's at its lowest. Less than a month after Andrea and I took our road trip, she informed me that she had broken it off with James. Although he talked a good game, he rarely made time to see her face to face. He always had an excuse as to why he couldn't see her, evenings or weekends. His actions began to speak far louder than his words, and Andrea had experienced all the rejection she could stand. She informed him they could no longer interact as a couple. Although the six-week relationship had been intense, it never grew emotionally intimate, and

Andrea realized that she would never experience the joy of feeling truly safe and secure in a relationship with someone like James. On the other hand, Greg is still by my side, as committed as ever.

The moral to the story is this: be careful not to mistake *intensity* for *intimacy.* Intensity fades as the newness wears off and familiarity sets in, but intimacy can continue to blossom the longer you know a person and the more familiar you become with each another.

INTIMACY REQUIRES WORK

Of course, intimacy doesn't just happen automatically. It takes a tremendous amount of time and effort. Our relationships only grow and blossom when we nurture them, feed them, and intentionally care for them with diligence. Greg and I have achieved this level of intimacy only as a result of many counseling sessions and many hours spent in painful, honest conversation and gut-wrenching prayer. I've often thought that our intimate relationship has required a lot of blood, sweat, and tears—Jesus's blood, Greg's sweat, and my tears. But the fragrant beauty of what the three of us have created during those tumultuous years was well worth every ounce of effort.

While writing this chapter, it occurred to me that marriages are a lot like my experience with growing strawberry plants. Several years ago I got the idea that I wanted to grow strawberries. I remembered how fun it was as a little girl to go out to my mother's strawberry bed (which was planted inside a tractor tire in our back yard) and pluck off the biggest, ripest red berries for dessert that evening. Initially I went all out on my endeavor. A friend offered me all the strawberry plants I wanted from her garden, and I went to her house and spent hours digging them up. I even got a tractor tire and filled it with dirt so my garden would be just like my mom's. I transplanted the delicate plants, then began watering them daily— for all of about four days. Then I forgot about the plants and neglected them for a few weeks. Weeds, insects, and dehydration killed them all within that short amount of time. I wanted the berries, but I didn't want them bad enough to tend the plants properly. I was *passionate,* but I wasn't *committed.*

A similar dynamic destroys marriages almost as quickly as my strawberry plants met their demise. Many marriages start off passionately with lofty goals, honorable intentions, and high expectations, but if a couple isn't committed to the routine care and maintenance of their relationship, love fades and eventually dies a slow death. It doesn't have to be that way. The initial passion in a relationship can wear off, and yet the commitment can remain as strong as ever. That's when passionate love evolves and matures into committed love. The long-term viability of a marriage is dependent upon a couple's successful transition from passionate love to committed, companionate love.

How unfortunate it is that so many couples never learn to make this transition. Once the flame of intensity dies, they do what I almost did—they throw dirt on the fire and move on to spark something new with someone else. But because you are reading this book, my hope is that your marriage isn't likely to contribute to a higher divorce statistic. You will be the kind of wise woman who longs for deeper levels of genuine intimacy within her marriage relationship rather than seeks the intensity of something new and superficial. Your love for your husband won't be based on butterflies or fireworks, but on familiarity, honesty, trust, safety, security, and commitment.

a greater gift than expected

While helping me decorate for my wedding reception, a high-school student tossed me a question I hadn't seen coming. "In a wedding ceremony, why do the bride and groom say 'until death do us part'? Why can't they just say 'until we no longer love each other' so that they can have the freedom to move on if they are not happy?" Elizabeth asked.

At first I thought she was kidding, but the look on her face told me otherwise. I was astounded by both the question and her courage to ask it. I don't recall my answer verbatim, but it was something along the lines of a girl not wanting just the ring or the wedding or the sex, but wanting the lifetime commitment.

However, when the going gets tough, many couples wonder, *Why does God ask us to stay together until death do us part? Why doesn't He give us the freedom to move on when the relationship no longer brings happiness?* These couples mistakenly believe that the ultimate goal of marriage is happiness. It is not.

The Ultimate Purpose of Marriage

God intended the marriage relationship to be a reflection of His relationship to us—a relationship that remains steadfast because it isn't based on fickle feelings or human worthiness but rather is based on uncompromising commitment. We find proof of this plan in Ephesians 5:31–32, as Paul reflects on God's creation of marriage:

> As the Scriptures say, "A man leaves his father and mother and is joined to his wife, and the two are united into one." This is a great mystery, but it is an illustration of the way Christ and the church are one.

Notice that the scripture doesn't say, "A man leaves his father and mother and is joined to his wife, and the two *will live happily ever after.*" Paul doesn't say anything about happiness. He says our relationship illustrates the commitment that Christ has to the church, and Christ's goal wasn't as much to make the church *happy* as it was to make us *holy.* Consider the words Paul spoke to the Ephesians just prior to the above passage:

> And you husbands must love your wives with the same love Christ
> showed the church. He gave up his life for her *to make her holy and*
> *clean,* washed by baptism and God's word. He did this to present her
> to himself as a glorious church without a spot or wrinkle or any other
> blemish. Instead, she will be holy and without fault. (Ephesians
> 5:25–27, emphasis added)

Did you catch that? Christ gave up His life for the church *to make her holy and clean.* While happiness is a great gift, holiness is by far the greater gift. Learning to be more Christlike while here on earth will result in even greater eternal rewards in heaven.

Marriage offers us an incredible opportunity to be made more holy, more Christlike. How? In two ways. The first is through what my pastor calls sanctification sessions—those conversations or events in marriage that spotlight our character flaws and convict us to change for the better. The second is through learning to offer our spouses the unconditional love and acceptance that Christ offers us in spite of our own imperfections. This receiving and giving of mercy is a vital element in marriage. It can exercise our spiritual muscles in an extraordinary way, providing spiritual strength beyond what we are capable of developing on our own.

Let's take a closer look at each of these two ways.

DEVELOPING HOLINESS THROUGH SANCTIFICATION SESSIONS

Each morning I put on my makeup and style my hair in front of the mirror above our bathroom sink. If I want to get a bigger picture of what I look like from head to toe, I have to look into the full-length mirror in our bedroom. However, each of these mirrors reflects only my physical appearance. To get a true reflection of my spiritual appearance, I require a different kind of mirror—a human mirror.

Greg often serves as a full-length mirror in my life by pointing out the embarrassing spiritual "spinach in my teeth," such as impatience, pride, greed, and selfishness—things I don't always notice about myself until I recognize that *he* notices them. When my husband gently brings these issues to my attention, our marriage can feel like a refiner's fire. These issues create incredible spiritual heat and bring my impurities to the surface and into plain sight. When this happens, I can stubbornly refuse to address these issues, pretending they are not really there, or I can humbly ask God to help me skim these impurities out of my life so that I am refined and can more accurately reflect Christ's perfection.

While we all hate to see the ugliness in our own lives, sanctification sessions can show us how we can grow spiritually and deepen our levels of personal holiness. When we strive toward more Christlike behavior, we are in essence saying to our spouses and to God, "You deserve better, so I'm going to try harder." Such an attitude honors both our spouses and God.

Gary Thomas, the author of *Sacred Marriage,* agrees that in marriage our flaws are made visible in a way that perhaps they've never been visible to us before, and they therefore can usher us to a holier place than we've ever been before. He explains:

> We must not enter marriage predominantly to be fulfilled, emotionally satisfied, or romantically charged, but rather to become more like Jesus Christ. We must embrace the reality of having our flaws exposed to our partner, and thereby having them exposed to us as well. Sin never seems quite as shocking when it is known only to us; when we see how it looks or sounds to another, it is magnified ten times over. The celibate can "hide" frustration by removing herself from the situation, but the married man or woman has no true refuge. It is hard to hide when you share the same bed....
>
> I wouldn't be surprised if many marriages end in divorce largely because one or both partners are running from their own revealed weaknesses as much as they are running from something they can't tolerate in their spouse.[1]

Indeed, many divorced people run from first marriages into seconds or thirds, only to discover that their own weaknesses continue following them from relationship to relationship. Until we deal with those weaknesses and character flaws, we'll never be happy in a relationship, primarily because we'll never be happy with *ourselves*. However, if we learn to see our own sin through our spouses' (and through God's) eyes, we'll perhaps discover the necessary incentive to pursue positive change.

When I recognize the magnitude of my own sin (such as temper tantrums, selfishness, and so on) through Greg's eyes, it becomes more real to me than ever before, and I don't like what I see. I strive harder to avoid that sin not only to please God and avoid self-destruction but also to avoid having Greg see me in that sinful condition. So I try to bite my tongue and not lash out in anger, or I at least try to soften my tone so I don't offend him with my words. I try to focus more on serving his needs rather than on trying to manipulate him into meeting mine. I respectfully communicate what I need from him out of a desire for us to understand each other rather than out of an attitude of expectation. Basically, I try to focus on treating Greg more like Christ would treat him if He were living in our house. As I become more Christlike in my actions and attitudes, I become more holy—and happier with myself.

Not only can marriage help us come face to face with our own sins and thus inspire us to strive for personal holiness, but it also affords us the opportunity to be Christlike in how we respond to our spouses' sins.

DEVELOPING HOLINESS THROUGH UNCONDITIONAL LOVE

What is the ultimate gift you and your husband could give each other? A bigger house? A nicer car? A day to yourself without children or household responsibilities? The list of possibilities is likely a mile long, but there's one thing you can offer each other that is far more precious than anything else. What is that gift? The same ultimate gift that God gave us through Jesus Christ—unconditional love and acceptance in spite of our sinful natures.

Just as Jesus laid down His life for His bride (the church), He asks us to lay down our lives for the sakes of our spouses. He asks us to love our husbands the way that He loves us. First John 3:16 says, "We know what real love is because

Christ gave up his life for us." He taught us how to love unconditionally—not "as long as I feel like it" or "as long as you deserve it." Based on His words, "My Father! If it is possible, let this cup of suffering be taken away from me. Yet I want your will, not mine" (Matthew 26:39), I can't imagine that Jesus *felt like* dying for us that day. Yet He chose to obey so we would know God's everlasting commitment of love for us.

Temporary or conditional love is simply not in God's nature. Therefore, temporary marriage commitments and conditional acceptance in our earthly marriages are not sufficient reflections of what God intends. As we remain committed to marriage during our lifetimes, we receive a foretaste of what heaven will be like when we enjoy God's faithful love throughout eternity.

Cathy's husband gave her the lavish gift of unconditional love, and his mercy inspired her to turn from adulterous relationships to pursue a more holy lifestyle for the sake of her marriage. Here is what she wrote in an e-mail about her husband's response to her sin:

> After engaging in multiple affairs, I knew I would never experience genuine intimacy with my husband until after I confessed to him. Even though I knew my adultery gave Brad every right to divorce me, I couldn't live a double life any longer. Two months after my last affair, I was overcome with guilt and a sense that I was unforgivable. As we drove down the road, I was wailing with grief over my own sin. Brad pulled over and just held me for a long time. When we returned home, he called me into our bathroom, offering to perform a "cleansing ceremony" to help relieve me of my guilt. He lit a candle, filled the tub with warm water, and removed my clothes from my trembling body. He ushered me into the tub, gently washed me and poured water over my head, and made me feel for the first time that I had truly been cleansed and forgiven. Although we are having to work on restoring trust, Brad's unconditional love is a lifeline that keeps me striving to truly be the person I really want to be.

Maybe you are thinking, *That's great that Cathy can have that kind of relationship with her husband, but my husband isn't as understanding and forgiving!* I don't share this testimony so that you can envy someone else's position as the recipient of such mercy and unconditional love. I share it to inspire you to *offer* such mercy and unconditional love.

Perhaps Maria's testimony of how she responded to her husband's sin will paint in your mind a more vivid picture of what such mercy might look like:

One Sunday afternoon my husband was napping, and it was getting close to time for us to be back up to the church for a potluck dinner. I tiptoed into our room with the intention of waking him gently but was disheartened to discover him masturbating to a pornographic magazine. Suddenly, some things started making sense, particularly why he hadn't initiated sex in weeks and why he had occasionally turned me down when I tried to initiate. I assumed it was stress at work that caused him to be disinterested. I knew by the look on his face that he was stricken with guilt and remorse. We didn't have time to really talk about it until much later that evening, but the Lord really worked on my heart in the meantime. God reminded me that Michael is only human, and I felt determined to give him the same mercy and forgiveness that I would want from him if I were caught in sin. I verbalized my hurt but also my forgiveness as soon as I could. This made Michael feel safe enough to open up with me about how this had been a struggle for him since his early teens and how he truly wants to be faithful to me rather than engage in such behavior. He attended an *Every Man's Battle* workshop and continues to see a counselor. I occasionally ask him how he's doing with maintaining victory, but he doesn't resent my asking because he knows I'm asking with a supportive spirit. I'm not just seeing progress in our bedroom (with restored interest in our sex life), but in all other parts of our relationship. This situation had the potential to destroy our marriage, but instead, it has ultimately brought life back into it.

I believe that because of Maria's merciful response, the quality of her marriage relationship ultimately improved rather than declined. Had she poured on the condemnation, I doubt her husband would have responded so humbly. Scripture tells us that it's God's *kindness* that leads to repentance (see Romans 2:4). Because Maria behaved as God would have, responding kindly out of concern for her husband, her heart remained soft toward her mate. Her response also created a soft heart in her husband as he repented and sought healing. If only all marital struggles ended this way—with both spouses acting in such a way that brings them both to a greater level of personal holiness and relational peace!

Of course, the sin a husband or wife needs to forgive may not be something as major as what we've discussed so far. Sometimes it's the "little sins" that cause bitterness and resentment to build a wall between spouses, hindering the pursuit of personal holiness in one or both partners because of their hardened hearts. How can those walls be torn down and turned into bridges that connect us instead? Through the building blocks of mercy and unconditional love.

Here are two examples from women who have had to implement such bridge-building strategies:

- "Because we both work full time, my husband and I take turns picking our children up from school. There have been a couple of times in the past year that he's forgotten that it's his turn and has left our sons stranded on the school porch. My "mama bear" instinct wanted to tear into him for being so forgetful, but before I lashed out, I recalled how often I forget to pick up the dry cleaning or something we need at the grocery store. Granted, laundry and groceries aren't nearly as important as children, but all of us tend to forget something on occasion. My husband asked our sons' forgiveness, and they offered it freely. And I've chosen to do the same rather than let it drive a wedge between us."

- "Since I have an accounting background, we agreed early in our marriage that I would handle the finances. However, there have been a few times that our checking account was overdrawn because Norm failed to tell me he'd made a significant ATM transaction. These mistakes have cost us about a hundred dollars in overdraft fees. Neither of us is happy about this, but harmony in our relationship is worth far more to me than a hundred bucks."

Sure, it's disheartening when our spouses disappoint us. It can be frustrating when they don't live up to our expectations. It can be shocking when we discover that they have dark sides that we were unaware of. On the flip side, it's also humiliating to confess that we have major character flaws or that we struggle with sinful issues of our own or that we fail to live up to certain expectations that our spouses have of us. But in these times we each have a choice to make—we can choose to make things *bitter* with resentment and condemnation, or we can choose to make things *better* by displaying God's character traits of unconditional love and acceptance.

TAKING THE HIGH ROAD TOWARD HOLINESS

God desires that we strive to become holy (set apart for His good purposes). Why? *Because He is holy* (see 1 Peter 1:13–16). In other words, He wants us to become like Him. The more like Him we become, the more we glorify Him and the more others are drawn to Him as a result. But we cannot pursue personal holiness without striving to respond to people and situations the way God responds. There are no shortcuts to holiness. We can't act any way our flesh wants to and expect that our spirits will be strengthened. We must take the high road and strive to act more like God and less like our sinful selves, especially in the face of marital strife.

To take the high road toward holiness and to choose to love unconditionally as God loves us unconditionally, we often need to learn to distinguish between the person we love and the behavior we loathe.

You've probably heard it said before that we have to love the sinner while hating the sin. This may be a real struggle for you. You are certainly not the only one who finds this difficult. Separating the sinner from the sin can be a real spiritual exercise for even the godliest of people. C. S. Lewis confessed that he, too, struggled with how to love the sinner while hating the sin. One day it suddenly became clear to Lewis:

> It occurred to me that there was one man to whom I had been doing this all my life—namely myself. However much I might dislike my own cowardice or conceit or greed, I went on loving myself. There had never been the slightest difficulty about it. In fact the very reason why I hated the things was that I loved the man. Just because I loved myself, I was sorry to find that I was the sort of man who did those things.[2]

Lewis makes a great point. If we can go on loving ourselves in spite of our own sin, surely with God's help we can find a way to offer the same unconditional love and mercy to others, especially our own spouses. In doing so, we make our homes better places in which to live, as well as improve society as a whole. After all, homes and society become more holy when individuals are fully dedicated to the pursuit of holiness.

Examining the Exceptions

Perhaps you're reading this book as a last-ditch effort at trying to make things work before you call it quits, and you're wondering, *Does God allow divorce?* The Pharisees of Jesus's day wondered the same thing. In Mark 10:2–9, they posed the question:

> "Should a man be allowed to divorce his wife?"
>
> Jesus answered them with a question: "What did Moses say about divorce?" Jesus asked them.
>
> "Well, he permitted it," they replied. "He said a man merely has to write his wife an official letter of divorce and send her away."
>
> But Jesus responded, "He wrote those instructions only as a concession to your hard-hearted wickedness. But God's plan was seen from the beginning of creation, for 'He made them male and female.' 'This explains why a man leaves his father and mother and is joined to his wife, and the two are united into one.' Since they are no longer two but one, let no one separate them, for God has joined them together."

Although divorce is certainly not God's desire for any of His children, Jesus acknowledges that there are concessions. I believe He acknowledges such concessions because He doesn't want to see His children continue hurting each other so deeply. Most theologians and counseling experts

A SACRED SOCIETY REQUIRES A SACRED INSTITUTION

God designed the institution of marriage not just as a means to our happiness but as the very foundation of society. Marriage isn't a temporary agreement made for our convenience or selfish intentions. It is a lifelong, blood-sweat-and-tears, come-hell-or-high-water commitment. When we marry, we pledge our entire lives to our

agree that there are three legitimate exceptions to the marriage commitment—abuse, adultery, and addiction.

But before you take these concessions as your excuse to file for divorce, please consider what I'm about to say. I'm not proud of it, but I've been guilty of all three of these—verbal abuse, emotional adultery, and relational addictions. I look back on a few seasons of our marriage when Greg had every right to toss me out on the porch and slam the door behind me. But he never did. I'm living proof that the mercy, unconditional love, and Christlike commitment of a spouse can truly change a person's heart and life such that there is hope for a harmonious marriage relationship.

Granted, if a man is physically abusive and you fear for your safety, you need to get out of harm's way. If he is unrepentant of continual philandering that puts you in danger of contracting a sexually transmitted disease, we do not believe you are bound by God to remain in that marriage. If your husband has a drinking or drug addiction that causes him to be a dangerous threat to himself or others, it may require "tough love" to wake him up and cause him to seek help.

But before you give up on your husband, prayerfully consider that you have the power to give him a gift that will perhaps influence him to turn his life around. If you respond to your husband's sin with mercy and unconditional love (and deal with your own), I believe you stand every chance of experiencing the marital miracle that Greg and I, as well as many others, have experienced.

spouses, "for better for worse, for richer for poorer, in sickness and in health, to love and to cherish, until we are parted by death."

Marriage is a sacred relationship that we should prize above all others and that we should hold on to for dear life. It's in this precious, sacred relationship that we can practice becoming more holy, exercising our spiritual muscles to become more like Christ.

the ministry of marriage

A few years into our marriage, I was proudly basking in numerous ministry roles. I was serving as a youth pastor, leading summer youth camps and developing their curricula, leading a weekly Bible study for teen girls, speaking at abstinence education retreats, and serving on several committees at our church.

Although Greg had been a youth counselor in our church when we first met, it dawned on me that he had no current ministry involvements other than attending church and Sunday school. Never mind that he worked fifty hours each week as a financial controller for one of Dallas's largest nonprofit Christian hospitals, I figured that was a job, not a ministry. I felt like Greg was slacking in his service to God and that he needed to be more like me. One day I had the audacity to approach him, saying, "Honey, you don't seem to be as ministry minded as I am. Why is that?"

Looking into my eyes, he replied, "Shannon, when we married, God told me that *you* were to be my sole ministry until He told me otherwise, and He hasn't told me to shift gears yet." *Ouch!* Once again, the truth hurt. I *was* Greg's full-time ministry, and as messed up as much of my thinking was back then, I needed to be. Had his energies been directed elsewhere, I probably would have felt even more desperate to have my emotional needs for attention and affection catered to in unhealthy extramarital relationships. Not only that, I was able to pursue healing and explore God's calling on my life. Greg worked hard to financially support our family, giving me complete freedom to be involved in church, study God's Word, see a counselor when necessary, pursue my master's degree, write, and teach.

During the first decade of our marriage, Greg felt he needed to exemplify to me that marriage *is* a ministry—one very worthy of focus. He writes:

Many people pray, "Lord, give me a ministry! Show me what I can do for you!" while the answer is right there under their noses. Yes, the world needs Jesus, but our spouses and children desperately need to be the primary recipients of our ministry efforts. If we save the world but lose our marriage or family in the process, what does that do to our witness? Can we really do more for others than we can do for those living under our same roof? As husbands and wives, fathers and mothers, we hold the power to minister to our own families in ways that no one else can.

Let's take a look at the three primary ways in which a wife can minister to her husband—bringing out the best in him, putting his needs before her own, and giving him her best time.

Bringing Out the Best in Each Other

Scripture tells us, "As iron sharpens iron, a friend sharpens a friend" (Proverbs 27:17). The process of sharpening both iron and other people, however, requires friction. In marriage we often come against rough edges that need to be smoothed out or dull places that need to be sharpened, both in our spouses and in ourselves. The problem is that some couples confuse *sharpening* with *stabbing*. I can be incredibly judgmental of what I perceive as Greg's failures, but with a concerted effort, I can lovingly encourage him to overcome those faults and become the best man, husband, and father he can be. Many times, this shift from being judgmental to being encouraging is simply a matter of the words I choose. Please see the sidebar on the next page for a few examples.

What about you? Do you have a tendency to stab your husband with judgment or sharpen him with encouragement? Can you always assume the best of him, even if you don't agree with his actions or with a decision he is making? Can you calmly point out your concerns without belittling him? If so, he'll see you as a precious gift from God, a true friend, and a valuable helpmate.

On the flip side, are you open to discussing what he perceives as your weaknesses so that you can become the person God wants you to be? Is your spirit humble enough that you can admit your flaws to your husband and ask for his guidance and prayers for strength?

If we treat our spouses as if we assume the worst of them, we usually get exactly that—*the worst*. However, when we always assume the best of someone, it's amazing how that's exactly what comes to the surface—the very best of that person's character.

In addition to bringing out the best in one another, marriage also involves placing our spouses' interests above our own.

PUTTING HIS NEEDS BEFORE YOUR OWN

On our first mission trip to Honduras several years ago, our family learned an incredible lesson about true service. Our team had geared up to minister at an all-girls' orphanage by building additional housing, pouring a concrete driveway, and setting up a computer lab where they could learn valuable skills. We were feeling so "selfless" because we'd taken an entire month out of our busy lives to do such work, and we couldn't wait to send out our newsletter with pictures that showed others what a difference we were making.

As we hopped off the bus the first day, cameras in hand, the team leader pulled Greg and me aside and said, "You never take pictures on the first day. There'll be plenty of time for that toward the end of the trip." We were flabbergasted. *What's the big deal?* we wondered. Later that evening, our leader had a chance to explain,

WORDS OF JUDGMENT	WORDS OF ENCOURAGEMENT
"Well, it's about time you called. I hate it when I don't hear from you all day."	"You must be really busy today, but I'm so glad you found a moment to call. I miss your voice."
"If you really loved God and this family, you wouldn't do that!"	"As much as you love God and our family, it must be really hard for you to struggle with this issue."
"If I know you, you are probably not going to follow through on this project, so why bother?"	"I know this isn't really your cup of tea, so I'm proud of you for trying to tackle this yourself."
"That's just like you, always doing stuff for others and putting our family last."	"I think it's wonderful that you want to help this person. Before you make a commitment, however, can we talk about what effect this might have on our time together as a family?"

"You need to have a relationship with these people before you go snapping pictures, or else they are going to feel as if they're just another notch in your missionary belt." *Whoa.* We hadn't thought of it that way. We were convicted by the fact that although our intentions were to serve *them,* our actions indicated that we wanted them to serve *our* needs first—our need for a good newsletter picture to send out to all our friends.

Don't many of us do the same thing in marriage? We serve our spouses, but it's really just a clever ploy to get our own needs met in the long run. While it's not wrong to want your needs met, genuine service is really about meeting the other person's need without selfish ulterior motives. Marriage isn't about receiving as much as it is about giving.

I was reminded of this just recently. Remember the story in chapter 2 about how I gave Greg extra time at work before leaving on our writing retreat, then delivered him dinner the next week as he had to work late several nights in a row? I confess it didn't take long for me to begin expecting that he would reciprocate in a big way. At that time, I was temporarily using an office near Greg's while our house was being remodeled. Upon returning from lunch one day, a florist van was parked at the entrance of the office building. "Do you work here?" the driver asked as I walked by.

When I responded positively, she asked if I would deliver some flowers on my way in. She emerged from the back of her van with a gorgeous spray of my favorites—fragrant stargazer lilies, pink roses, purple and white snapdragons, and more. My first thought was, *Well, how ironic that you would ask me to deliver these, because I think they are for me anyway!* But looking at the card, my heart sank to read *Jackie Ellis,* not *Shannon Ethridge.*

That evening, I noticed my heart wasn't nearly as warm toward Greg as it had been over the past week. To avoid being too crabby that evening, I slipped into the tub for a relaxing soak before dinner. I questioned why I was in such a bad mood, then I realized that I was still disappointed that those flowers weren't for me. I was feeling as if Greg wasn't working very hard to meet my emotional needs *again*! But then I realized that I was expecting something in return for all I had been doing for him. Oh, he had expressed his gratitude all throughout the week, but flowers speak much louder than words. As I continued soaking, however, I decided to stop sulking. I asked God to take away any sense of expectation that was hindering my selfless service to Greg and to help me love my husband simply for who he is rather than for what he does for me in return. I was able to put my selfish expectations aside and enjoy a relaxing dinner and fun evening playing games with my husband and children, which was an even greater gift to myself than any bouquet of flowers would have been.

Selfless service and true ministry to our husbands also involves freely giving another gift, the incredible gift of quality time.

GIVING HIM YOUR BEST TIME

Time is a precious commodity these days, so it's no surprise that busyness is one of the biggest intimacy killers. And now it has a medical diagnosis: the Hurried Woman Syndrome, which doctors believe is caused by the stress of doing too much. Symptoms include weight gain, low sex drive, moodiness, feeling overwhelmed, resentfulness, hostility, and depression.[1]

Several years ago when my children were preschool age, I made one of the hardest decisions I've ever made, but I believe it kept me from falling prey to this syndrome. I wanted to take a class or two to begin working toward a master's degree in counseling. The school closest to us was a very expensive, prestigious university, and a friend on staff there encouraged me to submit a scholarship application. Within a few weeks, I was notified that I had been awarded a 100 percent scholarship—both tuition and books. There was only one catch. I had to attend *full time* to qualify. Greg understood what an honor this was and how much I wanted to pursue this degree, so he said we'd make it work somehow.

But a few days later I was expressing my gratitude to God when I clearly heard Him say, *Don't go. Now is not the time.* My first response was to question God's sanity. "You want me to give up a 100 percent scholarship, Lord? Isn't it a gift from You?"

I sensed Him gently replying, *Yes, I gave it to you, but I'm asking for you to give it back. Do you trust Me to fulfill this dream when the time is more appropriate?* I also had a vision in my mind of a mama bird leaving her baby birds in the nest. I knew that God was telling me that our family was too young for me to embark on this endeavor.

Four years later, my youngest started kindergarten, and God gave me the green light to work on my master's degree through a school offering a distance-learning program where I could watch class lectures on video at home rather than traveling to a classroom several times each week. Although it took five years to complete my degree and a lot of money out of our pockets, I have no regrets about declining that scholarship during that season of our lives.

My writing and teaching ministries also require huge amounts of time and energy. Balancing marriage and motherhood with ministry hasn't been easy. I have to make a concerted effort to do my writing during the day while my kids are in school so I can separate work time from family time. Greg and I intentionally schedule date nights or "walking and talking" time together so we can stay emotionally connected. There are times when one of us has to travel, leaving the other one to play both the mom and dad roles for a little while. In strict moderation, this can be a good thing, because absence can make our hearts grow fonder as we grow desperate for our spouses to return (and we develop more grateful hearts for our mates' many contributions to raising children and running households). But the two of us have learned that we can't leave our marriage on the back burner for very long before one of us starts to feel slighted. Too many late nights at the office, too many "Fend for yourself" nights in the kitchen, and too many "Gee, honey, I'm just really tired tonight" responses cause our home lives to be neglected and our relationships to suffer.

Not long ago I received an e-mail that offers another great example of how we often forget that our husbands crave quality time with us. According to Tina, her busyness eventually caused her husband's heart to grow cold toward her. She was involved in MOPS (Mothers of Preschoolers), babysitting, playgroups, the library, the church nursery, and other Christian committees. At times she found herself running on empty and becoming frustrated that her husband, Chris, wasn't sharing more of the household responsibilities. But Chris was also becoming frustrated because of Tina's lack of energy and availability. She admits:

Unfortunately both of us were too lazy to bring up the issue with the other. Day after day we appeared to everyone that everything was okay, a perfectly in-step couple. But night after night we would spend our evenings becoming more and more distanced from each other. I assumed that I just needed to "suck up" my irritations and be the bigger person. So what if my husband spent his evening playing computer games, completely forgetting that I had asked him to throw his lunch together (because I didn't have time)? I would just need to make sure that I got up a little earlier to make it, of course with more than a little resentment toward him.

On the flip side, my husband was getting frustrated that I was not available to him. He would all too often find me on the phone after dinner, with me feeling as if I was simply taking care of business, but with

Bonus: Top Five Dating Guidelines

When marital bliss wanes, it's often due to forgetting the romance. Consider these best tips for dating your spouse adapted from *Good Housekeeping* (February 2009):

1. *Plan it.* Aim for smaller weekly dates to walk, talk, or share coffee, and at least every other week shoot for a "real" date with dinner and a shared activity.
2. *Accept your role.* It's great if you can both plan your dates. But if it's difficult for him to help, make it a gift to him and your marriage.
3. *Get creative.* Find the time of day and activities that work best for you as a couple, and decide to pursue what both of you can enjoy or, barring that, what the other enjoys most.
4. *Protect the time.* Agree to avoid rain checks, errands, and any conversation that can kill romance—such as home and family management duties—and focus on each other whatever you do.
5. *Double date.* Studies show that sharing some deeper conversation involving self-disclosure with another couple can strengthen your bond. So make an effort to connect and invest in friends together.

him feeling slighted and neglected. He would turn to something else, like computer games or television, to vent his frustrations. Once I got off the phone or finished my work, I would find him doing his own thing, so I would bury myself in a book or some other activity. We continually focused on ourselves, only thinking about how our own needs were not being met.

Tina brings up a good point—many husbands want to enjoy quality time with their wives, but we have to make ourselves available before that's ever going to happen. Your husband's probably not going to ask you to schedule him into your day, but it would make him feel cherished for you to put phone calls, e-mails, and household chores on the back burner so that the two of you could enjoy uninterrupted time together.

Of course, it doesn't take an educational pursuit, a career, or outside activities to cause a wife to put her husband on hold. Some women allow their children to consume so much of their personal time and energy that they have nothing left for the fathers of those children. Many men feel like Karl, who wrote the following in an e-mail:

> I think my wife is a great mom, but I have to admit that I can get pretty jealous of the time and attention she gives to our kids. She works outside the home so that we'll be able to afford to allow our kids to be involved in lots of extracurricular activities. Between car pool, ballet, piano, voice lessons, soccer, tae kwon do, scouts, and volunteering in their classrooms as often as possible, it seems her afternoons, evenings, and weekends are all booked with the kids' activities. Yet this is the only time I have with her since we both work during the day. I feel like our relationship suffers as a result, but I'm afraid my family will think I'm selfish if I tear my wife away from my own children to get the quality time that I crave.

While we all want to be wonderful moms who spend lots of hands-on time with our kids, we can't do this at the expense of our marriages. We have to be careful not to make idols of our children, bowing down to their every whim and allowing our lives to get absorbed into theirs.

One of the greatest gifts parents can give kids is to teach them that the world doesn't revolve around them. We need to instill in our children the importance of a balanced life (for everyone in the family) and demonstrate that moms and dads need their quality time alone together. So leave your kids at home with a sitter on occasion and go on dates with your husband. Limit their extracurricular activities to one sports team or one cultural activity, such as music or dance lessons, each season. Between school, church, Sunday school, youth group, and one outside activity, they get plenty of social interaction. When you limit their activities, you save both time and money because you aren't carting your kids around to every activity under the sun.

As you strive to make your marriage one of your top priorities, you'll be making an incredibly worthy investment.

No Greater Investment

Imagine all the important relationships in your life and how long you get to enjoy each of them. Only one will remain consistent throughout your life—your relationship with your spouse. Decades of living under the same roof, sleeping in the same bed, eating at the same table, and sharing a rich emotional, mental, spiritual, and physical history together places this relationship in a class all by itself. Surely, the more you invest in your marriage, the greater the return on your investment.

If you are ready to make your marriage the focus of your ministry efforts, read on as we explore in the next part some of the things that wives do to douse the flame of joy and passion that once burned brightly in their husbands' hearts.

how his flame of joy and passion dies

games women play

When my niece was a little girl, she would frequently ask, "Aunt Shannon, will you play a game with me?" If I agreed, Carye would run to her room and then quickly reappear with a board game in hand, explaining, "Now this is *my* game, so *I'm* going to win, okay?" As a preschooler, Carye wasn't mature enough to be able to say, "It would help me feel smarter and more grown up if you could let me win, okay?" Now Carye is in her twenties, and we still laugh about how she always had to win at her own games. But it's no laughing matter that many adult women are still playing games, insisting on winning at all costs.

Of course, I'm not talking about board games; I'm referring to the mind games that women play in marriage. Subconsciously, many of us can be really good at assigning the roles, making up the rules, and attempting to win so that we can somehow feel better about ourselves or get our own needs met. Some of these mind games have even cost women their husbands' respect and affection, or worse, their marriage relationships.

In this chapter, we'll examine several such mind games, starting with one of the most common.

THE MOMMY-CHILD GAME

One of our greatest attributes as women is our natural mothering instinct. Most women love taking care of others and making sure that everything goes smoothly. We're not afraid of rolling up our sleeves and diving into sibling squabbles, slumber parties, school field trips, vomit, poop, blood, or anything else for the benefit of our children. After all, we are responsible for their well-being until they are able to take responsibility for themselves.

It's one thing to mother our children, but it's another to mother a grown man.

Although husbands appreciate it when their wives do things for them, they don't appreciate it when we treat them like children. For example, Clifton explains:

> I like it when my wife does nice things for me, such as packing my lunch or pressing my shirt the day before a big meeting, but sometimes she talks to me as if I'm not capable of doing things myself or making decisions on my own. Sometimes she tells me to bundle up or else I'll catch cold (as if I can't tell how much outerwear I need that day), or she'll rudely insist that I change clothes because I'm not dressed appropriately for the occasion, when what I am wearing is perfectly fine. I resent being told what to do. I am a man, and I have a pretty sharp mind of my own. I don't need or want someone telling me how to dress. It's humiliating.

Peter's comments echo Clifton's:

> It's unnerving how my wife harps on me, like she harps on our children about doing something around the house. She can't just ask me once and trust that I'll do it. She has to keep bringing it up over and over until I give in and do it out of exasperation just to shut her up. It makes me feel like she doesn't have any more respect for me than she does for our preschoolers. When she treats me like a child instead of a man, the last thing I want to do is have sex with her. That would feel like having sex with my mother.

In light of these blunt comments, we'd do well to remember that only children, not grown men, need mothers. A man needs a wife. By all means, be helpful and offer your spouse your insight or advice when needed, but offer it as encouragement with no expectation that he is under any obligation to abide by it. Strive to be his loving peer, not his parent.

There have certainly been times when I fell into the mother role with Greg and expected him to simply obey me. I've insisted he be home from work at a certain time rather than trust that he'll come home as soon as he can. I've attempted to control what he eats and how often he exercises, as if he's clueless about living a healthy lifestyle on his own. I've created honey-do lists a mile long with the dates that I needed these things done by, as if his free time were completely mine to control. Like Peter and Clifton, Greg didn't appreciate it that his wife was trying to micromanage his life.

Perhaps you have fallen into a similar trap. Women frequently tell me, "I feel more like my husband's mother or boss than his partner," and that they they are always harping on their husbands about helping more around the house. If this sounds familiar, remember that you can't *require* your husband's cooperation. You can, however, *inspire* it. Because you want your husband to be internally (rather than externally) motivated to help out, try encouraging him with a nice comment, such as, "Would you mind running the vacuum cleaner for me sometime today? And when you do, remember how much I appreciate how hard you work both inside and outside our home." Or when you see him doing a particular chore, you might say, "I am so thankful to have a guy who is willing to do that!" He'll feel like he's your hero rather than your rebellious child, and chances are he'll be more likely to want to play that heroic role more often in the future.

While some wives are tempted to play the role of mom in their marriages, others may be more tempted to play the role of the child instead.

THE SPOILED CHILD—SUGAR DADDY GAME

Although we may not have gotten *everything* we wanted when we were growing up, some girls were able to wrap their dads so tightly around their little fingers that they could bat their eyelashes and get pretty much whatever they wanted. That may be fine for a little girl, but when a woman emotionally manipulates her husband to get her way, she creates an unhealthy dynamic.

I felt sorry for one woman's husband when she told me, "I can get anything I want from Dan, within reason, of course. All I have to do is cross my legs and stop cooking, and he'll cave in after a couple of days." Translation: "I'll withhold sex and starve him until he caters to my every whim."

Maybe you've played the spoiled child role in more subtle ways. Do any of these comments or thoughts sound familiar?

- "I've given my whole life to him, so the least he can do is buy me
  _____!" (You fill in the blank.)
- "You didn't mind wining and dining me when we were dating, so why
  won't you splurge on me now?"
- "I'd much rather stay in a nice hotel on the beach than with your rela-
  tives. Am I not worth it to you?"

Because money (or its lack) is one of the most common sources of marital
strife and divorce, it's important that we not place more of a financial load on our
husbands or on ourselves than we can reasonably carry. With the invention of the
credit card, creating an unmanageable debt load is as easy as a magnetic swipe and
a signature. You may find it shocking (or convicting), but according to an online
poll commissioned by *Redbook* magazine, 33 percent of spouses admit they have
excessive credit card debt that they keep secret from their partners.[1] It's hard to
imagine what stress this places on the spouse doing the spending and hiding, and
how the secrecy and the debt will affect the marriage when the other spouse dis-
covers what has been going on. Greg and I have a friend whose wife suddenly committed suicide several years ago, and no one understood why. The reason became
obvious within several weeks, though, as the credit card bills, reflecting thousands
of dollars' worth of debt that her husband knew nothing about, came rolling in.

To avoid unnecessary financial stress on your marriage, use a system of only
cash, check, or debit cards, especially if you are prone to spending money bor-
rowed with a credit card. Studies show that consumers spend significantly *more*
when using a credit card because it creates the "I can have it now and pay for it
later" mentality, deceiving us to believe that we can live outside our means without consequences. Although credit-card rewards can be tempting, there's nothing
we can buy from any store that is more valuable and fulfilling than the peace of
mind we get when living free of excessive debt.

Of course, handling finances isn't just a matter of avoiding debt. It's also a matter of stewardship. Sadly, I've known some women who have such high-paying
jobs that they feel justified in spending as much money as they want without
regard to how their husbands feel about such stewardship. I've also seen a few wives
who have almost made professions out of spending their husbands' paychecks.
They complain that their husbands are always at the office, so they feel justified in

their excessive shopping to fill the hours of loneliness. But these same husbands often say they feel they have to work longer and harder to keep up with their wives' shopping habits. These wives want bigger houses and nicer cars, but they aren't willing to scrimp, save, or cut corners to get them. Their demands can make their husbands feel more like bankers than life partners, and the husbands often work insane hours out of fear that the loss of a regular paycheck could ultimately mean the loss of their families.

Chances are, we have enough clothes in our closets and far more shoes than

Separate Money and Marriage

Several friends shared how the failing economy negatively impacted them. It seems everyone has been shaken in some way, and when individuals are shaken, marriages and families are too.

How do you keep financial concerns from wreaking havoc on marriage? Bank accounts may fluctuate, but marriages are far more important—and harder to heal! Here are a few ideas to keep your marriage from going down in tough times:

1. *Turn off the news.* Declare a news fast for a week or two and spend that time together focusing on blessings in your life together.
2. *Turn on the romance.* Don't let declining bank accounts cause your bedroom activities to decline with them. Soothe stress with a warm bottle of lotion and massage and see where that leads.
3. *Commit to date night.* If you haven't already done so, schedule regular date nights. Save the money you might spend on a restaurant or theater tickets to pack a picnic dinner, play a game, or snuggle to a favorite movie.

For better or worse, in good times and bad, there's no price tag on a strong, vibrant marriage. In trying times, get back to basics so you can look back with pride instead of regret.

we need. The cars we drive may not turn heads, but they usually get us to where we are going. We don't necessarily need a bigger house as much as we need to get rid of all the clutter that eats up so much space. Keep in mind that regardless of how much money either partner earns, husbands tend to mentally carry most of the responsibility for making sure the family is provided for, because that's how men are wired. We wives only increase that burden when we demand things that we don't really need.

So the next time you want to make a purchase that might have a major impact on the family budget, pray about whether it's really something you need. If it is, talk about it with your husband and consider what sacrifice you can make for a while to help shoulder some of the burden for the expenditure so that your husband is not overwhelmed by the request. For example, you might clip coupons, give up Starbucks coffee, or take your lunch to work each day rather than eating out.

If you don't get the response you were hoping for, deal with your disappointment without going into manipulation mode. Remember what James said in chapter 4: the desires that battle within us are often the source of quarrels, and we often don't have something because we've failed to ask God for it or because our motives are wrong. Try this three-step approach to remedying such situations:

1. Surrender the desire to God for a time and see if it disappears. Material desires are often fleeting, and garage sales full of last year's "must haves" often attest to this fact.

2. If the desire remains even after you've surrendered it, take the next step of praying that your motives be purified, and ask God to fulfill the desire according to His will.

3. If time passes with no answer, pray that God would change the desire in your heart or your husband's heart to be in accordance with His will.

Throughout this three-step process, regardless of the outcome of your prayers, keep unity and harmony in your relationship a priority over any purchase you wish to make. Nothing you can ever buy or possess will ever be as valuable to you, your marriage, or your children as a peaceful, unified relationship with your husband.

There are other times when a wife may be tempted not to play the child role but instead play the father role—the *heavenly* Father, that is.

THE HOLY SPIRIT–WRETCHED SINNER GAME

Have you ever experienced any of these thoughts, or worse, said them out loud?

- *My husband thinks he's a Christian, but I'm not so sure.*
- *My life would be so much better if my husband loved the Lord like I do.*
- *If our children grow up to know Jesus, it won't be any thanks to my husband!*

While I certainly don't want to minimize any woman's pain if she is living with an avowed nonbeliever, I do want to point out that legalism and self-righteousness are two things that Jesus spoke against more often than any other issue. Many of us have to admit that we often assign the bad guy role to our husbands while we wear the angelic halos. But what are we trying to accomplish when we do this? To guilt him into a more righteous lifestyle? Or to make ourselves look all the more holy by calling attention to his unholiness?

Every Christian woman longs for a husband who is a strong spiritual leader in their home. But sometimes it takes years for a man to mature into such a role. Unfortunately, many women stunt that growth process with their own self-righteous indignation, as Anthony explains:

> My wife thinks she's such a saint because she goes to church every time the doors open, but she can be such a mean-spirited person that I wonder if all this religion has done her any good. If the church is filled with hypocrites like her, I don't want anything to do with them. Spending time on Sunday mornings under my car alone with God is more my thing, but of course my wife thinks I'm going to burn in hell because I don't warm a pew every Sunday like her. "Faith without works is dead!" she says, but her cynical attitude tells me that her faith isn't exactly alive and well, either.

Anthony's response to his wife's approach is a graphic reminder that we can only *model* the abundant Christian life for our husbands, not *force* them to experience it. As much as you may desire for your husband to be more committed to spiritual things, remember that there's only one God—one Father, one Savior, and one Holy Spirit—and you're not Him. We might nag our husbands enough that they change their behavior slightly, but a deep, heartfelt change is only possible through the power of the real Holy Spirit, not the one we try to be in our husbands' lives. Simply pray for your husband, lovingly encourage him when appropriate, and let the Holy Spirit do in your husband's life what only He can do.

Finally, since so many of us come into marriage with unresolved issues, there's yet another mind game that's worth mentioning.

THE PATIENT-PSYCHOTHERAPIST GAME

Like many women I find it helpful to talk about some things out loud. When I verbalize my thoughts, I often gain clear direction on how to solve a particular dilemma. When our problems are solved that easily, our husbands can make great sounding boards. However, problems that can't be easily identified or remedied can become wedges between husbands and wives, causing frustration and confusion.

Such was the case with Wendy and Jeremy. In an attempt to be transparent with her husband, Wendy told him all about the sexual abuse she experienced as a child at the hands of a neighbor. They had been married about six months, and Jeremy was very sympathetic and understanding at first. He told her that he would work overtime to pay for counseling if Wendy would go. She didn't want to burden him with the expense, so she told him she was handling it okay. But Wendy was rarely interested in having sex because it reminded her too much of the abuse. Instead, she'd ask if Jeremy would just hold her while she talked about how she was feeling about the abuse.

Eventually, her husband got so frustrated and tired of hearing about the bitter memories and recurrent nightmares that he said, "Look, I don't mind listening to you, but unless you want me to go find this guy and beat him up for what he did to you, maybe it's best that you not tell me all this stuff." Although it wasn't what Wendy wanted to hear at the moment, it was actually a turning point in their relationship. She reports:

> For a while I took Jeremy's response as rejection, but the more I thought
> about it, the more I realized that even though he had never taken a psy-
> chology class in his life, I was trying to get him to counsel me, and that

had to overwhelm him. While I still feel I can be honest with Jeremy, I don't waste a lot of time telling him gory details about things he can't really do anything about. Those I take into my counselor's office instead of into my bedroom.

As Wendy discovered, men are problem solvers by nature. They love to be our heroes, remedy our predicaments, and rescue us from our distresses. But when our problems are incredibly complex and deeply rooted, our husbands can feel overwhelmed and frustrated by their inability to fix things. So if you need a problem solved and your husband can solve it, feel free to look to him. But if you need therapy to overcome an ongoing issue that your husband isn't trained to handle, do yourself and your husband a favor and go to a therapist.

Of course, the reverse is also true. If your husband has deep-seated issues he needs to work through, it's unrealistic to expect that you are all the counselor he needs. Encourage and support him, but don't try to fix him on your own. You're his wife, not his therapist.

PLAYING FOR KEEPS

What about you? Have any of these (or other) mind games been a flame killer in your marriage? Are you ready to give up these games so you can begin *inspiring* rather than *requiring* intimacy in your relationship?

If so, put a stop to playing games to get your needs or desires met. Granted, we all have times when we feel the need to nurture others, when we want to be nurtured by someone else, when we desire to help someone become a better person, or when we need to overcome issues to become better people ourselves, but game playing is never the answer. With God's help you can learn to recognize and verbalize those needs and desires such that your husband feels respected by you rather than manipulated.

The only way that you will ever truly experience relational fulfillment is by simply loving your husband for who God made him to be (rather than trying to make him play the role you want him to play). By recognizing and verbalizing your own needs or desires, you'll be setting the stage for *both* of you to feel like winners.

riding emotional escalators

My grandmother spent much of her life wandering around shopping malls and department stores looking for the hidden elevators. Why? Because she was terrified of escalators. I recall one time when my mom was trying to coax Granny onto an ascending escalator. Granny so resisted getting on that thing, you'd have thought that the second floor was on fire. She insisted, "There's got to be an elevator in this store somewhere, or at least some stairs that don't move!" She even stormed out of one store, claiming, "My goodness, I don't need new stockings from this store that bad. We can find them somewhere else that doesn't require an escalator ride to get to them!"

As a wife, I wish I could be more like my grandmother and intentionally avoid escalators. Of course, I'm not talking about physical escalators; I'm referring to emotional escalators, where one tiny step out of line on Greg's part gets escalated to a third-degree offense. Let me give you a few examples of what this has looked like in our house and in many other homes across the country.

Sweating the Small Stuff

Not all that long ago we were going on a camping trip in our travel trailer to enjoy some family time over spring break. We were due to leave on Thursday, so I asked Greg to bring the camper out of the woods and into the driveway on Tuesday so I'd have time to clean it out and stock it up with all the things we'd need. On Tuesday it was pouring rain, so Greg decided to wait until Wednesday to bring the trailer up. However, Wednesday night was hectic with getting the kids to and from their youth group and Awana activities and with Greg trying to tie things up at the office to be gone for a couple of days, so the trailer didn't get brought up Wednesday, either.

Greg finally brought it up Thursday morning, just a couple of hours before we were due to leave. He told me that we had accidentally left a watermelon on the kitchen floor the last time we had gone camping (which had been several months earlier), but that he had already cleaned up the mess. In a pinch, I resorted to just tossing all our clothes, bedding, toiletries, food, and activity items in suitcases and laundry baskets, and then I threw them into the trailer, thinking we'd clean and organize later.

However, "later" never seemed to arrive. Throughout the weekend we just kept shuffling suitcases and laundry baskets around from beds to table to floor and back onto the beds again. After two days of the chaos, this happy camper turned into a crabby bear. I snapped at Greg, "If *you* had brought the trailer up when I asked you to, we wouldn't be having this problem! I can't function like this! This is not fun for me!" It didn't seem to matter that Mom going off on Dad wasn't fun for anyone else. I was being inconvenienced. I was not comfortable. Rather than just bucking up, emptying the trailer, and getting everything situated to my liking, Mama Bear chose to pick a fight. Meanwhile, here is what Papa Bear was thinking:

> I resented the fact that Shannon was chewing me out, especially in front of the kids. For one thing, if we were going to get to the campsite in time to hook the trailer up to the utilities before dark, we had little choice but to throw things in and head off down the road. Besides, she just assumed that I had left most of the work to her. She didn't know all the work I'd had to do to clean the rotten watermelon residue off the kitchen floor, or else she'd have been thanking me rather than griping at me. I didn't think all the suitcases and laundry baskets were that big of a deal since we could just move them out of the way when necessary. Obviously, they were a big deal to her, but griping at me didn't solve the chaos. It only created more.

Sometimes things simply don't go the way we plan or hope. At those moments when we feel disappointed or offended by life's circumstances, we can choose to allow our emotions to escalate into anger, frustration, resentment, or deep depression—any of which usually makes the scene worse—or we can roll with the punches and make the best of a bad situation. If absolutely necessary, we can always express our concerns later, when the time and place are appropriate and when we can talk in a calm and loving manner.

Of course, it's not always life's circumstances that can send us into emotional tailspins. Sometimes it's our husbands' little quirks that we allow to drive us crazy!

LETTING HIS QUIRKS DRIVE YOU CRAZY

We all have our own unique set of quirks, and one of my husband's is that he has a poor sense of direction. He once arrived three hours late to an important business meeting in east Texas because he accidentally wound up in Oklahoma instead. He didn't find it funny, but his coworkers got a big kick out of his being horribly late because he had turned north when he should have turned south.

It was easy for me to laugh about that incident too, because I wasn't inconvenienced by it at all. But one particularly hectic morning of trying to get everyone up, dressed, fed, packed, and out the door for school and work, I let Greg's poor sense of direction put me on a high-speed emotional escalator. We pulled out of our driveway and stopped at a four-way intersection. Greg, as if on automatic pilot, turned left to go toward his office, even though we were en route to the kids' school, which required a right-hand turn. My tension had already been building all morning, and this was the little push that sent me right over the edge. I slammed my foot onto the imaginary brake pedal on the passenger floorboard and yelled, "*Where* are you going? Would you get your head out of the clouds and *pay attention,* for crying out loud?" As soon as the words came out of my mouth, I was flabbergasted by my own behavior, especially since my outburst had been in front of our kids.

Another one of Greg's quirks, which I've actually come to appreciate (much more than his poor sense of direction), is his inability to get riled up. Rather than yelling right back after my outburst at that four-way intersection or sarcastically asking if I wanted to do the driving instead, Greg looked calmly at me and said, "Could you have a little more patience with me? I wasn't thinking, but that doesn't give you the right to yell at me." Of course, he wasn't calm on the inside. He admits his heart felt incredibly hardened toward me in that moment. I had already eaten breakfast, but the situation called for a big helping of humble pie for dessert.

Like many men, Greg hates to ask for directions. I've heard that the Israelites wandered in the desert for forty years because Moses refused to stop and ask directions to the Promised Land. While that may be a gross exaggeration, a woman who's been trapped in a wandering vehicle with a man who refuses to admit that he's lost knows how this aversion can drive a person crazy. I used to let this minuscule issue about Greg bother me to the point of frustration and anger. By the time we arrived at many of our destinations, my badgering him to ask for directions or to let me drive left us both so angry that neither of us could enjoy the evening.

Now, instead of yelling at Greg, I put my hand on his thigh to get his attention, give him a cute little grin and an eyebrow raise, and ask, "Where are you going?" This approach enables him to laugh at himself with me. Even if we're running short on time, I tell myself, *What difference is it going to make to anyone's salvation if we're a couple of minutes late because Greg accidentally took a wrong turn?*

If we do get lost, I've learned not to bring it up to others once we arrive, because it can come across as if I'm ragging on his poor sense of direction. I've also learned that if we are truly in need of directions, I'll get a lot further if I say, "I need to go to the restroom anyway. If you'll stop at this convenience store, I'll check to make sure we are headed in the right direction." This way, he's my hero for stopping to let me go to the restroom, not a dunce for getting us lost.

Now Greg and I have a new way of ensuring our timely arrival—a global positioning navigation system (GPS). The story of *how* we got it is another good illustration of how we wives can either choose to hop on yet another emotional escalator or we can choose to respond to disappointments calmly and rationally.

REFUSING NO AS AN ANSWER

As mentioned in the previous chapter, sometimes we try to manipulate our husbands into giving us what we want, and refusing to accept no as an answer is often the method we use. While I've certainly been guilty of this in the past, this is one emotional escalator I've learned to avoid. Greg explains:

A few months ago we decided to order a new Toyota hybrid to replace our fourteen-year-old Camry and to alleviate some of the strain on our wallets created by our gas-guzzling Suburban and rising gas prices. When we placed the order, we were told it would take a minimum of six months before we could take delivery of the car. Shannon suggested we consider the higher-priced package that included a navigation system because of my membership in the "I refuse to ever stop and ask directions" club. But I thought that the GPS wasn't worth the extra money. Ten years ago, Shannon would have pouted, insisted on her way, or somehow manipulated the situation in order to win. Instead, she simply said, "Okay, whatever you think." I wonder if she didn't turn around and pray that God would change my mind, though. It was only four weeks after we placed the order that I called her one day and said, "I've been thinking maybe we should have ordered the navigation system."

She didn't rub it in or say, "I told you so." She just pleasantly replied, "Then you would *never* have to stop and ask directions! Do you want me to change the order?" I agreed to the upgrade, mainly because she was so agreeable to accepting my no that I really wanted to give her a great big yes, knowing how much she wanted the GPS.

Did you catch that? Because I accepted his no, my husband wanted to give me a wholehearted yes whenever possible. I suspect that your husband is probably a lot like mine. When you pout, cry, or pitch a royal fit, it only makes him want all the more to dig his heels in the dirt. But if you take his no for an answer and respect his feelings, you will motivate your husband to consider seeing things from your perspective. I offer this not as a way for you to manipulate your husband more effectively but as a way to maintain unity and harmony, fueling the joy and passion you both desire and inspiring a more cooperative spirit in each of you.

You can also maintain unity and harmony in your marriage by refraining from the emotional escalator of thinking that everything is about you.

TAKING THINGS TOO PERSONALLY

When Barbara and Andy were dating, she often asked him what he was thinking. Nine times out of ten, he was thinking of her. But after twenty-some-odd years of marriage, it's not that way anymore, which isn't necessarily a bad thing. However, if Barbara asks Andy what he's thinking and he responds, "I'm not thinking about anything," she takes it personally and becomes self-conscious about what she's doing wrong. She begins questioning him about why he rarely thinks of her the way he used to. Andy has decided that "Nothing" is always the wrong answer to the question "What are you thinking?" even if he's not thinking anything at all. He admits:

> If Barbara does catch me thinking about something, it might be about what I need to be doing at the office or how I want to have the guys over to play poker some Saturday night soon. But if I told her that's what's on my mind, she'd sulk and complain about how I'm married to my job or that I never take her out on Saturday nights anymore. I love my wife, but do I really have to be thinking of her every minute to prove it to her? Should I lie to her and tell her that I'm thinking of her even if it's not true? This seems like a ridiculous quandary for a grown man to be in.

The moral of this story is that we need to take our husband's words literally rather than taking them personally. If he says he's not thinking of anything, then he's probably not.

I remember a time when I expressed disappointment over one of Greg's "I'm not thinking anything" responses. He sincerely explained, "Shannon, I'm not smart enough to be having deep thoughts every moment of the day. Sometimes I'm really not thinking about anything. My mind is blank. I'm vegetating. At work I have to think all the time. At home, I want the freedom to let my brain chill. Please don't take this as a sign that I don't love you or don't think about you often."

Perhaps you ask your husband this question occasionally, simply because you want to know him better. While this is understandable, try to refrain from having any expectations about what his answer *should* be when you ask what he's think-ing. If you expect that he should be thinking about you and this is your reason for asking, you are fishing for affirmation or a compliment. But when you ask with pure motives (simply wanting to feel a connection with him in a given moment), you'll be able to accept any answer he gives, regardless of whether it's what you hoped to hear.

Or perhaps you, like Barbara, ask this question as a way of seeking affirmation that your husband still loves you. A more effective way of getting this affirmation is by recognizing your need and inviting him to meet it by telling him something like this: "I am feeling a little insecure right now and need to hear you say that you love me. Will you tell me what you love about me?" He might respond better if you also ask him some direct questions, such as: "Do you remember what you were thinking when I walked down the aisle at our wedding? Do you still feel that way? What's your best memory of our married life?" You get the idea. Don't take it personally if his words don't match up to the imaginary script you dream of in your own mind. Let him connect with you in his own words and in his own special way.

Finally, when we take little things too personally (and get bent out of shape as a result), we can find ourselves creating major issues in our relationship, especially in one room of the house—the bedroom.

A Sigh Is Just a Sigh

This example is a bit personal, but based on the conversations I've had with other women and how we sometimes overreact to the little things in bed, Greg and I feel it's a worthwhile offering.

Six months into our marriage, late one Saturday morning, we had indulged in a big breakfast of bacon, eggs, biscuits, and gravy and were both feeling the overwhelming temptation to unplug the phone and just go back to bed for a postbreakfast nap. As I disrobed, however, Greg got that look in his eye—the look that says, "Ooh, baby! Come over here!" I slipped between the sheets and into his arms, and we began making love.

Afterward, Greg drifted off to sleep while I drifted into a deep depression. The problem? I just knew he was growing tired of me and bored with our sex life. What gave me this impression? Greg had *sighed* in the middle of our lovemaking! It wasn't any sort of passionate sigh, like you'd expect to hear from your spouse while making love. It seemed to me more like a "Gee, I'm tired and wish this were over" kind of sigh. What gave me that impression? Women's intuition. A girl just knows these things, right? Wrong!

When I told Greg how I was feeling, he could hardly contain his disbelief. Here are his thoughts:

A *sigh* is just a *sigh*! I don't understand how one little independent sigh on a very slow morning after a big breakfast could be translated as "I'm not excited about our sex life anymore." When I awoke from my mid-morning nap to find Shannon bawling into her pillow, I was scared that something was really wrong. But when she explained why she was crying, I couldn't believe that she would even entertain such a thought!

We share this incredibly intimate detail of our marriage because it's a perfect illustration of how Satan can take something as tiny as a sigh, blow it way out of proportion in a person's mind, and cause a huge downward spiral in the relationship as a result. Something is said, and the hearer takes it out of context. The speaker is maybe just having a bad day, or is tired, or is feeling stressed because of something happening in the background of life. We are tempted to take it personally, and rather than keeping a short account of offenses, we build a case in our minds to prove that the person really doesn't love us, or respect us, or like us, or appreciate us, or want to be around us. With every negative incident that we let add up in our minds, we stack another brick between ourselves and that person, creating mental walls that only serve to separate us. But it doesn't have to be that way.

IMAGINE THE POSSIBILITIES

Consider how it might impact your marriage for the better if you simply refused to take a small incident, blow it way out of proportion in your mind, and get overly emotional about it. What if you never sweated the small stuff and instead rolled with whatever unexpected punches life throws your way? What if you learned to laugh about your husband's poor sense of direction (or whatever little personality quirk he has that can drive you insane with frustration)? What if you could accept his no without any manipulative drama? What if you learned to give your husband the grace to have his own thoughts and you refused to take things personally? What if you held firmly to the belief that your husband loves you like crazy and desires to be intimate with you whenever possible? Wouldn't it be much easier to ignite and maintain incredible joy and passion in your relationship?

You bet it would. So do yourself (and your husband) a favor and try to remain grounded whenever you sense the temptation to take another emotional escalator ride.

leaving his sidelines

I was recently visiting a friend in Colorado who was born on the same day I was. We frequently compare notes about how we are aging, and the subject came around to how our physical fitness level just isn't the same now that we're rapidly approaching the big 4-0. "You were a pretty active teenager, weren't you?" I asked Kia, also mentioning how I remembered looking at her cheerleading pictures on her mother's wall of fame. She laughed and said, "Remember, I grew up in Samoa. There, anyone could be a cheerleader. Every girl who wanted to was automatically on the team. When I came to the United States to a high school with over a thousand students, I knew there was no way I could make the cheerleading squad. I couldn't even do a cartwheel."

This struck me as funny at the time (and familiar—I never mastered the cartwheel either), and hours later I couldn't get her story out of my mind. How great that those Samoan girls were allowed to be cheerleaders, regardless of their abilities. There was no performance pressure. Joining the squad was no popularity contest. They just did it because they wanted to.

While not every girl aspires to be a cheerleader, there was certainly a time in my life when I did. However, I didn't want to work out every day or attempt those daredevil gymnastic stunts, so I never even tried. But if getting on the team was as simple as raising my hand, showing up for practice, and cheering my team on from the sidelines, I'd have done it in a heartbeat.

Well, guess what. I've discovered it's not too late to fulfill my dreams of becoming a cheerleader. All that's required is that I have the desire. No performance pressure. No popularity contest. No daredevil stunts expected. The only prerequisite is that I want to cheer my man on to victory, in both his on-the-clock and off-the-clock pursuits. Let's look at both types of these pursuits and at some of the ways that a wife can be either a burden or a blessing to her husband.

ADDING TO HIS STRESS

While women often have a mind-boggling number of responsibilities to tend to, we can't forget that our husbands also face a whirlwind of challenges every day. Not only do they need to bring home the bacon, they need to make enough money to save for the future. Not only do they need to get the job done, they need to impress the boss and coworkers and meet quotas and deadlines in a way that shows they are capable, decisive, and efficient.

Your husband faces a plethora of daily pressures, and every hour of his day can sometimes feel like an uphill battle. He needs to know, beyond a shadow of a doubt, that someone is on his side, regardless of how well or how poorly he feels he's doing that day. He needs someone who is committed to rooting him on to success both at work and at home.

Unfortunately, not all men would describe their wives as their biggest cheerleaders. Consider these comments from men we surveyed:

- "I just wish my wife understood that my job is not your typical nine-to-five routine. Rebecca resents me when my pager goes off and I have to leave for work, especially on a day when we have special plans. I can understand her disappointment. I'm disappointed to have to leave my family too. But it doesn't make it any easier when I have to walk out the door knowing my wife is angry with me."

- "I invite Kate to go with me on out-of-town work trips whenever possible, but she says she'd rather stay home than be with me and feel ignored because my attentions are so focused on the event or people I have to interact with. She seems jealous of the time I spend with clients, but it's just part of my job, and that's how I make a living for our family. I wish she didn't feel she had to compete for my time and attention. It tears me up to leave her at home sulking over my having to be out of town *again*."

- "I have really sensed God calling me to leave my practice as an orthopedic surgeon and serve as a missionary in foreign countries. Laura refuses to even pray about it or consider that God may be leading us in this direction. She says she wants me to put my family first, but I think this would ultimately be a very good thing for our family to travel and help incredibly needy people. I can't help but wonder if it's not really about the big salary we'd be giving up to serve as missionaries, and that makes me feel as if she wants me to serve her rather than serve God."

As these quotes indicate, men crave their wives' support, understanding, and encouragement when it comes to their chosen careers or ministry callings.

What about you? Are you ever resentful of your husband's job? jealous of things he gets to do? adamant that he change or not change careers because of how it may affect you?

I realize that there are situations when a wife needs to gently speak up, especially if her husband is a workaholic or regularly ignores the needs of his family. But if you are like me, there are times when your dissatisfaction is born out of selfishness or of jealousy of the time and energy your husband pours into his career, because it takes him away from you.

During those times, consider this scenario: If your husband were unemployed and you had no salary to live on, would his current situation be a welcome change in your wondering how your family would keep a roof over its head and food in the pantry? I don't mean to be melodramatic, but let's put things into perspective. The next time you feel resentful of your husband's career, ask yourself if you have a legitimate complaint and if adjustments can be made. If so, discuss your concerns calmly and respectfully. For example, you might start off with, "Honey, can we sit down and assess how our lives are going right now and talk about what's most important to each of us and to our family?" If you realize that adjustments can't be made for whatever reason, know that your husband needs your encouraging support far more than he needs your resentment. Do what you can to let him know that you are his biggest fan and that you want him to succeed at work and to feel good about his ability to provide for his family. That's the kind of cheerleader he's going to want to come home to whenever possible.

Of course, there are increasingly more stay-at-home dads these days as more and more women are earning salaries big enough to be sole breadwinners. If your family fits this description, I hope you'll lovingly encourage your husband the same way you would want him to be supportive of you if you were staying at home. Don't expect a picture-perfect house, and be willing to help him out when necessary during your off hours. Be sensitive to the fact that his stay-at-home status may be difficult for him to deal with at times (just like it sometimes is for women), and praise him for his willingness to buck traditional roles to serve the needs of your family more wholeheartedly.

With that being said, are you eager to see your guy succeed in the workplace, whether he's routinely in a high-rise office, out on a job site, on the road, or on the home front? Do you want him to feel good about his contributions to society? Do you wish to see his career dreams come true for the benefit of his self-esteem and for his family? We sure hope so.

A husband needs a cheerleader to support him, not just in his on-the-clock responsibilities, but also in his off-the-clock passions. Do you know your husband well enough to know what sorts of activities and interests excite and renew him? what he needs to feel fully alive and excited about life? Sadly enough, I had to learn this lesson the hard way.

STEALING HIS JOY

Greg and I first connected during a Sunday-school outing to a Texas Rangers baseball game. We hadn't known each other long, but I knew I was attracted to him. I'll never forget the look on his face when I said, "I have to run back to the church van for something, but save me a seat *next to you,* okay?"

"Oh, uh, okay!" he responded with a surprised look and a cute little grin. When I took my seat next to him in the stands, Greg was already almost up to his ankles in peanut shells, and he offered to share his peanuts with me. During the first inning he warned me that he'd have to leave early because he had his own softball game to play that evening. I replied that I had a doctor's appointment very early the next morning and said I might leave early with him, if he didn't mind giving me a ride home. Instead of dropping me off at my apartment, he asked if I'd like to come along and watch his game. My subliminal plan worked. A group outing was quickly turning into a one-on-one date.

In awe I watched him play first base. At six-feet-seven inches with an amazing wingspan, Greg kept one toe on the base and reached what seemed like halfway to the pitcher's mound to catch those balls and tag the opposing team's runners. During our courtship, I spent most Saturdays and at least one evening each week in the bleachers rooting Greg's team on. He loved having his own personal cheerleader in the stands, and I loved watching him play.

But all that changed after we married and had children. In hindsight, I was probably resentful that Greg had a recreational hobby that he loved, and I, well, I had the kids to take care of. When I attended his games, my attentions were turned away from first base to make sure that my toddler son didn't fall through the bleachers and onto the concrete below, or to watch my daughter to make sure she didn't stray in pursuit of a hug from Daddy onto the field at a dangerous moment. I even changed diapers on those cold steel bleachers, which my babies didn't seem to mind, but I did. I began to dread going to games.

There was also another reason why I lost my fervor for sitting on the sidelines at Greg's games—one that I'm embarrassed to admit, but I know was definitely a factor. My attentions weren't just turned away from Greg toward my children, but they were also turned toward my own insecurities as I compared myself to all the other softball wives, especially the ones who didn't have children yet. Their bodies were untainted by postpregnancy pounds and stretch marks. They wore cute little outfits that flattered their toned bodies, sleek curves, and tanned skin, and I felt frumpy and intimidated. I didn't like what I saw when I mentally compared myself to the other wives, so I just didn't want to be around them because of the negative emotions that my jealousy aroused.

I began staying home and letting Greg go to his games by himself more and more, even though he urged me to come each time. I thought I was making a point by refusing to go, but after a while, I dreaded the sound of the door closing and the car driving off while I stayed at home with two kids. I didn't like him going to games because I wanted him to stay home with me, and I made sure he knew that before he left. I felt as if softball was a much higher priority to Greg than our family was, and I felt cheated. I came to see softball as a mistress that he was more faithful to than he was to me. I couldn't recognize that softball was the outlet my husband desperately needed to recharge his physical, mental, and emotional batteries.

Then one Saturday night it all came to a head. Greg's team was in the final tournament, which meant that as long as they kept winning, they kept playing. I secretly wished they'd lose so he'd come on home to be with us, but he was gone all day. Finally, he walked in at 9:00 p.m., covered from head to toe with red dirt and wearing a big grin on his face. He quickly announced that he wasn't home to stay. He was just there to grab a sandwich because they had another game at 10:00 p.m. There was a good chance they'd win the championship game and take the first-place trophy. I couldn't muster up any excitement over his news. All I could think about was the fact that he was about to leave *again*. Instead, I announced, "I'm going to my parents', and I'm taking the kids! You love softball more than you love this family, so fine! Just go hang out with your buddies and have a ball!"

Greg's enthusiasm melted into devastation. He couldn't imagine that I'd actually leave him out of anger over this situation and go to my parents' house to spend the night. He begged me not to walk out the door. When that didn't move me, he sprawled his entire length on the floor in front of the door and said, "I will not let you leave me because of this! We can work this out and we will!" I was blown away that he would be so humble as to throw himself in front of the door before he'd let me walk out on him.

When the next softball season began, Greg told his buddies that he had too many things going on to commit to being on the team. He even gave up watching sports on television, which was a drastic change. He used to watch football every Sunday afternoon, but he disengaged from the sport to the point that he didn't even know who was in the Super Bowl from year to year.

Over the next several years, Greg was a teetotaler, not playing or watching any sports out of submission to my desires. But he was also dying on the vine. Without the relief outlet he'd found in softball, he was more stressed about his work and less excited about life. At the time I didn't connect the change in Greg to his withdrawal from sports. But if I had been more committed to seeing Greg's heart and to meeting his needs, I would have seen that even though I had succeeded in getting him to spend more time with our family, I had belittled him for his love of sports and made him feel guilty. I may as well have literally ripped out his heart and stomped on it.

A few years later when our seven-year-old son developed a love for basketball, I frequently encouraged them to go out and shoot some hoops. I wanted Greg and Matthew to bond by spending quality time together. When they wanted to watch a college basketball game on television, I didn't complain about the decorating show on Home and Garden Television (HGTV) that I'd have to miss. I even happily joined Greg and our kids at several professional basketball games.

Then one day it hit me, and I asked Greg, "How hard was it for you to give up sports altogether during those years when I nagged you about it? Is that why you lost your zest for life for a while but seem to have it back now that you and Matthew are enjoying sports together?" Bingo. I hit the nail on the head. Greg explains here how my jealous demands affected him:

I had played a lot of softball before Shannon and I met. It was a fun part of my life and gave me an outlet for pent-up aggression and an opportunity for some male bonding. It's hard to explain how quitting sports affected my life, but I don't think it helped our marriage. It may have shown Shannon that she was, indeed, my first priority, but I became much harder to live with. If anything, it started a downward spiral of resentment in my heart toward her because she just couldn't understand what a vital part of my life sports was. I felt misunderstood and hurt. It felt as if my wife had done a bait-and-switch number on me. Why did I have to crucify my love for softball to keep her happy if my love for softball was one of the things that drew her to me in the first place? It was very confusing to me. The first year that Shannon began attending my softball games was my best year ever. I hit my first home run and loved having my girl in the stands, focusing her attention on my performance.

But when Shannon stopped coming to my games, much of the joy was gone. On top of that I had to deal with the fallout of coming home to a bitter, angry wife. At first I tried to argue my case, but my debating skills were never very good, and Shannon's were supreme, so I could never get her to understand my frustration. She seemed to care only about *my* understanding *her* frustration.

Even though I gave up softball, I felt forced to do so, and while I was spending more time at home, I was not there with a willing heart. There was no joy in Mudville. Casey had struck out.

I greatly regret robbing Greg of the joy of playing softball during those years of our marriage. I was condemning him for loving something passionately and doing it well. How sad is that! In addition, I cringe to think of the many wonderful memories our children would have collected had they grown up watching their dad hit as many home runs and stop as many players at first base as I had witnessed in our earlier years.

While I can't rewind the tape, I can make sure that Greg knows he has my full support when he wants to play or watch sports now. Things are very different these days. He plays basketball on Mondays and Fridays regularly, but he does it during his lunch hour so that he doesn't take away from precious time with our family. This group of players consider their court time as "men's fellowship" that is crucial to their week. If Greg misses a game or two, he feels the stress building up and has to get out and chop down trees or do something else that week to compensate. Like many men, he has a genuine need to engage in some sort of intense physical activity on a regular basis.

I recently drove to the gym during Greg's lunch hour to sit on the sidelines and watch him play. He told me that just knowing I was watching and admiring him helped him shoot better that day—even better than he had shot when he was in his twenties! The guys joked about how he was showing off for his own personal cheerleader, and then afterward several commented that they wish their own wives would come and watch them play (which is a surprise we arranged a few weeks later!).

Greg also watches an occasional game on television, but we try to make a family affair out of it with popcorn and snuggles on the couch. This year he watched his first Super Bowl in ten years and enjoyed every minute of the game, because I wasn't trying to make him feel guilty about neglecting me.

Obviously, if your husband is playing softball several times a week and on weekends or is spending all day every Saturday on the golf course, his love of sports is out of balance. But in most situations, the two of you can reach a compromise if you state your concerns in a calm and respectful manner.

Perhaps your husband doesn't have a passion for sports but rather some other activity that gives him a sense of joy and satisfaction. Perhaps he retreats to the outdoors to hunt, fish, or dig around in the garden, or immerses himself in a new computer software program, or hides out in the basement with his guitar or other musical instrument. Whatever your husband's hobby, I encourage you not to take his passion for it personally. Don't be his opponent by assuming that he uses these hobbies as an escape from his family (which is more than likely not true). Instead, encourage him to do the things he loves and is energized by. When we allow our husbands this time, we inspire them to return to us as much happier campers, with greater desires to connect emotionally with us.

One of the quickest ways a wife can douse the flame of passion in her husband's heart is by leaving his sidelines. So do what you can to help your husband feel your love and support, whether he's at work, at home, or doing something he loves. Be the one who knows him best, loves him most, and cheers him on at every turn.

comparing apples to oranges

Whether it was in a high-school home economics class or as a starving college student, most of us learned early in life how to comparison shop. As a teenager, I remember going from dealership to dealership searching for just the right car, returning a pair of blue jeans that I found cheaper at another store, and even reading *Consumer Reports* magazine before buying my first computer. Learning the art of comparing and contrasting makes us much more savvy shoppers.

However, the art of comparing can be a curse upon our relationships, especially in marriage.

WHY CAN'T YOU BE MORE LIKE...?

One of the most shameful mistakes I've ever made was once saying to Greg early in our marriage, "You just don't seem to approach me with as much whirlwind passion as I'm used to. If you could be a little more enthusiastic in sweeping me off my feet and into bed, I'd be more willing to go there."

He responded kindly but firmly, "Shannon, don't ever compare me to another man that you had no business being in a sexual relationship with in the first place."

It was another *Ouch!* moment in the life of Shannon Ethridge but a much needed wake-up call, pointing out that I had been unfairly comparing Greg to a past lover. If the tables had been turned and Greg had said something along the lines of, "You know, you aren't as thin or beautiful as some of the other girls I've been attracted to. If you would lose a few pounds and fix yourself up a little more, I'd be much more attentive," I would have been cut to the core. I'm sure that in that moment, he must have felt the same way.

After much reflection, I realized that while the guy I was comparing Greg to was a smooth talker, I certainly wasn't the only woman he was smooth with. This man had years of experience wining and dining women, along with several ex-girlfriends and ex-wives to show for it. Had I remained in that relationship, I wouldn't have been able to trust him any further than I could have thrown him.

Greg, however, was a virgin when we married. He didn't have previous sexual experience, but that's because he was saving himself for *me*. Everything that he may have lacked in the suave and debonair department, he more than made up for in the trustworthiness department. When we were dating I never had to worry about Greg looking at another woman or about whether I was just another notch on his relationship belt. He proved himself to me when he watched me walk down the aisle wearing a white gown that gracefully masked all the bitter sexual mistakes I had made before he came along. He hadn't flinched when I confessed all my sordid past to him prior to our engagement. And I had stooped so low as to compare him to a man who didn't value sexual purity at all—his or mine. *Yuck!*

Unfortunately, I'm not the only wife who has fallen into the trap of comparing her husband to other men. Consider these comments and ask yourself if you have ever alluded to such a sentiment in any way:

- "Her husband still takes her out on a date each week and sends her cards and flowers often. How come you don't do that for me anymore?"
- "Why can't you be as handy around the house as my dad? He would have had that problem fixed in no time!"
- "It really makes me feel special when the guys at the office will take a few moments just to talk to me and ask how my day is going. Why can't you show such an interest?"
- "He must really love his wife the way he takes such good care of their yard. How do you think the way our yard looks makes me feel?"

Of course, comparing our husbands to other men is only part of the problem. Sometimes we put ourselves under the microscope of comparison as well.

"I Wish I Were As Pretty As..."

Most of us have someone in our lives who drives us to unhealthy comparisons, whether it's the perky personal trainer at the fitness club, the happy little homemaker next door who has all her photos in a Creative Memories scrapbook and cuts her kids' sandwiches in the shape of stars, or the sexy glamour queens who grace the silver screen. For Jamie, the temptation to compare can come from all angles. She writes:

> When my husband takes me out on a date, I can't help but notice the other women in the restaurant and if they are bigger, smaller, or prettier than I am. If I measure up, then I feel a little puffed with pride. If I don't, I am extremely self-conscious and become focused on myself rather than on my husband. Then he usually takes me to a movie, but I really hate how I feel about myself after the show. Women like Julia Roberts and Sandra Bullock look fantastic, even in their roughest

Boundaries in Friendships

Here is one of the most common questions I receive from married women: "Can I be friends with a man other than my husband?" Talk about a loaded question! First, it all depends on who the man is. If he's a flirtatious type, someone you dated or slept with in the past, someone who cries on your shoulder about how unhappy he is in his marriage or love life, then the answer is *no*! I don't recommend being friends with a man like this.

The best situation is for you and your husband to be friends with an appropriate man and his wife. Both spouses need to know about the friendship and feel comfortable with it. Where there are no secrets, there can be no lies and no grounds for suspicion or jealousy.

Another consideration is your definition of friendship. I have several men in my life I consider friends, but they're not like my girlfriends. I don't call them, and I generally stick to business with them. I don't go to dinner or hang out with them without spouses, and I don't make specific efforts to see them without Greg. I never share anything intimate; my husband is the only man I have those conversations with.

on-screen moments. When I was younger and thinner, female celebrities didn't intimidate me much. But now that I'm in my forties, it's hard not to get depressed when I look in the mirror and imagine that this is as good as I'm ever going to look.

Even when I go to the gym and try to do something positive to change my body (for the one-millionth time), I can't help but notice all of the lean, tight bodies that only remind me why I wish I had taken better care of myself in my twenties and thirties.

Women of all ages can sympathize with Jamie's sentiments. It's easy to compare ourselves to other women and to ruminate on all the ways that we don't measure up. As I mentioned earlier, that's one of the main reasons I didn't want to go to

Nationally known Rabbi Shmuley recommends the following boundaries:

- No dinners together. Public lunch is okay, but no alcohol.
- No long drives or flights together, even for work. Don't place yourself in any situation where romance can grow, such as being alone or sharing secrets.
- Share no information you don't share with your spouse. Do not create exclusivity with someone other than your spouse.
- No ex-lover friends.

If this area has been a challenge for either of you in the past, or if your marriage is shaky, forgo any lunches with male friends as well. Time alone away from others creates intimacy and reason for suspicion in any relationship.

Also remember, time in someone's presence is no longer necessary for an affair. Emotional affairs now come via cell phones and the Internet, so pay close attention to what you do and say in all communications. Here's a good rule of thumb: if you wouldn't say it in front of your husband or pastor, don't say it!

Greg's softball games anymore—because I didn't feel I measured up to the other, "prettier" wives. When we do this, we rob ourselves of our peace, our joy, and our confidence. We also put our husbands in an incredibly tight spot as we fish for the affirmation we need with such questions as "Am I as pretty as she is? as good a cook? as good a housekeeper?" Most men are smart enough to know that the answer to any such question should always be "Of course, dear!" so don't bother asking your husband. It only magnifies your own insecurities in both your eyes and his. It also places the burden of responsibility on his shoulders to make you feel good about yourself, but feeling good about yourself is a gift that only *you* can give *yourself.*

Of course, we'd be doing a great disservice to husbands if we didn't address another comparison that drives many men crazy.

KEEPING UP WITH THE JONESES

Greg has often felt caught between my conflicting desires. From one side of my mouth I'm telling him I want him to spend more time with our family, and from the other I'm telling him that I want a better standard of living. Greg describes here how this impacted him and our relationship:

> One of my greatest challenges as a husband and father has been finding a healthy balance between spending time with my family while still investing enough time in my career to provide the standard of living that Shannon desires. When we had our first child, Shannon wanted to be a stay-at-home mom, and I wanted to make her dream come true. I worked hard to make sure I was climbing the corporate ladder high enough to financially keep up with the ever-increasing expenses of parenting. We established a tight budget and managed just fine. But after baby number two came along, Shannon wanted to move to a bigger house. Our current house had plenty of room for a young family of four—three bedrooms and two bathrooms—so I thought we just needed less stuff, not more space.
>
> When the most charming house in the neighborhood went up for

sale, I knew I was in trouble. It had four bedrooms and two living areas. But it was also fifty thousand dollars more than the house we were in. When we went to look at it, I knew Shannon had her heart set. It was owned by an interior decorator who had fashioned every detail of that house after a quaint Williamsburg cottage. The house was her "calling card" to attract clients. Again, I wanted to make Shannon's dreams come true, so we took the plunge and bought it. Once we were in, we realized that our décor didn't exactly coordinate with the colonial charm of the house, so piece by piece we began replacing furniture, which strained our pocketbook even more. With two babies at home, it didn't make much sense for Shannon to pay a sitter so she could work to help out financially, so the burden fell on my shoulders alone.

Then in the second year of owning this house, Shannon approached me singing the "You don't meet my emotional needs!" song. I was caught in the middle of her expectations. How could I meet her emotional needs when I had to work longer hours to pay for the standard of living she wanted? As beautiful as that house was, I have very few fond memories of living there. Shannon was miserably lonely because much of the time she had only two young children for company, and I was miserable at work worrying about how we were going to buy the furnishings we wanted and still stay afloat financially.

I have to agree with Greg. I loved the look of that Williamsburg cottage, but the three years we lived there were by far the most painful of our sixteen years together. The craving for more stuff to fill that house and the pressure this placed on our budget resulted in far too many disagreements and emotional disconnections.

Remember, most men don't need a lot of stuff in order to be happy. Greg was perfectly happy in a next-to-naked apartment for two years before we got married. While I've learned to decorate on a tight budget, the most important lesson I've learned is that genuine happiness doesn't come from having nicer stuff or a bigger house. Happiness is found in the love we have for one another and the memories we make together as a family.

THE KEY TO CONTENTMENT

How can you refrain from the kind of comparisons that feed discontentment? The opposite of comparing and complaining is, of course, to be content with where you are and what you have, to refuse to let unrealistic dreams of the future rob you of the realization that today really is pretty good. We're not saying that it's wrong to want to improve your current situation, whether it's helping your husband become a better person, improving yourself so that you can be more at peace, or updating your living environment to make it more conducive to happy memory making. Striving for positive change is a good thing—as long as it doesn't come at the expense of marital unity, such as in the cases we've shared in this chapter.

The key to contentment isn't trying to make your husband more like Mr. So-and-So or trying harder to be more like Mrs. So-and-So or having as nice a house as someone else down the block. The key to contentment is avoiding unhealthy comparisons and being thankful for what you *do* have.

Chances are, if you are reading this book, you do have a husband—something most single women would love to have. If you are able to get up and exercise, do so with a happy heart, thanking God for your good health. If you have children of your own, be grateful that you aren't one of the multitudes of women who struggle with infertility month after month. If you have a roof over your head, food in your pantry, and gas in your car, you are actually among the wealthiest people on the planet compared to those in many other countries.

The next time you are tempted to compare apples to oranges, or to compare your own situation to a seemingly better one, remember that God has custom-tailored these blessings especially for you, especially for this season of your life. He has given you a unique size, shape, and personality, all to be used for His glory rather than your own. He has given you a marvelously unique husband and perhaps children, complete with a few character flaws that serve as great reminders that no one is perfect in every way. He has blessed you with a comfortable home where you can take refuge from the world and make memories that will warm your heart more and more with each passing birthday.

Absolutely nothing can compare to the joy of finding contentment in these

Giving Yourself the Gift of Affirmation

Rather than looking to others to make us feel good about ourselves, try looking up to God for His opinion, then looking inward to recognize the things we like and enjoy about ourselves. Also, try one of these exercises:

- Make a list of ten things that you like about yourself. Try focusing on a variety of things, such as your physical, mental, emotional, and spiritual attributes.

- Read through several verses in Proverbs, highlighting the positive scriptures that you feel describe you (focus on encouraging passages, such as the Proverbs 31 woman, rather than discouraging passages, such as the adulterous woman in Proverbs 5!). Thank God for the wisdom He has given you as His own daughter.

- Make a list of the most amazing of God's blessings in your life (things He's done for you, special people He's placed in your life, and so on), then create a "Garden of Blessings." I like to use rocks around a tree, but you might want to use flowers in a planting area somewhere. For each blessing, strategically place one rock or flower in a pretty pattern, or place them around a tree. Each time you walk by this area, smile and remember what a blessed woman you are!

- Carve out an afternoon or evening to do something you absolutely love doing, but do it by yourself. Some ideas are walking, reading, listening to music, enjoying a favorite hobby, and so on. Bask in the quality time with your most intimate earthly companion (yourself!).

- Next time you exercise, think of all the things you do with the particular muscle group you are working on. For example, your arms may pick up children or hug your husband. Your legs may walk you into church. Your eyes read God's Word and make others feel good when you look their way with a smile. You get the idea. With every muscle worked, thank God that He's allowed you to be a temple of the Holy Spirit. Thank Him for accomplishing His work through you.

remarkable gifts that the Lord lavishes upon us. And displaying that joy is the secret to fanning your husband's flame for you. Just ask any husband whose wife has learned the art of contentment rather than the craft of comparison, and he'll more than likely tell you that he is one happy man.

married to Mrs. (Always) Right

One of the most memorable wisecracks I have ever heard came from an elderly man in a nursing home who joked, "Sixty years ago, I married Mrs. Right! I just didn't know at the time that her first name was 'Always'!"

While his comment struck me as cute at that moment, it has since come back to convict me many times because I wrestle with wanting to control the things and people in my life. I even used to jokingly tell friends, "Greg rules the roost, but *I* rule the rooster!" Greg was by far the primary breadwinner. He paid all the bills and tended to the odd jobs around the house, yet I wanted to have the final say in just about everything. I desperately *wanted* control, often because I felt so *out of control.*

DOES THIS SOUND FAMILIAR?

Although I've grown much more secure with myself and my marriage relationship over the years, I can't honestly say that control issues are completely a thing of the past for me. That's why I felt a sense of conviction as I read these e-mails. Marty, married eight years, writes:

> My wife seems to think that her way is the only way to do something,
> especially when it comes to housework and taking care of the children.
> She doesn't even allow me to have my own ideas for getting something
> done. It's *her* way or the highway. She's come unglued when I used a dif-
> ferent kind of dusting cloth than she normally uses. Does it really matter
> as long as I get the dust off of the furniture? One time I put a scented
> air freshener in our bathroom, but it wasn't the scent she normally uses

in that room, so she sharply asked me not to "mix" different scents. How was I supposed to know? I'm also kind of a neat freak and occasionally will take the time to organize the pantry, but then she gripes about how she can't find anything. I feel like the only way to please her is just to shut up and let her tell me what to do and how to do it, but what man can feel good about himself when he's acting like a pushover?

Marty makes a good point. Our husbands aren't mind readers, and they may have their own ideas about how they prefer to accomplish various tasks. As long as things get done, do they really have to get done *our* way? Only if we want to make our husbands resent having to help us.

Here's another example of a typical complaint from men. Brent, married thirteen years, explains:

My wife, Alicia, seems to enjoy a good argument and always has to have the last word, even if it means mumbling it behind my back as I'm leaving the room. Some of her comments make me furious—"I told you so!" or "We'll just see about that!" or even mocking my last words in an incredibly juvenile way. If I respond, I know the argument will just go on longer and make matters worse, but I can't help but wonder, why does she feel the need to have the last word every time?

Does this sound familiar? If so, what might be the reason you seek to win arguments every time or to get that last word in? Is it so you can feel superior? more intelligent or articulate? Are you merely resorting to childish behavior because you've not learned to respond to strife like a mature adult? Or do you try to inflict harm on your husband so that there's some sense of justification or revenge for your own pain?

When we insist on getting the last word, we don't resolve any disagreements. We only cement them in our husbands' minds as they leave the room feeling disrespected and resentful. I'm sure you'll agree with me: winning an argument isn't nearly as important as ultimately winning your husband's admiration and affection. Jack, married less than three years, writes:

My wife often hides behind a spiritual mask. When we disagree on how something should or shouldn't be done, she'll say something like, "Well, I've prayed about this, have you?" or "I really sense God saying…" I do believe she can hear from God, but she treats me as if I can't. I certainly want her to submit to God to a greater extent than she submits to me, but I hate it when she plays the "God card" on me.

Beware of ever playing the God card, as Jack so perfectly phrased it. For many women this is simply a spiritualized form of control over our husbands. If such is the case, can you imagine how God might feel about us using His name to justify our attempts at controlling our husbands? In humility, we need to remember that our believing husbands can usually hear from God as easily as we can, and there's always a possibility that God may give our husbands a word that we've not yet received.

Finally, if you insist on having everything "just so" prior to company arriving, you might also feel a twinge of conviction as you read Rick's words:

The thing that frustrates me most about my wife is that she freaks out if everything's not absolutely perfect when company is coming. It makes me dread opening our home to anyone. She usually has me running around like a mad man doing a ton of chores, but if I'm not going fast enough or if, God forbid, I forget one assignment, she goes berserk. It doesn't make me a lousy husband if something slips my mind on occasion, does it?

No, Rick, it doesn't. Greg had to chuckle when he read this e-mail. Unfortunately, he is painfully familiar with a wife's precompany perfectionist standards. One time I shouted, "Stop leaving a trail throughout the house!" just because he had left an imprint in our bedspread after he sat down on the bed to take off his shoes. Another time I got miffed because Greg kept turning off lights that I had turned on to create a certain ambiance in the room for our company. Yet another time, I came unglued because he forgot to scoop a pile of animal poop off the patio before our guests arrived. I'm not proud of these outbursts, but I've learned a secret. If it's so important to me that certain chores get done before company comes, I make Greg a list the day before. Then he can budget his time accordingly and not have to worry about forgetting something I've asked him to do.

But why do we become so controlling when company is due to arrive? Because we want our guests to feel special, but I also believe it can be a pride thing. We want others to think we are a perfect family who lives in a perfect house. But the reality is, we all have occasional dust bunnies on the floor, toothpaste in the sink, or imprints on the bedspread. Maybe we should focus more effort on developing a hospitable frame of mind before company arrives instead of obsessing over every detail of our houses and every neglectful act of our husbands.

When your husband fails to accomplish a chore you've asked him to do, chances are it's merely a sign that he's human and can forget things (just like you can), *not* a sign that he doesn't love, respect, or appreciate you.

Complaining when things aren't done *our* way…insisting on having the last word…playing the God card…demanding perfection prior to company's arrival: does any of this sound familiar? If so, let's explore more deeply what's behind this relational dynamic.

Understanding the Desire to Control

What's usually behind a woman's quest for control? Experts agree that an overwhelming need to control is actually an outward manifestation of the inward insecurities we feel. When we're good with ourselves, we're usually good with almost everyone around us. But when we're not feeling so good about ourselves, we often seek to assign the blame to someone outside of ourselves, ruminating on such thoughts as, *If my husband were more attentive… If my kids were better behaved… If my home were more in order… If my coworkers were more appreciative… Then my world would be a better place and I'd feel and act like a better person.*

Of course, controlling women will tell you that they *must* be controlling for anything to get done because their husbands are so passive. But it's worth asking ourselves, *Am I controlling because he's so passive, or is he passive because I'm so controlling?*

The roots of male passivity and female control can be traced all the way back to the Garden of Eden. If you'll remember in Genesis 3:6, Adam was actually standing right beside Eve when she took a bite of the forbidden fruit. She was grasping for control of what she thought God was withholding from her. Adam passively allowed Eve to rebel and even followed her example. I have often wondered if, in Adam's mind, not submitting to God's request to abstain from eating the fruit seemed to be the lesser evil than not submitting to his wife's request to partake of it. Regardless of his motive for sinning, Adam's passivity left a lasting mark on humanity, as did Eve's quest for control.

We are following in Eve's footsteps when we seek control rather than submissiveness. When we seek control, we sometimes *create* the exact behavior in our husbands that we abhor. I confess I've been guilty in the past of insisting that Greg do things my way, and then resenting him for not being a stronger leader in our home. I've dragged him into counseling for his "passivity issues" when, in fact, my control issues were ultimately the real root of our problems. When this dynamic is present, it's like what Jesus said in Mark 3:25, "If a house is divided against itself, that house cannot stand" (NIV). It creates a Catch-22 situation for both spouses. She wants him to lead, but she doesn't want to let go of the reins. He feels damned if he gives up control and damned if he doesn't. No one wins when spouses are in a power struggle. We can't complete each other as helpmates if we are competing with one another for control.

Therefore, when women ask, "How do I get my husband to take the wheel and be the leader?" I tell them, "By getting out of the driver's seat!" In most cases, as long as a wife is trying to manipulate and control, her husband will usually ride along in the backseat for the sake of unity and in an effort to keep her happy. But if a wife will trust her husband and follow him, even when she doesn't necessarily agree with how he's driving or where he's taking her, he might just develop the courage or the desire to become the leader that she wants him to be.

A MODEL OF MUTUAL SUBMISSION

Of course, when we talk about trusting and following your husband, we're not talking about blind submission to someone who abuses his leadership privileges and demands that you obey him regardless of the emotional or spiritual cost. That's like a slave-master relationship. Neither partner should seek to control the other.

That's why Scripture teaches us to *mutually* submit to one another and to work together as a team toward a common goal—harmony and oneness. Paul explains the model of mutual submission in Ephesians 5:21–25:

> And further, you will submit to one another out of reverence for Christ. You wives will submit to your husbands as you do to the Lord. For a husband is the head of his wife as Christ is the head of his body, the church; he gave his life to be her Savior. As the church submits to Christ, so you wives must submit to your husbands in everything.
>
> And you husbands must love your wives with the same love Christ showed the church.

Again, notice Paul is charging *both* husband and wife to submit to *one another*. It's a two-way street. And these charges aren't conditional. We can't wait until we feel the other partner has earned that submission before we start doing our part.

Perhaps reading this passage stirs up bitterness because you feel that your husband fails to love you like Christ loved the church. Maybe you are thinking, *Well, if he loved me like that, I wouldn't have any problem submitting to him!* I want to gently remind you that this is not a book on how to change your husband. This is a book on how a woman can change her way of relating so that her husband will respond the way she longs for him to. With that goal in mind, let's think about submission in terms of how it might play out in the corporate world.

AN EXAMPLE FROM THE CORPORATE WORLD

Consider the example of a chief executive officer and a chief operations officer. (For simplicity's sake, we'll refer to the CEO as "he" and the COO as "she.") Ultimately, the CEO is the leader in charge, but he delegates the authority to lead the day-to-day operations to the COO. The COO is free to set goals, direct the staff, make decisions and suggestions, offer feedback, and so on, but she does it as an *extension* of the CEO, not because she feels the CEO is incompetent or unwilling to do it himself. She constructively controls many areas of operation, but she always respects the fact that she's under the CEO's umbrella of authority. Her position isn't a threat to the CEO at all, but rather a benefit and a blessing.

Now apply this same relational dynamic to marriage. Ultimately, God has charged husbands with being spiritual head of the household, but God also created woman as a "helpmate" to man. Think of woman as a COO of sorts who is under her husband's authority, the CEO of their family. She may be the one setting certain goals, calling many shots, directing the staff (or children), making decisions, and so on. But rather than doing so begrudgingly because her husband's not around all day or because she feels he's incapable of doing it himself, she operates in this role with excellence as an extension of him. She's under his authority, but she willingly receives the delegation of certain realms of responsibility as a vital part of his team.

Many women complain that their husbands don't initiate family devotions or prayer time together. So what's wrong with the wife acting as the COO and cheerfully *offering* to read a devotion or say a prayer, or respectfully *inviting* the CEO to do so? You may be amazed at how well received such an invitation, offered with the right attitude, may be. Remember, just because a wife thinks of the idea or initiates more often doesn't mean that she's the spiritual leader. It simply means she's a great helpmate. Here is Greg's two cents' worth on this issue:

> I can't stress enough how important it is for a woman to approach this topic with great sensitivity. It can be a real blessing to a husband when his wife initiates family devotions and prayer time with a happy heart. But when she does it with disdain for him, it makes him feel humiliated and resentful of her. Let me show you what I mean by giving you two different examples.
>
> We send our kids to bed thirty minutes before lights-out with the expectation that they'll read their Bibles or have some sort of quiet time with God. However, one evening Matthew's bedtime of 8:30 came around, but there was less than two minutes left on the clock in a Dallas Mavericks game (which, granted, can go on for more like ten minutes). Matthew would never have understood if I had been legalistic enough to say, "No, you have to go to your room and have your quiet time right now. I'll tell you who wins when I come tuck you in." So I decided to

let him stay in the living room until the game was over. At 8:40, Shannon called me into our room where she was doing something on the computer. With an incredibly condescending tone, she said, "Maybe the kids' quiet times are not a priority to you, but they are to me. How much longer are you going to ignore his bedtime?" She assumed that I was so engrossed in the game that I had lost track of time. But I was well aware of the time and doing what I thought was best, given the situation. I left the room disgusted with her attitude.

Fast-forward several months. One evening as we were going to bed, Shannon looked into my eyes and very sweetly said, "Greg, do you ever worry that we don't spend as much time as we should discussing spiritual matters as a family? I know we take our kids to church and they attend Christian schools, but sometimes I wonder if we could focus more on their spiritual growth here at home. What do you think?"

Shannon's attitude this time was completely different. She wasn't pointing a finger at me. She was looking into the mirror and questioning the reflection, a reflection that I couldn't deny needed improvement. I agreed, thanking her for bringing it up, and together we prayed that God would help us make our kids' spiritual growth more of a priority.

A woman's attitude and approach truly make all the difference in how it will be received and what kind of results she is going to get.

When we wives behave like Mrs. (Always) Right, our rebellion and quest for control only serve to push our husbands away from us and interrupt the connections that we long to have with them. On the other hand, lovingly submitting to our husbands will draw their hearts closer to us.

EXERCISING THE BEST FORM OF CONTROL

If you don't want to douse the flame in your husband's heart by coming across as Mrs. (Always) Right, use the following principles to help you exercise the most constructive form of control—*self-control.*

- *Don't assume right and wrong.* If he approaches a task differently than how you would do it, don't assume that your way is right and his way is wrong. Keep a teachable spirit and see if there is something you might glean from his way of doing things.

- *Focus on the right goal.* The goal isn't perfection or getting things done your way; the goal is to work as a team, maintaining oneness among the teammates. Things certainly have to get done, but not at the expense of harmony in your relationship.

- *Accept* no *for an answer.* If you want him to lead, you have to follow. If he's not leading the way you want him to, don't nag. There's a reason why Scripture says, "A quarrelsome wife is like a constant dripping on a rainy day" (Proverbs 27:15, NIV). By taking no for an answer, you'll be showing him respect—and you may be surprised how much more often you'll get a yes.

- *Disagree agreeably.* In situations where you simply can't see eye to eye no matter what, agree to disagree without personal attacks or manipulation. We have to choose our battles. Before making a big deal out of something and insisting on having your way, ask yourself, "Is *this* the hill I am willing to die on?" If the matter is very serious, consider professional counseling or mediation to help you sort through the issue while maintaining the integrity of the relationship.

- *Commit the matter to prayer.* Rather than manipulate, argue, or try to control, simply pray and ask God to help you see the issue clearly, and seek His guidance on how you should proceed with further discussions. Remember, you may not be considering all the facts. Ask God to help you see the big picture and the role He wants you to play.

- *Don't play the God card.* If God can impress something upon you, He can also impress it upon your husband. Rather than telling your husband that he should do something because God told you (and not him), ask your husband to pray further about a matter before making a final decision, and that ultimately you will submit to whatever he thinks is right.

- *Compliment rather than criticize.* There is a huge difference between criticizing and offering affirming, constructive feedback. Consider the "Oreo cookie" approach—a compliment, followed by constructive feedback sandwiched in the middle, then another compliment. For example, you might say, "I really appreciate the way you help out around the house when I ask you to. In the future, you might find that this dusting rag works better than the one you used, but you did a great job and I love you for it!"

The desire to control things can be a constructive drive in such tasks as maintaining order in a household, managing bills, and juggling schedules for multiple children. But the most constructive use of a woman's tendency to try to control things is to direct those energies inward rather than outward.

We can't control other people. However, we can be very effective at controlling ourselves and maintaining peaceful relationships. You may wish that your husband could think more like you do or be more like you in certain ways. You might get frustrated by his personality quirks. You may want to bite off his head for not doing something when or how you think it should be done. But try biting your tongue instead. Control your temper before it controls you. Wait until you are calm enough to discuss the matter without elevated negative emotion. Then solutions can be discussed while hearts remain soft. And as a result, you remain Mrs. Right in his eyes.

PART IV

igniting
his flame
once again

what men (really) want most

Do you think you know what men really want most? Actually, you might be pleasantly surprised to find out. I'll give you a hint. This deep desire was conveyed in the words of a popular song many years ago.

No, I'm not referring to George Michael's "I Want Your Sex." Although men certainly want sex, that's not what most men say is their number one desire. Nor am I thinking about Aretha Franklin's "R-E-S-P-E-C-T." That's certainly every guy's wish as well, but it's still not numero uno. According to the responses from many of the men polled and interviewed for this book, these song lyrics from James Taylor's "Your Smiling Face" reflect what they want most: *"Whenever I see your smiling face, I have to smile myself."*

Your husband's greatest desire doesn't revolve around sex, sports, sandwiches, sitcoms, or success, but around putting a smile on your face.

What He Sees in Your Smile

I've asked Greg to tell you why this is so—at least from one male's perspective:

A few years ago, Shannon asked what attracted me most to her while we were dating. I remembered thinking how pretty she was the night we first met while playing Twister at a single's game night at church. As we started spending more and more time together, I enjoyed her outgoing and fun-loving personality. I loved the way she jumped in alongside me and started volunteering with the youth group at our church. She has a beautiful face, body, personality, and spirit, but none of those things are what attracted me *most*. What attracted me most was that Shannon was happy whenever I was around (and relatively unhappy whenever we had to be apart). Her smile made me feel really great about myself and my ability to make a woman like her happy.

If you don't believe me, think about it. Pretend for a moment that you meet a guy who is everything you could ask for, gorgeous both inside and out. But if you feel intimidated by him or awkward around him, chances are you are not going to want to spend every waking moment in his presence. Everyone wants to be in the presence of someone who makes them feel good about *themselves*—it's just human nature.

Of course, there were seasons in our earlier years of marriage and parenthood when Shannon's happiness faded into disillusionment and eventually into deep depression. It's no coincidence that during those times, I struggled to feel good about myself. A man's self-esteem is wrapped up in how good of a husband, father, provider, friend, and lover he is. When we're not making the grade and we see the disappointment on our wife's face as a result, it's like looking into a mirror and seeing the loser we've always feared becoming.

When your husband looks at your face, what does he usually see? Does he most often see a smile or a scowl when the two of you are together? Does he see tenderness in your eyes or distance and disillusionment? Based on what he sees, how do you think he feels about himself?

YOU HAVE THE POWER TO TURN NEGATIVES AROUND

Perhaps you are reading this chapter and thinking, *I would be happy if my husband were just more* _____ (you fill in the blank). However, your happiness does not have to depend on your circumstances. In his book, *The Be (Happy) Attitudes,* Robert Schuller tells of a remarkable man whose life is a powerful testimony to the fact that happiness is a choice:

> Dr. Viktor Frankl, an eminent psychiatrist and author of the famous book, *Man's Search for Meaning,* is a living example of [having a] Be-Happy Attitude.

Dr. Frankl, who is a Jew, was imprisoned by the Nazis in the Second World War. His wife, his children, and his parents were all killed in the Holocaust.

The Gestapo took Viktor and made him strip. He stood there totally naked. But they noticed that he still had on his wedding band. As they removed even that from him, he said to himself, "You can take away my wife, you can take away my children, you can strip me of my clothes and my freedom, but there is one thing no person can *ever* take away from me—and that is my freedom to choose how I will react to what happens to me!"[1]

Later Dr. Frankl used his experiences to develop many writings and lectures, as well as a form of counseling (called logotherapy) that has helped thousands of people deal with whatever life brings their way.

Indeed, happiness is a choice, and being happy can simply be a matter of smiling more often. In fact, some studies indicate that our facial expressions are not so much a reflection of our feelings, but that our feelings are largely a reflection of the facial expression we wear.[2] I've experimented with this theory, and it works. The more I smile, the happier I feel. We are free to choose both our facial expressions and our attitudes in any given situation.

When we choose negative attitudes, we radiate negative feelings and can expect to be the recipient of such negativity as well. When we choose positive attitudes, we radiate positive feelings and will receive the same from others. Let me show you how this works. Let's say your husband is in sales and his job involves traveling for two weeks out of every month. How will you choose to respond? You could focus on the downside and complain that you have to carry the load of managing your household without him. And whenever he calls you while he's on the road, you could tell him about all the problems you have to deal with and that you don't know how much longer you can take the stress of his travel.

Or you could choose to be happy. You could deepen his love and appreciation for you by sending him off with a smile on your face as you tell him that you understand how hard it is for him to be traveling so much and that you are proud he is such a good salesperson. When he comes home from a trip you could do something special to celebrate his return—make his favorite dinner and dessert or get a baby-sitter and have a date night. This is the kind of thing that will make him want to come home and stay home as often as possible.

A friend of ours recently faced a huge marital challenge with an "I'm going to smile and make the best of this!" spirit. Jill's husband and a small group of workers were under a tight deadline to renovate an entire hotel building within just a few weeks' time. When he told her, "I'm going to have to work late most nights and work many weekends for a while," she had two choices. Jill could get disgruntled over the situation (not that it would change what was being required of him), or she could do whatever she could to make things easier on her husband.

Fortunately, Jill chose the latter. She put on her work clothes and showed up many evenings to work alongside him, just so they could be together. Other nights she prepared food and took it to him so they could enjoy a dinner break together. Rather than complain, she was a continual source of encouragement. When the project was completed, they both shared in the sense of accomplishment, and they appreciated all the more their return to free evenings and weekends together.

While you may not be able to join your husband at his workplace or go to these extents to be with him whenever possible, you get the idea. The better you make your husband feel about himself (and his responsibilities), the better you'll both feel about your relationship.

Let's be sources of strength and joy for our husbands. Let's choose to be happy, regardless of life's circumstances. I realize your husband more than likely has a few rough edges that can make "happiness" a challenge sometimes. Mine does. But I have rough edges too, and I'll bet you do as well. Truth is, we all do. But we can't wait until everyone's rough edges are all smoothed out before we can be happy. We must choose happiness now, not just for ourselves but especially for our husbands and for our children as well. Consider this passage from *The Proper Care and Feeding of Husbands*:

When it comes to home and relationships, women rule. [It is our responsibility to] rule wisely and lovingly. If a woman does not marry a sociopath or narcissist, then she's got her basic "male package"...a decent creature with simple desires: to be his wife's hero, to be his wife's dream lover, to be the protector and provider for his family, to be respected, admired, and appreciated. Men live to make their women happy.

The cruelest thing a wife can do to a husband is to never be happy. And don't forget, being happy is more an attitude than a reality.[3]

You—more than anyone else—have the power to make your husband's day. You may find it helpful to sit down and make as long a list as possible of things you can be happy about. Even when I'm in the bluest of moods, I can always rattle off a long list of blessings that God has bestowed upon me, such as my salvation, my marriage, my children, good health, a loving extended family, great friends, ministry opportunities, healing for the past, security for today, hope for tomorrow, and so on.

What about you? How long a list can you think of just off the top of your head? Enough to bless your husband with a smile and a warm look of contentment?

THERE'S NO TIME LIKE THE PRESENT

It's been said that the best time to plant a tree is twenty years ago, but the second best time is today. It's the same with choosing to be happy in our marriages. It's a choice that we all wish we had made from day one; but even if we failed to do it then, the second best time to do it is now.

If you're ready to give your husband what he desires most, then take a moment to whistle Bobby McFerrin's old familiar tune, "Don't Worry, Be Happy." But don't just whistle the tune, live the lyrics out loud in front of your husband, and then he'll be happy too!

r-e-s-p-e-c-t

I was surprised when our ten-year-old son, Matthew, came into the room as I was writing this chapter and said, "Mom, I finished my homework. We had to write the exact words that we'd want people to read on our tombstone some day." When I asked what he wrote, he responded, "Matthew Thomas Ethridge: A Respected Man of God."

Out of curiosity, I asked, "How about 'A *Beloved* Man of God'?" to which he replied, "No, I want it to say *respected*." Though still a child, my son was expressing the same deep longing for respect that I have heard over and over again from men of all ages. Sadly, many men feel like a zero around their wives. Consider these comments:

- "I hate it when my wife talks to me like I'm just one of the kids instead of the man of the house. It's humiliating and infuriating."
- "I don't mind a little teasing now and then, but when my wife does it in front of my friends or coworkers, I cringe. It embarrasses me when my wife just blurts out all my faults in front of everyone without considering my feelings or the effects her comments could have on others' opinions."
- "I like it that my wife is an independent thinker and has her own views. I wouldn't want her to change that. But I've often felt like she *never* agrees with anything I say. If I say, 'It's so nice to have clear skies,' she'll say, 'What do you mean clear skies? Can't you see that cloud?' On top of that, her tone of voice implies that I must be a complete idiot. I want her to be her own person, but I also want her to value my perspective on things. Is that too much for a husband to ask of his wife?"

I don't think so, nor does Shaunti Feldhahn, author of *For Women Only*. She concurs that respect is an overwhelming need among men. She conducted hundreds of personal and written interviews, the results of which reveal what men really struggle with internally. Feldhahn writes:

While it may be totally foreign to most of us, the male need for respect and affirmation—especially from his woman—is so hardwired and so critical that most men would rather feel unloved than disrespected or inadequate....

If a man feels disrespected, he is going to feel unloved. And what that translates to is this: If you want to love your man in the way *he* needs to be loved, then you need to ensure that he feels your respect most of all.[1]

If your husband doesn't feel that you respect him, there is no way that you will be able to ignite joy in his heart.

HOW DO YOU REGISTER ON HIS RESPECT METER?

Webster's dictionary defines *respect* as "to consider worthy of high regard." In the book of Ephesians, where respecting our husbands is a biblical mandate for wives (see 5:33), the Greek word Paul uses for "respect" is *phobeo,* which means "to be in awe of" or "to revere."[2] Do you consider your husband worthy of high regard? Does he inspire awe in you? Do you make the choice to revere him?

If you really want to know the truth about how you are doing in this area, ask your husband. Several times throughout the writing process, Greg would ask me to include in this book a principle that he felt was important for wives to understand. I'd often reply, "Ooh! That's good! Have I done that (or not done that) in the past?" He'd usually just smile with his eyebrows slightly raised, as if to say, "How do you think I learned that that's an issue for men?" I suspect that if Greg and I hadn't written this book together, I may never have realized that even though I do respect him, I sometimes do and say things that cause Greg to feel disrespected. My voice gets snippy, or I give him the evil eye in response to something he says. Or I do something I know he won't appreciate, such as spread one of my projects across his desk and leave it there so that he has to clear my things off before he can begin working in his sacred territory. There have been times when I have overexplained something to him, going into far more detail than necessary about things such as what he can make for dinner. He gets a certain look on his face that tells me, "Okay, enough detail, Shannon. I'm a grown man, and I think I can figure things out from here."

What's another surefire way a wife can determine how she registers on her husband's respect meter? Shaunti Feldhahn goes on to offer us this insight into how we can usually tell if we've done something that causes our husbands to feel disrespected:

So how do we know when we've crossed the disrespect line? Thankfully, there is one easy barometer: Check for anger....

Rest assured, if he's angry at something you've said or done and you don't understand the cause, there is a good chance that he is feeling the pain or humiliation of your disrespect....

Notice that one of the main biblical passages on marriage—in Ephesians 5—never tells the wife to love her husband, and it never tells the husband to respect his wife (presumably because we each already tend to give what we want to receive). Instead, over and over, it urges the husband to *love* his wife and urges the wife to *respect* her husband and his leadership. Women often tend to want to control things, which, unfortunately, men tend to interpret as disrespect and distrust (which, if we're honest with ourselves, it sometimes *is*).[3]

Yes, it is unfortunate that sometimes when we are telling ourselves that we are trying to be helpful, what we are really doing is trying to take control and "fix" our husbands. Even though we may tell ourselves we are just trying to bring out the best in him, our efforts to "improve" him send a message of rejection.

If a wife wants to meet her husband's need to be respected, two things are absolutely essential: she must accept him for who he is, and she must choose her words wisely.

ACCEPTING HIM FOR WHO HE IS

Intimacy is risky. As a husband and wife over time reveal to each other who they really are, they both hope that the other person will be unconditionally loving and accepting. If both spouses feel accepted and loved, then emotional, spiritual, and physical closeness usually results. But if one spouse feels unaccepted and unloved, that person will retreat, resulting in emotional, spiritual, and physical distance. To be free to open up and be ourselves in any relationship, we must first feel safe. If we feel unsafe, we will most likely withdraw into ourselves rather than risk trying to connect with the person who causes us to feel rejected in the first place. That's why acceptance is a key factor in building the kind of intimate marriage relationship we long for.

One of the most helpful analogies I've heard is Gary Smalley's "open spirit closed spirit" analogy. Smalley uses a clenched fist to illustrate what happens emotionally to people when we hurt their feelings—their spirit closes. Then his fist blossoms into an open, flat palm to illustrate what happens when we affirm people and make them feel good about themselves—they open up.

Does your attitude toward your husband cause him to shut down toward you or to open up with you? Do you consistently affirm him and encourage him with a spirit of complete acceptance? Or does he feel closed off emotionally from you due to the spirit of rejection he senses from you?

We all have to guard our hearts, and rightfully so, as Scripture tells us, "Above all else, guard your heart, for it affects everything you do" (Proverbs 4:23). God placed in all of us the ability to discern when our hearts are being treated tenderly and when they are being trampled. Human nature causes us to gravitate toward relationships that make us feel good about ourselves. Human nature also leads us to avoid relationships that cause us to feel bad about ourselves.

Remember back to when you and your husband were dating. Chances are, he couldn't get enough of you because your attentions and affections made him feel really good about himself, and vice versa. Of course, marriage can't be one big, long, romantic date, as pointed out earlier. Reality sets in and responsibilities pull us away from each other more frequently in marriage than during courtship. But if you feel an emotional disconnection in your marriage and you sense that your husband is intentionally avoiding you at times, you might ask yourself if he could be feeling a sense of rejection from you.

If so, you might want to carve out some time for an attitude check. Ask God to reveal to you specific times when you were too harsh, too judgmental, or too demanding. If you recognize a spirit of rejection, confess your sin to God and to your husband. Being humble enough to admit that you have failed to show acceptance and respect is the first step in rebuilding his trust.

You also might want to talk with your husband about giving both of you permission to lovingly pull the other aside whenever one senses an attitude of rejection. Both of you need to feel the freedom to say, "My heart is beginning to feel closed toward you, and neither of us wants that. What's really going on here, and how can we get back on track?" or "I sense that your heart is growing cold toward me. Is there something that I've done or said that has caused you to feel this way? I really love you, and I want you to feel fully accepted, so help me treat you the way you deserve to be treated."

Greg and I have given each other permission to say these kinds of things to each other, and as a result we've been better able to keep short accounts with each other and to remain spiritually connected.

In addition to learning how to show acceptance toward one another, we've also had to learn to respect that we are *very* different.

RESPECTING YOUR PERSONALITY DIFFERENCES

The things that draw us toward someone while we are dating are usually qualities that we don't have ourselves, but these opposing qualities can also drive us crazy in marriage. When Greg and I were dating, I loved the way he chose his words so carefully. But after several years of marriage, I began to see this quality as a weakness rather than a strength. I often felt that Greg was shutting me out or was disinterested in connecting with me emotionally simply because he wasn't as talkative as I wanted him to be. When I asked him questions, he would sometimes think about the answer for so long that by the time he responded I forgot what I had asked!

This difference in our personalities made arguing with him incredibly frustrating. I would bark out a question, expecting a quick answer so that I could bark out another question or make my point, but I found myself having to wait so long for Greg to respond that it exasperated me. I would also get frustrated with his preference not to attend social engagements where he'd be expected to mix and mingle with people. He claimed he had "mingle-itis." The more I tried to change him into the person I wanted him to be, the more he sensed that I disapproved of who he really was. Greg couldn't help but feel disrespected, unloved, and less attracted to me as a result of his feeling rejected.

Greg and I can testify to the truth of this passage from Dr. John Gray's *Men, Women and Relationships:*

> When partners do not respect and appreciate their complementary differences they lose their electricity, i.e., they are no longer turned on by each other. Without the polarity, they lose the attraction.
>
> This loss of attraction can happen in two ways. We either suppress our true inner self in an attempt to please our partner, or we try to mold them into our own image. Either strategy—to repress ourselves or to change our partners—will sabotage the relationship....
>
> Every time you try to alter, fix, or improve your partner, you are sending him the message that he does not deserve to be loved for who he is. Under these conditions love dies. By trying to preserve the magic of love through [attempting to reform our mate], we only make matters worse.[4]

Our marriage was suffering because Greg was feeling the pressure to suppress his true self while I was trying to mold him into my image. I couldn't understand why he couldn't be more like me (outgoing and talkative), and I would drag him to parties and places where he could "practice" being more sociable. He would return home drained, not understanding why I thought it was necessary to try to change his more introverted personality. The problem, of course, wasn't *his,* but mine.

My breakthrough came when we studied six unique personality traits in our Sunday-school class—the Harmonizer, the Achiever, the Catalyzer, the Persister, the Dreamer, and the Energizer.[5] I immediately recognized myself as a classic Achiever, but the real revelation came the week I realized that Greg is a Dreamer. Dreamers are cautious and reserved. They never feel the urge to talk, and they need to reflect on things before they can discern what they really think. They get drained when they are around a lot of people, and stress causes them to want to retreat. As I read the description of this personality type, I realized it summed up my husband. The description went on to point out that Dreamers are also out-of-the-box thinkers.

They can often come up with insightful solutions to the problems around them, solutions that others have never imagined. Dreamers are also great under pressure because they never get rattled.

As I made note of all these characteristics that described Greg so perfectly, I realized that his careful, contemplative choice of words was not a fault or shortcoming, but a reflection of the personality that God had gifted him with. Many of the books I have written on sexual issues are filled with the reflective and contemplative insights that Greg has shared with me over the years. His mind is able to juggle an international nonprofit organization's complex finances, my ministry, our church, and our personal accounts. One of Greg's strongest attributes as a Dreamer is that he doesn't get angry, which is good because if I were married to someone more like me, I'd be making him angry all the time, and our kids would grow up in a war zone. These insights into Greg's personality type have helped me better appreciate him for who he is instead of trying to turn him into something he's not.

How has my acceptance of Greg affected our marriage? Here's what he says:

It's great not to feel as if I have to force myself to be more outgoing like Shannon in order to have her approval and respect. Now, rather than insisting that I go places and mingle with people, she asks without any expectations if I'd like to join her somewhere. Most times I go just because I want to be with her, but I appreciate her allowing me to make the choice on my own. When I'm there, she sometimes senses I'm feeling awkward. But rather than drag me into conversations like she did before, Shannon will sometimes wink and remind me about Albert Einstein. He was also a Dreamer and often mistaken for being dumb because of his introverted personality. Because Shannon respects my Dreamer personality, loves me unconditionally, and thinks of me as brilliant, I can find the courage to walk into conversations more than ever before.

Here are a few more words of wisdom from other women who've learned to accept their husbands' unique personality traits and natural drives:

- "I know Phil loves to travel and interact with people. I'd love for him to have a job where he sticks closer to home, but he also wishes I'd be willing to travel with him more often, which is possible now that our kids are grown and gone. But I'm more of a homebody, so I usually tell him to go on without me. The times we are together seem very precious because he feels I respect his need to be 'out there' and he understands my desire to remain 'right here.'"

- "My husband is very much a detail person and feels the need to be in control of our finances. On the other hand, I make more money than he does and can be pretty free with my spending without feeling the need to create budgets and reports of where our money goes as long as we are making ends meet. But because it makes Jim feel better, I try hard to keep track of all my receipts and let him know what kind of major purchases I need to make. He rarely complains that I'm spending too much; he just likes to know where our money is going. I've realized that by my helping him track our spending, I'm respecting the fact that this is a need for him."

If you have struggled with understanding why your husband does the things he does or feels the way he feels about certain things, I recommend that you find out more about personality types. Check with your local library or go online to find books or resources that can help you identify and understand both your husband and yourself better.

Besides embracing her husband's unique personality, what is the best way that a wife can demonstrate that she respects him, both publicly and privately? By choosing her words very carefully.

CHOOSING WORDS WISELY

When Julie met Eric in high school, she thought he was everything she wanted. He was patient, understanding, warm, gentle, and fun. But as time went by, those assets turned into liabilities. She felt as if she had to be his mother to get anything done. She came to view his patience as procrastination, his hard-work ethic as workaholism, his gentle nature as weakness, and his willingness to help others as a lack of boundaries that frequently cut into family time. Rather than respecting her husband, Julie had contempt for him, and she let him know it. She says:

I didn't respect Eric (respect is *deserved,* right?), wouldn't give him verbal admiration (I didn't want to *lie*), withheld sex (*share my body* with a man I didn't respect?!), threw angry tantrums (it was his fault I was mad), nagged and dictated (*someone* had to be responsible), compared him constantly to the men in movies and fiction romance novels (it's always good to aim high!), and gave him the silent treatment for however long it took to get results (well, it was the only thing that worked!).

I actually thought all our problems were his fault. He wasn't doing what *he knew* I wanted him to do. He wasn't making me happy. Isn't that why people get married—to find someone they can count on to make them blissfully happy? But he just couldn't do it. Buckling under the pressure of my attitudes and his own insecurities, Eric emotionally deserted the marriage after seven years, and we divorced six years later. When I look back at my disrespectful behavior, it's amazing that he lasted *that* long!

Unfortunately, sometimes the realization of the part we play in the dance of discontentment isn't clear to us until after the divorce is final.

Julie is certainly not the only wife to use words and tones of voice that demean and devalue her husband, which only serve to push him away.

She Says	He Hears
"Why don't you do it this way? It makes more sense!"	"You're stupid and can't do anything right."
"Why don't you just call a handyman to fix it?"	"You're not smart enough to figure this out."
"Why don't you just stop and ask directions?"	"You're incapable of getting us there by yourself."
"Why don't you stand up to your boss?"	"You're a wimp."
"Why can't you just do what I need you to do?"	"You are an inadequate failure of a husband."

Do any of these sound familiar? We need to remove such phrases from our vocabularies and replace them with words that show acceptance and respect. For example:

- Rather than saying, "Why don't you do it this way? It makes more sense!" a better approach would be, "I'm amazed at how differently we approach tasks. I would have a tendency to do it this way, but I'm glad that way works for you."

- Instead of bemoaning, "Why don't you just call a handyman to fix it?" try, "I believe that you can do anything you put your mind to, but if you decide you need to call a handyman, I completely understand. I wouldn't have a clue how to fix it myself, but I applaud you for trying."

- Avoid complaining, "Why don't you just stop and ask directions?" Instead, simply say, "You love the challenge of navigating foreign territory, don't you? Okay, Columbus, but if for the sake of time you decide we need directions, I'll be happy to go in somewhere and ask."

- Rather than demanding, "Why don't you stand up to your boss?" try building him up with, "I wish your boss understood just what an intelligent person you are and what a valuable part you play on his team! Too bad he doesn't appreciate you like we do around here."

- Instead of, "Why can't you just do what I need you to do?" a better approach would be, "I really need a hero to take care of this for me. When you have an opportunity, could you be that hero?"

If you want to ignite your husband's joy and passion for you, you'll carefully consider your words to ensure that they communicate acceptance and respect. Ask him to tell you what things you say to him that cause him to feel disrespected— and then determine not to use those words again. Think about what respectful words you could use in their place, and then do so.

When you choose your words wisely and demonstrate respect for your husband, you'll reap many benefits. Not only will he feel good because he knows he pleases you, but your children will also grow to revere him all the more, and they will revere you as well. You'll feel much more satisfied with your attempts to be the wife that you want to be. Your marriage relationship will be enhanced, and your family will benefit from the security of a respectful atmosphere at home. Most of all, you'll please God with your attempts to show the respect that your husband, His beloved son, deserves—not because he does everything perfectly to deserve such reverence, but because he is divinely and uniquely created in his heavenly Father's image.

Not only do we need to choose our words wisely in our everyday communication with our husbands, we need to do so even more in the heat of conflict, which is the topic of the next chapter.

a fair fight

Robert, the first boy I had a crush on, hurt me terribly. We met at camp the summer after my sixth-grade year, and we enjoyed hanging out with each other during meals and swim times. One afternoon while playing water volleyball on the same team, we both reached for the ball and grabbed it at the same time. He began trying to wrestle it away from me with great force, so I responded in kind, refusing to let the ball go. In the struggle, I accidentally hit him in the crotch with my knee. Doubled over in pain, Robert eventually regained his composure and proceeded to give a swift kneecap to my pubic bone, just so I could see how it feels. The intense pain brought tears to my eyes and an immediate end to my schoolgirl crush.

Why all this talk of hitting and getting hit below the belt? Because many couples fight this way, hurling insults and killing their affections for one another. When wives choose to hit below the belt emotionally, men feel emasculated, disrespected, and hurt. And how do these feelings affect our husbands and our marriage relationships? Pretty much with the same effect as it had on my relationship with Robert—it causes our fond feelings for one another to fade quickly. Just ask Jennifer.

When she and Jeff first got married, she vowed that he would be the head of their home. But she wanted the best marriage possible, and so she started giving him advice about everything: money, spiritual matters, jobs, friends, hobbies, his role as a husband and father, and sex. When they would get into arguments, she threw darts from past hurts, flung stones of suspicion and insecurities, and hit below the belt about intimate issues. She writes:

One day I got a two-by-four upside my head. We were driving with our three children asleep in the back (or so we thought) down the road discussing a past vacation, something that should not have caused a huge fight. We began yelling, I began crying, and I got sharp-tongued trying to prove my point and prove him wrong. Then Jeff said, "I can't live like this. There is no reasoning with you or pleasing you. I have to walk on eggshells all the time."

You would think that would wake me up, but it took an even bigger two-by-four before I caught on that the problem was really mine. After sleeping on the couch that night, Jeff left for work the next morning silently, with no kiss or good-bye. My oldest daughter woke up crying that morning. I walked in her room and asked what was wrong. She asked if her daddy and I were not going to be married anymore. She said that I talked very mean to daddy. She said it sounded like I didn't love him. *Knock! Knock! Hello, Jennifer!* Not only was I killing my husband's love for me, I was sowing insecurities into my daughters' lives.

If our goal during conflicts with our husbands is to win (change their behavior or viewpoint to match ours) rather than trying to see their points of view, we have the wrong goal. Why? Because then we'll do whatever it takes to win—and we'll either play manipulation games (see chapter 6) or we won't fight fair. Claire, whom we heard from in the first chapter, admits that this dangerous dynamic has already permeated her marriage after only one year:

Last night my husband and I had one of our big fights. He was trying to help me do something, but I got irritated and called him a jerk. Then he called me a witch, and it went downhill from there. That's often the case with us—something little turns into something enormous and insurmountable. After our nasty interchange last night, we didn't speak to one another, and we both went to bed miserable with each other and with ourselves—again. I keep thinking if he were a better husband, I'd be a better wife. But it's not solely his responsibility. One of us has to grow up, and then the other will follow. But I want him to change first!

When it comes to learning to fight fair, I hope you won't hesitate to become the leader if necessary. Regardless of how long you've been married, it's never too late to improve the dynamics of your communication, beginning with avoiding any below-the-belt behaviors.

AVOID BELOW-THE-BELT TACTICS

A significant part of learning to fight fair is avoiding below-the-belt tactics like these:

- *Involving a third party.* One of the worst things you can do is call your mom or sister or best friend and complain about your husband rather than going straight to him with your concerns. Others are powerless over the situation, so you're wasting emotional energy talking about it when you could be pouring that same energy into resolving the conflict with your husband.

- *The silent treatment.* Refusing to talk with your husband rationally about an issue you are angry over accomplishes little except to cause him even more confusion and allow you to build up even more steam over the situation. If you feel you aren't ready to talk calmly yet, take some time to sit and write down your thoughts. This will allow you to let off some steam, process your emotions, and get your thoughts in order before bringing the issue up in conversation with your mate.

- *Yelling or crying.* A calm, rational discussion will get you much further than yelling or crying. Such tactics will likely make him want to retreat altogether. Chances are, you wouldn't resort to yelling or crying with your boss, so use positive tactics in your marriage as you would in the workplace.

- *Criticism.* If you have suggestions for positive behavior that you desire from your husband, present them in a loving, encouraging manner. However, refrain from complaining, criticizing, and, especially, name-calling. Mom's advice will serve us well in marriage—"If you can't say anything nice, don't say anything at all."

- *Sarcasm.* Though often masked with humor, sarcasm is usually intended to cut people down and causes them to feel belittled or even stupid. The truth is, sarcasm is sometimes a more socially acceptable form of bullying, but no one likes to feel bullied. Make every attempt to avoid sarcasm and speak with sincerity when interacting with anyone, especially your mate.

- *Threats and ultimatums.* Don't make a promise unless you mean to follow through with it or else you'll lose your credibility. There's a big difference between "If you can't find more time to spend with your family, you may come home one day to find us gone" and "I fear that if we can't find more time together as a family that we'll drift further and further apart." The first statement puts the hearer on the defensive, whereas the second encourages a compassionate response.

- *Getting defensive.* If your husband expresses a concern, applaud his courage in bringing up the issue and don't get defensive. Pray for God to help you consider his point, and humbly choose an apology over an argument whenever possible.

- *Using buzz words.* Some words should be off-limits in the heat of a discussion—words such as *always* ("You *always* work late!"), *never* ("You *never* talk to me anymore!"), *hate* ("I *hate* the way you procrastinate!"), and *divorce* ("If that's the way you feel, then maybe we should consider *divorce*!").

- *Expecting him to read your mind.* Forget what your mother said when she taught you, "Never ask for something—wait until it is offered to you." In marriage, you often have to ask for what you desire or else he has no idea. Of course, to communicate your wishes, you have to know what you want. Whether it's going out to dinner, taking a walk together, or having some other desire met, feel free to initiate with him rather than getting upset that he's not taking the initiative.

- _____. Ask your husband how you should fill in this blank. Are there any tactics you use during disagreements that he considers below the belt? Is there something you say or do that only makes matters worse when the two of you disagree about something? If so, write it down here.

Of course, fighting fair isn't just about refraining from certain things. There are also tactics we can adopt that will minimize hurt feelings and maximize a quick and constructive resolution. Healthy conflict resolution involves setting some ground rules so we can express our emotions calmly, validate one another's feelings, and work toward a compromise.

SET GROUND RULES

Try to maintain the following guidelines for successful conflict resolution:

- *Limit the discussion to one issue.* Rather than dredging up old issues and previously unresolved arguments, focus your discussion on one issue at a time. This will allow the two of you to concentrate your energies in that one direction and come up with a quick resolution. If you are unable to do that and you still feel the need to punish him for past deeds, it's a sure sign that unforgiveness is a problem in your relationship.

- *Establish a proper time and place for discussion.* We've learned that there are places and times when we have to postpone our discussions for the sake of peace. For example, we try not to argue in our bedroom because it should be a loving place of relational harmony (the place where we make love, not war). We go for a walk instead, where there are no distractions or children present.

  I also have learned not to argue while I'm experiencing PMS. I try to say, "I'm not in the best frame of mind to discuss this now, so can we maybe talk about it this weekend?" For the sake of peace, Greg is happy to put it on the back burner until my hormones level out.

- *Agree to disagree when necessary.* Winning an argument isn't nearly as important as winning his heart. There have been times when Greg and I have disagreed on boundaries for our children, particularly with how much time is too much to spend playing computer games. Matthew knows that when I'm at home and in charge, he can't play computer games for more than an hour per day. But Greg is a little more lenient and will even play computer games with Matthew for extended amounts of time. Greg and I couldn't agree on what we felt was a reasonable time limit, so rather than fuss and fight about it, we simply decided to agree to disagree. We feel it's okay for our kids to know that we disagree on certain issues and that this disagreement isn't a hill that we're going to allow our relationship to die on.

Of course, conflict is inevitable in any close relationship. It's not a matter of *if,* but simply a matter of *when* disagreements arise. Conflict doesn't mean we have a bad relationship or that we are unhappily married. Conflicts are simply opportunities for couples to grow in understanding of each other and to work out amiable resolutions. However, *how* we handle the conflict does have a bearing on the ongoing quality of the intimacy we share. So, in those moments when we don't see eye to eye, it's important not to let our emotions get out of control.

EXPRESS EMOTIONS CALMLY

One of the worst things we can do when we disagree about something is to let our emotions take one of those escalator rides we discussed in chapter 7. Most men find emotional tantrums annoying and will dig their heels in deeper rather than be manipulated by screaming or unnecessary crying.

So keep your voice at a normal level, face your husband, maintain eye contact, and even hold hands or have some part of your bodies touching. This kind of body language is much more effective than a turned back, folded arms, or rolling eyes. Remember, actions speak louder than words.

Whether you are expressing anger, fear, resentment, hurt, or frustration, you can do so effectively without becoming emotionally manipulative. Rather than making accusatory statements ("*You* were the one who spent that money!"), limit your expressions to your own feelings and use only "I" statements ("*I* am worried that we're spending too much money lately"). Instead of saying, "Why do *you* always feel the need to correct me in front of the kids?" say, "*I* feel embarrassed and angry when you correct me in front of the children."

Remember, it's not always *what* we say, but *how* we say it that causes the hearer to be either defensive or cooperative. LuAnn's conversation with her husband, Kurt, demonstrates this point perfectly:

> I've had to learn a lot about fighting fair over the past fourteen years of marriage. For example, I've learned that if something is really important to me, one of the worst things I can do is insist on having my own way and getting emotional if I don't. For example, a few years ago I started thinking about buying camping equipment—a tent, sleeping bags, and everything a camping family would need. Camping was something we

had enjoyed when we first married but hadn't done much since we had had our daughter. When she was about eight, I mentioned a couple of times that I'd like to buy some camping equipment, but Kurt finally said that he didn't see the point since we didn't camp all that often. I was disappointed, but wisdom and experience told me not to press the matter.

However, every time I thought about it, I'd get upset all over again. After praying and asking God what to do with this yearning for camping gear, I finally realized what bothered me so much about his no. I had always dreamed of being a camping family, and I saw buying camping gear as an investment in quality family time together. When I realized that and calmly explained it that way to Kurt, he immediately saw my point and agreed. It was so affirming and satisfying when he didn't pull a power play but was open to seeing my point and coming alongside my vision. If I had approached it any other way or gotten overly emotional about it, I'm not sure the results would have been as positive.

LuAnn is likely correct in her assessment. Insisting on having our own way and emotionally beating up our husbands to get it may be successful in the short run, but in the long run it destroys what we really want most—a happy marriage partner.

VALIDATE EACH OTHER'S FEELINGS

Women often say they want their husbands to communicate more on an emotional level, but for most men to feel comfortable doing that, they must know we honor their feelings, whether we agree with their assessments or not. If your husband shares his feelings, try not to get angry with him for having them. Again, applaud his courage to confront the issue.

Greg and I were out on a date recently and saw a bumper sticker that read, "Men have feelings too! But then, who cares?" I was saddened by the expression because I think it says what many men feel, not just because of the world we live in, but because of the women they live with.

I'm sure that Greg would have to say that he's felt that way on more than one occasion. For example, he has always had a personal aversion to the word *stupid*. Of course, I've never called him stupid, but I have made the mistake of impatiently saying something along the lines of, "Why would we want to spend money on more life insurance? That's stupid!" From Greg's perspective, I may as well have said, "You are stupid for thinking we need more life insurance!" I share this example because one of the main ways I believe we can validate our husbands' feelings is by intentionally avoiding the things that we know would hurt them in any way.

Of course, Greg has had to learn this lesson as well. In our early years of marriage, we'd occasionally go to my parents' house for family get-togethers, where my father and older brother would inevitably wind up picking on me about some petty little something just to get a rise out of me. As the baby of the family, I was used to their teasing, but when my husband chimed in and gave them a little ammunition to use against me (disclosing something I had done or said that simply reinforced what they were teasing me about), the situation wasn't so funny to me anymore. It was all part of the game to Greg, but to me it felt like betrayal. I communicated my feelings to him, and although he didn't really understand why it was such a big deal to me that he not join with my family in poking fun at me, he apologized that he hurt me and agreed not to play that game anymore out of respect for my feelings.

Validating someone's feelings is simply a matter of somehow communicating, "I'm not sure I would feel the same way in this situation, but you have a valid right to feel the way you do, and I can respect and appreciate that." Validation is our way of saying to our spouses, "I'm in your corner. I've got your back. I won't twist this knife or use this information against you or think any less of you because you feel this way. If anything, I think more highly of you for trusting me with your feelings."

And when we can validate each other's feelings rather than take opposing stances, working toward a compromise is much easier.

WORK TOWARD COMPROMISE

In times of conflict, avoid taking the offensive or getting defensive and going head to head against each other. Remember that you are on the same team, fighting for victory over the opposing forces of anger, bitterness, unforgiveness, and so on.

Sadly, most of us enter conflict with one main goal—to win! And we usually assume that for us to win, the other person has to *lose*. But if you are familiar at all with Stephen Covey's *Seven Habits of Highly Effective People,* you'll more than likely recall his success strategy to develop a win-win mentality. To think win-win rather than win-lose is not only more effective in business but also in personal relationships, especially marriage. The most favorable strategy to maintain joy and passion in the midst of conflict is to figure out what kind of compromise can be had so that you both walk away feeling like a winner.

Sometimes achieving a win-win can be challenging. For example, there was a time in our household when I put my foot down, insisting that there will be no more pets indoors! I even felt I had the backing of Dr. Phil, as I watched a show where he asked one husband, "If something is so important to your wife, why can't you make that important to you simply out of love for her?" So that's the song I

Cut Each Other Some SLACK

I have found Randy Fujishin's formula[1] for constructive conflict resolution quite helpful and use a familiar saying to remember it, "Cut each other some SLACK," which stands for:

Sit

Listen

Ask

Compromise

Kiss

Sit down together to put the two of you on the same level and to help set the stage for a focused conversation without distractions. *Listen* to each other with a desire to understand the exact nature of the problem at hand. *Ask* nonoffensive questions to clarify your perceptions of your mate's concerns and provide assurance that you hear what your spouse is saying. Remember you are on the same team, so the goal of every conflict is to find an acceptable *compromise* that both spouses can live with and feel good about. Finally, seal the deal with a *kiss* or expression of affection, confirming your continued commitment to the relationship.

sang to Greg one night—"If it's so important to me not to have indoor animals that shed like crazy and leave pet hair all over the furniture, why can't that be more important to you out of love for me?" I wasn't prepared for Greg's response. He very respectfully and sincerely explained that he had many fond memories of growing up with his cats in the house, and he wanted our children to experience the same. Of course, the kids jumped on Dad's side of the fence, and it was three against one—not good odds.

I decided I'd better get creative and come up with a win-win so I didn't walk away a total loser. I suggested that the cats could remain indoors throughout the year without my complaining *if* everyone else would agree to keep them outside during the heavy shedding months of April through September. I also asked what they'd be willing to do to help me in the house throughout the six months that the animals were free to come inside so I didn't have to spend so much time cleaning. Greg offered to sweep and vacuum. Erin offered to dust the furniture. Matthew offered to feed the animals and sticky-roller the pet hair off the couches and drapes. Everyone in our house won that day, including the cats.

As beneficial as it is to follow these guidelines in resolving inevitable conflicts, there's an even greater measure we can take to maintain peace and harmony in our relationships—learning to prevent conflicts altogether.

TRY TO PREVENT CONFLICT

If couples make time (notice I said *make* time, not *find* time) to connect with each other on a regular basis, we can actually prevent conflicts from forming, or at least prevent them from becoming any more of an issue than they really need to be. Professional counselor Tom Haygood and his wife, Nan, have discovered this secret, and it seems to be serving them well:

As a couple, we made a choice about fifteen years ago. It has made a difference.

Almost every night we sit facing each other and communicate, sometimes for only thirty minutes, sometimes for hours. We talk about our schedule, our plans, our previous day's events, but mostly we relish in our relationship, how we feel, think, hope, etc. We deal with any conflict, keeping a "short account." If a conflict does not get settled, we agree on another time we will bring it back to the drawing board. We keep in touch emotionally with each other.... Does this time spent together come naturally? No. We plan for it, protect it, cherish it, and sometimes labor through it! True love that lasts does not just automatically happen.[2]

Indeed, we don't grow close or remain connected simply by coexisting in the same house and sleeping in the same bed. Lasting love takes tremendous effort. Strong relationships require work. Conflict is bound to come, but it can actually make our marriages stronger if we choose our words carefully, express our emotions calmly, respect each other's feelings, and work toward compromise.

ADOPT A NEW MOTTO

You're likely familiar with the motto "All's fair in love and war." This saying insinuates that there are no rules, boundaries, or guidelines that can't be broken to serve our own agendas. However, if one or both spouses have this perspective, it's lethal to the relationship. Without a strategic plan for maintaining peace and harmony in our relationships, especially during times of conflict, love can certainly begin to feel more like war. We may find ourselves on opposing sides, both battle weary, and wondering how we'll ever win.

Rather than an "all's fair in love and war" attitude, I encourage you to adopt Jesus's motto instead: "If a house be divided against itself, that house cannot stand" (Mark 3:25, KJV). If you learn to flow with conflict rather than allow it to divide you, your family can stand united as you remain strong in your commitment to one another.

The following story from Randy Fujishin's *Gifts from the Heart* paints a beautiful picture of what married life could be like if we learn to fight fair:

From my bed I could see down the hallway into the kitchen where my parents were talking. Dad looked upset as he whispered to my mom across the little table.

Although I couldn't hear the conversation, I could tell they were having a disagreement. After talking for a while, my mom smiled, got up from her chair, and walked over to my father. She hugged him from behind as he laughed to himself....

In junior high I remember asking my mom if she and Dad ever fought with raised voices or fists.

"No," she told me. "I always have a choice when differences arise with your dad. I can become harder, or I can become softer. Marriage is a long haul," she continued, "and I decided during our first years together that I didn't want to harden, so I chose to soften and flow."[3]

Isn't that a great goal for all of us? Let's choose to soften and flow with conflict, building each other up rather than tearing each other down. When words and hearts remain soft and commitments remain strong in spite of any conflicts that may arise, the "happily ever after" part of marriage doesn't seem like such an unattainable dream after all, does it?

a safe haven

Our son, Matthew, and his friend, Oliver, both nine years old at the time, were riding in the backseat of the car. Oliver suddenly leaned over and in all sincerity asked Matthew, "Do you think you'll ever get married?"

Matthew replied, "Someday, I guess. Why? Are you gonna get married?"

Oliver replied, "No way. I don't think I'll ever find a girl who'll let me have deer heads on the walls and a fishing tackle box for a coffee table, so I guess I just won't get married."

It was all Greg and I could do to contain our laughter. Obviously, there must have been a few disagreements over the living room décor at Oliver's parents' house. Greg winked at me and said, "Oliver sounds like a man whose house will be his castle!"

I replied, "Sounds like it will be more like his *cabin* rather than his *castle*."

Greg responded, "To a guy, it's the same thing."

When he spoke those words, a mental light bulb came on. It suddenly made sense to me why Greg had been so adamant that we were never moving again. We live in a guy's paradise—a rustic log cabin home in the middle of over a hundred acres of wooded land, with a creek and multiple trails running through the middle and a pond full of fish just waiting to be caught.

I, on the other hand, could find every excuse in the world why I wanted to find a different house. We had lived in the cabin six years and, being addicted to change, I felt like it was time to find another place and move on. I'd whine, "But Greg, this place is just not me!" I wanted some place lighter and brighter and closer to civilization (shopping). In spite of Greg's feelings, I even set up an appointment with a real-estate agent, thinking that if I found the perfect place, Greg would surely cave in and agree to move, just to make me happy.

When I told him about the appointment, he was bewildered but agreed to go with us to look at a few houses that were more suited to my taste. However, as we explored several possibilities that day, I could read the looks on his face. No other place was as Greg as the log cabin we already lived in. Here's what was going through his mind:

I had this sinking feeling that history was about to repeat itself. Remember the house we occupied in Dallas—the one decorated like a Williamsburg cottage that was the envy of the neighborhood? Shannon loved the house, but I was miserable living in it. I never felt like I could exhale, prop my feet up, and relax—even though it was my own home. What's worse, I had no workshop area to escape to, just to go tinker and let off steam. But to make Shannon happy I had agreed to buy that house, and I would never have suggested moving because I knew how much the place meant to her.

So I was actually relieved when she felt prompted by God to move to the country. Finding an old log cabin home on a large piece of land with such potential was a dream come true—a dream I wasn't ready to give up just because Shannon now thought the house was too small, dark, and rustic to suit her. But I also realized that by insisting that we stay in the cabin, I was essentially doing to her the same thing that had made me so miserable. I wasn't happy living in a froufrou colonial cottage in the middle of the city, but Shannon wasn't thrilled about living the rest of her life in a rustic cabin in the woods. Surely there had to be a compromise.

It may sound silly, but we believe that God used HGTV to save our marriage. I began watching remodeling shows where little dark houses were transformed into wonderful, light, and bright living spaces, and I realized that with some modifications to our log cabin home, maybe it could become a reflection of *both of us*. The spark returned to Greg's eyes when I brought up the idea of staying in our home but renovating it to address the things that I disliked. I wanted to change some rooms to make them much lighter and more colorful than the dark brown interior log walls that I found so depressing and that frequently caused episodes of cabin fever.

The more Greg and I talked about this, trying to be sensitive to each other's needs and personal tastes, the more we realized that our desires for a home were actually more alike than different. Even though shopping trips were few and far between for me, I had to admit that our home was a writer's paradise—perfectly secluded from the distractions of city living. I also realized that the land was far too important to Greg to ask him to give it up. Chopping down trees, blazing new trails for family explorations, and fishing on the weekends were forms of therapy for him. So the obvious solution was to turn the house into a place we both could love, with a delicate balance of masculine and feminine elements. Although there are no deer heads adorning the walls and our coffee table is not a fishing tackle box, Greg loves that his home feels more and more like a castle to both of us.

What Men Want in a Home

Greg's certainly not the only man who desires a home in which he can be himself, relax, and spend quality time with his family. Here are what some other husbands have to say about what they want in a home:

- "All my stuff gets relegated to the garage, the attic, or the trash can. It's my home too, but I don't feel as if our house is any reflection of me, my passions, or my hobbies. When I asked my wife if I could display my hockey trophies on the bookshelves in our den, she looked at me like I'd lost my mind and replied, 'You're kidding, right?' Rather than pick a fight, I pretended that I was kidding, even though I was serious and genuinely wanted them to be displayed somewhere in our home."

- "My wife recently started her own business as a sales consultant for a popular line of kitchenware. While I appreciate her entrepreneurial spirit and willingness to help out with the finances, all her kitchen stuff has taken over our home! She keeps displays set up in the living room so that as people come over, she can pique their interest in the products. It seems like every evening the phone is ringing off the wall, or there are people coming over to look at her displays or to get a catalog. She uses a small desk in our bedroom as her office, and I go to sleep at night and wake up in the morning staring at catalogs and paperwork everywhere. When product shipments arrive, they sit in our garage for days before she gets them all delivered, so I have to park on the street. Sometimes I feel like all this stuff is in *my* way, but other times I can't help but feel like I'm in *her* way. How can I encourage my wife in her business, yet draw some sort of boundaries so that I can enjoy my home once again?"

- "I appreciate how my wife takes great pride in our house, but at home I feel like I walk on eggshells all the time. She wants things kept so immaculate that if I leave a glass in the living room, I am scolded for not putting my dirty dishes in the dishwasher. Does home really have to be a place where everything is kept absolutely perfect? If so, it will never be a place where I feel completely comfortable."

You can't blame a guy for wanting his home to reflect a little of *his* personality and hobbies, wanting to have some territory in the house that *he* can control, and wanting to have the freedom to relax and not worry about keeping everything spotless at all times. Women want the same thing. We want to reflect our tastes in our décor, to arrange rooms to suit us, and to have at least some space where we can just close the door and not worry about it being presentable all the time.

Of course, creating a comfortable home that our husbands can enjoy isn't just about the physical environment, but also about the emotional environment.

EGGSHELLS VERSUS OIL WELLS

There's something so stressful about the block of time between 5:00 and 6:00 p.m. that it's been called the bewitching hour around our house. Maybe you know what I'm referring to. You've worked hard all day, either inside or outside of your home, and now you're faced with the overwhelming decision of what in the world you can throw together for dinner. The kids have either been at your feet all day or are home from school and perhaps lagging behind on getting their chores and homework done or arguing over who gets to watch what on television. The phone begins to ring incessantly—usually annoying telemarketers wanting to sell you vinyl siding or storm windows or to send you on a free vacation that's anything but free, which doesn't sound like an altogether bad idea in this whirlwind moment. You realize that you not only have to prepare dinner and do dishes, but you also have to pay bills, start laundry, attend a committee meeting at church, and create your child's makeshift costume for tomorrow's school play, all within the next three to four hours. The stress is overwhelming, and suddenly your husband walks in, not sure of whether he's stepping into eggshell or oil well territory. Greg explains:

I hate to admit it, but for many years, I often dreaded coming home from the office, fearful of what kind of "door prize" I may get upon my arrival. While our young children were always happy to see me and ran into my arms, Shannon sometimes looked at me with contempt, as if I was the source of all the stress she was feeling at that moment. I entered through the back door, intent on avoiding upsetting her more than she already appeared to be. I often wondered, *What did I do to tick her off? I've not even been here all day!*

Occasionally, though, I would come home to an oil well rather than an eggshell environment. Shannon would just be gushing with sweetness, the table overflowing with my favorite foods. I finally figured out the pattern. After several consecutive eggshell days, Shannon would feel bad and try to make up for it all by going to the opposite extreme. While oil well evenings were far nicer than eggshell evenings, what I really wanted was for Shannon to simply find some balance—a happy medium where she didn't feel the pressure to be Julia Child or Martha Stewart but wasn't feeling like the Wicked Witch of the West, either. It wasn't a big deal to me if I walked in and the house wasn't clean and dinner not on the table. Those things were secondary to just wanting to walk in and find everyone in a good mood. Rather than feeling pressure to have everything perfect for my homecoming, I needed Shannon to be less stressed when I got home.

I think it's safe to say that the mood inside our homes is probably the most important part of their ambiance. We can have it decorated beautifully and immaculately clean, but as the saying goes, "If Mama ain't happy, ain't nobody happy!" Even Scripture supports this theory. Proverbs 21 says, "It is better to live alone in the corner of an attic than with a contentious wife in a lovely home" (verse 9), and "It is better to live alone in the desert than with a crabby, complaining wife" (verse 19). Are there days when your husband would rather be in the corner of an attic or alone in the desert than with you? If so, try to turn your home from a place of strife to a place of sanctuary.

CREATING A SANCTUARY

Home should be a place of sanctuary for the family—a place of peace and rest where our souls and bodies can be fed and healthy relationships fostered. To create such an environment in your home, try some of these ideas:

- *Schedule a daily, fifteen-minute quick clean.* It may not bother some husbands, but most don't enjoy walking into a cluttered house. If you work and have a sitter, ask her to tidy up the house before you get home. Or, if you are home all day, do it yourself. Don't stress about cleaning; just focus on straightening things and making the place more inviting and relaxing. Enlist the kids' help by handing each of them an empty laundry basket so that they can walk through each room and gather any out-of-place items that belong to them. Set a timer for fifteen minutes (ten or even five minutes will work if that's all the time you have), and make it a game as everyone races against the clock to get ready for Dad's homecoming. This is not just for his benefit but for your own sanity and peace of mind as well.

- *Make dinnertime special.* There's a good reason why people are often willing to pay twenty-five dollars for a meal at a nice restaurant rather than five dollars at a fast-food place. It's incredibly nourishing to both the body and the soul to simply slow down, soak up the ambiance of some candlelight and soft background music, eat a nice meal together, and enjoy each other's company. You can create such an atmosphere anytime you want (for even less than fast-food prices) simply by turning off the television, turning on the stereo, and setting an elegant table. Don't save your nice dishes and candlesticks just to impress company a couple of times each year. Who better to make feel special than your own husband and children? And you don't have to spend a lot of money to make a simple, nutritious, home-cooked meal. On occasion I've served Hamburger Helper on china and chocolate milk in crystal goblets, just to create a special feel to our family dinner rituals.

- *Make it easy on yourself.* If you are like me, finding time and energy to cook nice meals is hard to come by. Whenever possible cook a double recipe and freeze half, so the next time you don't feel like preparing dinner, you can just heat up your home-cooked meal. Also, as soon as your kids are old enough, designate one evening each week when they are expected to create the family meal. This can take a load off you and teaches them the art of hospitality at the same time.

- *Give him his space.* Most men want at least a small area of the house that they can call their own and not have to worry about keeping it presentable or decorated to suit others. Whether it's the garage, a home office, a media room, or just a corner of the bedroom, let your husband have a say in what goes in the space and how it's decorated (or not decorated).

- *Welcome him home.* One of the reasons why we love coming home to our children is because they usually make a pretty big production about welcoming us with squeals, hugs, kisses, and wrestling matches. How would you feel if every time you walked in the door, your husband made a point of acknowledging you with a big smile and a warm hello? You'd feel loved, wouldn't you? He feels the same when you welcome him home. Even better, drop what you are doing to wrap your arms around him and give him a welcome-home kiss.

- *Show an interest in his day.* If you ask him how his day was and he responds with more than just "Fine," listen carefully to what he tells you before changing the subject to talk about your day. Chances are, he's giving you clues as to how he's feeling right then, and you need to pick up on those clues.

- *Don't make him your target.* If you've had a difficult day or if something is bothering you, don't take it out on your husband when he walks in the door or when he doesn't jump to do the things you were expecting him to. Try to use him as your sounding board rather than your dartboard, and ask if there's some time during the evening when you could talk to him about what's bothering you.

  If you are just in a bad mood and don't really want to talk, it's okay to simply say, "I'm afraid I'm not going to be very good company tonight, but please know that it's not about you, okay?" He'll more than likely be happy to give you the space you need. If you need a day or a night off to relax and de-stress for the sake of harmony in the house, ask for it!

- *Praise his partnership.* Whenever your husband does something to help out in the house or with the kids, express sincere appreciation. It's easy to think, *Well, it's his job isn't it? Why do I have to thank him for simply doing his part?* But remember, we all like to be appreciated and applauded for doing our parts. It's only natural that such praise spurs us on to want to serve others to an even greater degree.

- *Care more about peace than perfect order.* Don't allow petty things, such as dirty socks on the floor, an overflowing trash can, or a dirty dish in the living room, destroy your peace or the unity in your relationship.

- *Make quality time a priority.* Don't let other people rob you of precious family time! Politely decline invitations to be a part of a group or serve on a committee if it's going to translate into significantly less family time or significantly more stress on you. In the evenings, limit distractions by letting the answering machine screen your calls; you can return calls at more opportune times. Give your family the gift of undivided attention.

The Real You

Creating a safe haven for my family isn't always easy, and I don't succeed at it on a daily basis. But because I love my husband and kids, I always *desire* to succeed at it. It takes time and energy and focus, but it's a ministry that is very worthy of all these things.

It often helps me to remember that the real me isn't the person whom others see teaching from a stage or speaking in front of a camera. That's the public side of me. The *real* me is the *private* side of me, the person with whom my husband and children have to live. If I minister to the world yet neglect my family's needs or harden their hearts toward me because of how busy I am or how difficult I am to live with, what have I gained? Paul answered that question two thousand years ago:

> If I could speak in any language in heaven or on earth but didn't love others, I would only be making meaningless noise like a loud gong or a clanging cymbal. If I had the gift of prophecy, and if I knew all the mysteries of the future and knew everything about everything, but didn't love others, what good would I be? And if I had the gift of faith so that I could speak to a mountain and make it move, without love I would be no good to anybody. If I gave everything I have to the poor and even sacrificed my body, I could boast about it; but if I didn't love others, I would be of no value whatsoever. (1 Corinthians 13:1–3)

"No value whatsoever." Those are strong words, but they paint the picture of just how vital love is, especially in our homes. So, may the love we show our husbands and children through our simple acts of creating safe havens for our families be the kind of love Paul calls us to in the next part of this passage:

> Love is patient and kind [especially when we're home alone with our family]. Love is not jealous or boastful or proud or rude [not even when we can do something better than the person doing it]. Love does not demand its own way [especially when someone else's way is perfectly acceptable, even if different from our own]. Love is not irritable, and it keeps no record of when it has been wronged [or how many times dirty socks are found on the floor]. It is never glad about injustice but rejoices whenever the truth wins out [and whenever he says, "I'll do the dishes"]. Love never gives up, never loses faith, is always hopeful, and endures through every circumstance [even during the "bewitching hours" and PMS]. (verses 4–7)

PART V

throwing fuel on the flame

setting his heart ablaze

A few years ago I attended a beautiful outdoor wedding where the young couple exchanged vows under a towering oak tree. They weren't your typical vows; they were carefully crafted sentiments that the bride and groom had written especially for each other. I don't remember exactly what words were said, but one eloquent line in particular will remain in my mind forever. Looking deeply into her groom's eyes, the radiant bride proclaimed, "And I will freely *worship you with my body.*"

I could tell these words created an undercurrent of surprise in the audience as people turned to look at one another with raised eyebrows and little smirks. I can't say what was going through everyone else's mind, but I was thinking, *What a gift that girl will be to her husband!* My friend obviously agreed, as she leaned over and whispered, "Look at the grin on his face! He knows he's one lucky guy!"

Most brides felt as this bride did on their wedding days and perhaps for months or even a few years afterward. But maintaining such a passion for sex with our husbands can be a challenge. And most men can't deny that this is a challenge they desperately wish their wives would overcome.

SEX ON A SILVER PLATTER

While some women assume it's enough that they are willing to go through the motions once or twice each week to meet their husband's sexual needs, men confess that they crave far more from their wives. Consider these statistics:

- Ninety-eight percent of men said "getting enough sex" wasn't, by itself, enough—it was important to feel wanted and desired by their wives.
- Eighty-six percent of men said that even if their wives offered all the sex they wanted, but offered it reluctantly or just to accommodate their needs, they would not be sexually satisfied.

- Eighty-six percent of men said that it would give them a greater sense of
  well-being and satisfaction with their lives if their wives were interested
  and motivated sexual partners.[1]

These statistics demonstrate that men desire what I've come to call silver-platter sex. They want to feel special and welcomed when making love. They want their wives to sexually desire them.

When a wife loses interest, her husband feels shortchanged. It's really no different than how a woman can feel shortchanged by her husband when he seems disinterested in meeting her emotional needs. Meeting each other's needs, both sexual and emotional, is definitely a two-way street. Our husbands want us to be as excited and passionate about fulfilling their sexual needs as we want them to be about fulfilling our emotional needs.

As I've sought to become a more eager sexual partner for Greg, I've had to learn that sexuality comprises four unique components that are intricately intertwined. I've discovered that by pursuing a physical connection with him, I'm opening the door to a more intimate emotional, mental, and spiritual connection with him as well. This revelation has helped me look forward to our lovemaking as much as I look forward to walking, talking, or worshiping with him. I've been delighted to find that my eagerness to connect with Greg physically has inspired him to connect with me on the other levels as well.

To help you understand your own sexuality so that you can become a more eager lover, let's return to an analogy that I have shared in each of the books in the Every Woman series.

TABLETOP SEXUALITY

Just as a table has four legs that support it, we have four distinct components that comprise our sexuality: the physical, mental, emotional, and spiritual aspects. These four parts combine to form the unique sexual individual who God designed each of us to be. In other words, our sexuality isn't *what we do*. Our sexuality is *who we are*, and we were made with a body, mind, heart, and spirit, not just a body. If one of these legs is neglected, the table gets out of balance and quickly becomes a slide instead. And where might that slide lead? To the pit of marital discontent, or even to sexual compromise, as we may feel tempted to get one of these four needs met outside of our marriage relationships.

When we become disconnected from one of these components and fail to attend to it in a healthy way, the storms of life can wreak havoc on the stability of our marriage relationships. Perhaps you've already experienced such storms and have felt that things are out of balance. Perhaps you are one of the many women who feel their marriages are trapped under a dark cloud, as you've not experienced marital ecstasy in a long, long time. I pray that as you read the chapters in this part, those clouds will give way to new rays of hope and that moments of marital ecstasy will soon return.

In the following pages we'll explore ways you can fulfill your husband's deepest sexual desires by getting more in touch with your own sexuality. We'll look at some attitudes, thoughts, and behaviors that can break one of the "legs" of your sexual desire and damage your marital relationship. We'll also discuss how you can

Erasing (and Embracing) Our Pasts

One day while walking on the beach, my husband and I came across a wedding party. The bridesmaids were making designs in the sand with their bare feet. The next day, the evidence of their art had been completely erased by the tide. No trace remained—only the memory.

At that point I wished that the thousands of women who've confided in me about their struggles over their sexual pasts could be there. I wanted to tell them that whatever they've done in the past, it's been washed away! The tides of time and God's forgiveness have erased it.

If you're still living with the ghost of your promiscuous past, know this: it's gone, girlfriend! Don't let memories of your sexual mistakes haunt you. Yesterday's pain can't be allowed to rob you of today's pleasure. Your past can be erased, and you can use those memories to mark how far you've come in your spiritual journey.

So forget the past, celebrate your progress, and learn what you can from those lessons to become the wife God wants you to be.

strengthen each of those legs, ensuring that you relate with your husband in ways that will bring you closer together.

Please remember that the primary focus of this book is what a woman can do to ignite joy and passion in her husband. If you'd like your husband to learn more about meeting *your* deepest desires, lovingly suggest that he read *Every Man's Marriage*.

SETTING THE STAGE

Genuine sexual and emotional fulfillment can only be discovered within a marriage relationship, not through an extramarital fling, solitary masturbation, lustful fantasies of other people, and so on. God designed the perfect plan of one man and one woman coming together in one unshakable union called marriage, where they can be naked and unashamed, just as Adam and Eve were before sin entered the picture and caused them to hide in shame (see Genesis 2:25 and 3:7).

According to this perfect design, your husband has the starring role, and God has cast you as his leading lady. Perhaps this passage from John Eldredge's *Wild at Heart* about how Ruth used her God-given feminine charms to set Boaz's heart ablaze will help you envision this magnificent role you've been given:

> The church has really crippled women when it tells them that their beauty is vain and they are at their feminine best when they are "serving others." A woman is at her best when she is being a woman. Boaz needs a little help getting going and Ruth has some options. She can badger him: *All you do is work, work, work. Why won't you stand up and be a man?* She can whine about it: *Boaz, pleeease hurry up and marry me.* She can emasculate him: *I thought you were a real man; I guess I was wrong.* Or she can use all she is as a woman to get him to use all he's got as a man. She can arouse, inspire, energize…seduce him. Ask your man what he'd prefer.[2]

Are you ready to ignite the flame of your husband's passion? to inspire and energize him? to lovingly seduce him and be the sexual helpmate that he yearns for? If so, then read on to learn more about how to become a more eager lover and a sexually satisfied wife.

the mental-physical connection

It's late in the afternoon and the telephone rings. Rather than the telemarketer you were expecting, you are surprised to hear that the caller is your husband. He wants to know if he can bring home a baby-sitter so he can take you to your favorite restaurant for a relaxing evening of good food and great conversation. He has no ulterior motive. He just wants to spend time with you and fill your emotional love tank simply because he loves you. Sound too good to be true? Maybe. But then again, maybe not.

Erase that scenario from your mind and envision this one. You pick up the phone and call your husband to tell him that you just sent the kids to a friend's house for the evening. You tell him you don't want to get all dressed up to go out—you'd rather get *undressed* and stay *in* with him! You tell him if he'll pick up a pizza on the way home, you'll set the stage for a wonderful evening of making love together. Do you think he'll be eager to get out of the office? Do you think he'll be experiencing a little joy and passion on his way home to you? You bet.

Now let me ask you: Are you willing to go as far to meet your husband's sexual needs as you desire him to go in meeting your emotional needs?

Many women think that our emotional desires are by far superior to our husbands' sexual desires. We view our needs for emotional connection as legitimate and good. After all, God is exceedingly loving and wants relational intimacy with us. But we may have a hard time imagining that a man's need for sexual connection is just as legitimate and good. And that's where our theology goes awry.

Your husband, and all men, are made in the image of God, and God declared His creation "very good." Did God know Adam and all his male descendants would be visually stimulated and crave physical touch? would so deeply desire frequent and passionate sexual encounters? Yes. God designed men to be this way, and we cannot call unholy that which God has created and called good.

I can't explain this mystery, but I believe that when we get to heaven we'll say "Aha!" when we are able to understand the connection between male sexuality and God's spirituality. In the meantime, we must believe that the wife's role as the sole source of her husband's sexual satisfaction is a high and holy calling.

To fulfill that calling, we must recognize the connection between the mental and physical aspects of our sexuality. If, when we think of being sexual with our husbands, we hit a mental wall that feels impossible to climb over, we are going to quickly extinguish their flames of joy and passion (along with our own flames). But if we learn to scale that wall, on the other side we'll find joy and passion awaiting both us and our husbands.

A Cure for the Common Headache

"Not tonight, honey. I have a headache." It's the old standby excuse, and only she knows for sure whether she really has a headache or not. If we've been married very long, we've probably used that excuse before. But one morning, I really did have a headache. A bad one. I felt the left side of my brain might explode, especially when my husband crawled back in bed with me and started kissing my ear.

I winced and said, "Oh, please be careful. My head is killing me." He snuggled up beside me and got still. I felt so much love and appreciation toward him for taking the kids to school and letting me have a little extra sleep, and I wanted to be intimate with him, but I figured I was out of commission. But then I thought, *I wonder if having an orgasm would help my headache?* I proposed the theory. Greg was happy to be my lab partner. Fourteen minutes later, I was amazed at how much my headache had improved! So much so that when it came back later that afternoon, I proposed another round of therapy.

Many other women tell me they've had success with this theory as well, so next time you have a headache, try this out instead of aspirin.

HITTING THE WALL VERSUS SCALING THE WALL

Many women tell me that they love their husbands and even enjoy an occasional orgasm, but when their husbands try to initiate sex, these wives are often not all that interested. Some have even confessed that they wish sex wasn't a "requirement" in the relationship because they really don't feel much need for it.

If you've had similar thoughts, let me remind you that God created women, as well as men, to be sexual beings. So even if sexual stimulation and satisfaction aren't as strongly felt needs for you as they are for your husband, they *are* needs you have. Perhaps these needs are deeply buried or masked in you, but they're there nonetheless.

There have certainly been times when Greg was interested in having sex but I wasn't mentally prepared for it. I would entertain the thought in my brain for a second or two, just to see if I could muster up any desire whatsoever. If I felt as if I were hitting a wall and couldn't work up enough energy to get over that wall, my response was usually, "No, not tonight," followed by some lame excuse.

However, I have come to understand that a man can take his wife's sexual rejection very personally. It feels as if she's not just saying no to sex but no to him, and no to his love, his attention, his affection, and his desire for connection with her. I also discovered that even if I felt no desire whatsoever at the moment Greg initiated, desire would quickly blossom if I engaged in certain sexual activities out of love for him and out of my desire to receive the love he wanted to give me. In other words, I can choose to scale the wall instead of allowing it to keep me from the oneness that Greg and I can experience.

And what do I usually find on the other side of that wall? Euphoria. Some of our most intensely pleasurable moments have been experienced during times when my brain had initially told me I wasn't interested. I've even thought (and verbalized) several times something to the effect of, "I want you to do this to me every night!" While Greg's sex drive has never been strong enough to take me at my word, it sure sets his heart ablaze to know that I enjoy his sexual partnership enough to sincerely desire such a thing.

Are you ready to learn how to scale mental walls so that you, too, can find euphoria on the other sides? If so, then let's look at the preparation required for such wall-climbing adventures.

PREPARING YOUR MIND AND BODY FOR PASSION

It's been said that for a woman, sexual pleasure and orgasm are 95 percent mental and 5 percent physical, emphasizing the key role that mental preparation plays in women's lovemaking. While no one can assign an exact percentage to the importance that each component plays in creating a pleasurable sexual response, I believe it's true that preparing yourself mentally can result in more frequent and incredibly satisfying sexual encounters.

How can a woman prepare herself mentally for a passionate sexual experience with her husband? Here are a few ideas to inspire you:

- *Think ahead.* Many times we can't work up the energy to do something simply because we have failed to plan ahead. For example, if I know what I'm preparing for dinner tonight and have all the ingredients I'll need, cooking doesn't seem too difficult. But if I've failed to prepare and plan, I will walk into the kitchen at 6:00 p.m. and feel overwhelmed and clueless as to what to serve my family. A similar thing happens with sex. If I walk into the bedroom at 10:00 p.m. with no plans except going to sleep, the idea of having sex before I doze off can feel like a mountain that's simply too high to climb. However, if earlier in the day I've been thinking about how I'd like to thrill my husband (or get a thrill of my own!) and have anticipated such an experience, I can walk into the bedroom at 10:00 p.m. with energy to spare.

- *Tune out distractions.* Mental distractions in the bedroom can be real passion killers. Perhaps it's the telephone that rings in the midst of a magical moment, the television that drones on and on, or the computer announcing, "You've got mail!" Or worse, perhaps it's the kid who gets out of his bed and walks in wanting a glass of water. Do whatever you need to prevent such distractions so that you can focus wholeheartedly on your husband. Lock your bedroom door to prevent surprise visitors, turn off the television and the computer, and take the phone off the hook. This is *your* time, so don't feel bad about tuning out any potential distractions.

- *Create a mood.* It's hard for a woman to feel romantic if she's in a room that is cluttered or that she dislikes tremendously. Spend a few minutes straightening the room regularly so that you have a sense of peace and tranquillity. Consider lighting a candle or turning on some soft music. If you find the décor incredibly uninspiring, ask your husband if you can spend a weekend doing an extreme bedroom makeover. If he knows your motive is to feel more inspired to have sex more often, he'll probably hand you the credit card with a smile and offer to drive you to the paint store.

Of course, mental preparation is only part of the battle plan. Preparing yourself physically is equally important, so here are a few more practical ideas to inspire you:

- *Save some time and energy for him.* Whenever possible, budget your time and energy so that you'll have something left to give your husband that night. Don't put things off until evening if you can do them that morning or afternoon. Carve out free time in your off-hours to just be together as a couple. If you have kids, this can be a challenge. We tell our kids, "We don't do tuck-ins after 10:00 p.m." If they want time to talk with either of us, they have to do it before their bedtime so as not to interfere with Mom and Dad's sacred hour between 10:00 and 11:00 p.m.

- *Pamper yourself!* Don't feel guilty about stealing away for thirty minutes of pampering time to help get you in the mood for sex. If I feel sticky after a long day in the Texas heat or if my legs feel like a porcupine, it's kind of hard to work up much sexual desire. But if I've just stepped out of a warm tub full of Calgon bubble bath with freshly shaved legs, Greg doesn't have to do much talking to get me mentally and physically ready to connect with him. I also recommend you make personal hygiene a part of your daily routine. Regular use of a cleansing product, such as Summer's Eve Feminine Wash (which is a mild soap to use on the external parts of your vaginal area), will give you the confidence to engage in spontaneous sexual play anytime either of you is feeling frisky.

- *Make physical touch a priority.* Even if you don't necessarily feel like having sex for whatever reason, somehow make skin-to-skin contact with your husband as often as possible so that he can delight in your physical attentions. Take a walk together while holding hands. Or sit next to him on the couch with your hand on his thigh while watching your favorite television show. Offer him a back massage, or ask him to rub your feet with lotion. Often just engaging in one of these activities will put you in the right frame of mind to feel more playful and affectionate with your husband.

Preparing yourself mentally and physically can not only help you become a more eager lover, but it can also help free you of any unwarranted inhibitions you may feel.

INHIBITION VERSUS EXHIBITION

When there's no one around but you and your husband, what subconscious thoughts drive your behavior in the privacy of your bedroom? Are you generally inhibited, embarrassed by your body, and more inclined to cover it up so that your husband doesn't see things that you feel shamed by? Or are you generally exhibitionistic, feeling the freedom to let your husband drink you in through his eyes whenever he wants? Excessive inhibition can be a real intimacy buster for both the husband and wife, whereas reasonable exhibition can be an intimacy booster.

Most men crave visual stimulation almost like they crave air and water. When they lay their eyes on something sexy, their bodies experience an immediate, pleasurable reaction. Fred Stoeker calls this a chemical pop in *Every Heart Restored,* a book he wrote with his wife, Brenda. In a conversation that Fred had with his pre-teen son, he explains:

When we look at women without clothes on, there is a chemical reaction that happens in our brains that some say is much like the reaction the brain has to taking cocaine [it's addictive].... When our eyes lock onto images of nude women, pleasure chemicals bathe the limbic pleasure centers in the brain, and because it feels good, we want to come back for another hit (look). Quite often then, our addictive behaviors [to pornography or looking at other women] are not rooted in some lack of love for our wives. Rather, they're linked to the pleasure highs triggered by the images entering the eyes....

[This] chemical pop is not a choice and may not always be conscious. What happens is that the beauty of a woman's body simply hits the eyes and then the pleasure centers of the brain....

Most guys will admit they understand the little pop quite well. It's just a quick little hit...bringing a natural curiosity about women.[1]

Let's face it. As women, we will never understand what these chemical pops feel like. We will never fully understand what it's like to crave visual stimulation. We can see a handsome, toned guy in a Speedo and think, *Oh, yuck! That's disgusting! Put on some clothes!* But rare—very rare—is the man who would be grossed out by seeing a beautiful woman in a string bikini. A man may look away, but probably out of discipline, not disgust. Most men have to learn to cope with and to train their naturally wandering eyes to remain focused on their wives. It's a discipline that requires great determination for a man, and you can help by inspiring him to keep his eyes focused on you.

One of the most wonderful gifts you can give your husband is a "for your eyes only" look at your naked or scantily clad body anytime he wants. Greg recently confirmed this for me in a big way. I hadn't done laundry in a while and was out of clean bras to wear to a church gathering one night, so I put on jeans and a spaghetti-strap camisole that had a built-in bra, with the intention of putting on my shirt when I finished curling my hair. Greg came home from work and saw me in the bathroom in nothing but jeans and that camisole, and we wound up being late to church because he wouldn't stop groping me. Did I mind? Absolutely not! I was very flattered that he thought I looked so sexy. I've come to understand that physical touch is my husband's way of saying, "Woman, I love you!" and I felt *very* loved in that moment.

That night Greg and I saw another woman wearing a similar style camisole, but she wasn't wearing any sort of shirt over it. I noticed that Greg avoided looking at her all evening, but he couldn't keep his eyes off of me in that camisole after

I took my shirt off when we got home. We made love that night, and Greg melted my heart with the words he spoke. Here's his take on the conversation, which I think represents how Christian men feel:

> I am so thankful that my wife dresses modestly in public because I would never want other men gawking at her, but I'm equally as thankful that she's not inhibited at all in the privacy of our own bedroom. I was so overwhelmed by this feeling that night that I couldn't resist telling her, "Shannon, I love how you always let me look at your body! I know I can come home to you and drink in your beautiful body all I want to! And the best part of it is that I don't have to feel guilty about it!"

I encourage you to give this gift to your husband as well. You don't have to dress like a prostitute. Your husband may prefer seeing you in a T-shirt and panties, pretty lingerie, or the workout attire that's too revealing for the public gym but perfect for workouts on the bedroom floor while he's looking on. Just find out what kind of attire (or lack thereof) arouses him most, and then let him catch you in it as often as he catches you in bulky sweats or flannel nightgowns.

I'm going to go even further out on the vulnerability limb here and tell you how Greg's and my conversation continued that night, because I hope it will help you overcome any inhibitions you may have about becoming more exhibitionistic for your husband. When Greg gave me such a sweet compliment about how I light his fire by letting him look at me so often, I responded, "I'll bet you'll love looking at me a lot more when I lose these extra ten pounds!" He looked at my body and said, "Shannon, I can't imagine that you could ever look more beautiful to me than you do right now."

There's a powerful, liberating message in Greg's words, girlfriends. We can't let a few extra vanity pounds cause such inhibition that we rob our husbands of one of the things he craves most—visual stimulation. Your husband is not as concerned with your dress size as he is with your willingness to let him look at you in (and out of) that dress. Most husbands will tell you that they don't need or even want their wives to look like anorexic celebrities. They want to gaze upon their wives' curves, regardless of their size. Your husband wants you to feel good enough about yourself that you are willing without hesitation to let him drink you in through his eyes anytime he wants.

If excess weight is destroying your sexual confidence, seek counseling and get to the root of your weight problem. Usually there is an emotional reason why we overeat, and these reasons are often deeply rooted in our childhood or early sexual experiences. Understanding these emotional connections can free you to make proper nutrition and a healthy lifestyle a priority. And when you feel better about yourself, you'll be much more excited about sharing your body with your husband.

Of course, it's unrealistic to think or expect that a wife will *always* be ready and eager for sex. There will be times when you really are sick or too tired, and that's okay. However, your response to his sexual overtures can either fuel or extinguish the flame of his passion for you.

PROCRASTINATION VERSUS INITIATION

Consider these e-mails from men in response to reading *Every Man's Battle*:

- "It just seems so much easier to masturbate than to face the possibility of my wife's rejection. I've heard no so many times that I've given up much hope of ever hearing yes."
- "I have more confidence asking my boss for a raise than asking my wife for sex. And if my boss rejected my request, it probably wouldn't cut me near as deeply as my wife's rejection."

Do you find these e-mails as sobering as I do? When you are aware of how your lack of interest in sex can hurt your husband, it can motivate you to be more sensitive about how you respond during those times when it's really *not* a good time. So, rather than a cut-and-dried no, consider a more promising reply, such as, "This is not a good time for me right now, but can we carve out some time in the morning or tomorrow night? or this weekend?" Let your husband know that you are interested in connecting passionately with him (ideally within the next day or so), but that you prefer to wait until a more opportune time so that you can be more mentally and emotionally present or physically energized. Then make that time a priority, just as you would want him to make a date night with you a priority. Rather than perceiving this as procrastination or rejection, your husband will feel honored by your conscious effort to seize a more opportune moment in the near future for a passionate physical connection with him. Then he will melt when you make yourself ready and *you're* the one doing the initiating.

Also let him know when you *are* mentally thinking about being sexual with him, even if connecting physically isn't a possibility. Occasionally Greg will be out of town or tied to his desk all day, but I'll call him just to say, "Thinking of you today has put me in the mood! I wish you were here right now!" When a man knows he has an interested partner waiting at home, he's not going to work late unless he absolutely has to.

If you do not feel the freedom or desire to initiate or engage in sexual intimacy with your spouse, then take some steps to remedy this roadblock. An easy first step is reading together with your husband a great book called *A Celebration of Sex* by Dr. Doug Rosenau. He is an excellent Christian counselor and sex therapist, and many couples (ourselves included) have found his book to be incredibly insightful, nonshaming, and beneficial to their sexual relationships. Also, don't hesitate to call 1-800-NEW-LIFE to locate a good counselor or sex therapist in your area if needed. That's what they are there for, and your sexual relationship is far too important an aspect of your marriage to ignore any issues that inhibit sexual intimacy.

I want to close this chapter with an inspirational analogy that illustrates how eager lovers approach lovemaking.

LIGHT-BULB SEX VERSUS LASER-BEAM SEX

Consider for a moment two objects: a light bulb and a laser beam.

The power of a single light bulb is limited because it sends light rays in many different directions. A light bulb in one corner of a dark room lights that corner relatively well, but it doesn't provide ample light for any other corners of the room. Its power is simply too limited.

However, with a laser beam, light rays are parallel to one another and focused in a single direction instead of fanning out in all directions. Such a beam of light can travel great distances because of its focus and strength. We've even figured out in this modern day that the light rays of a laser beam are so powerfully concentrated that you can cut metal or perform surgery with them.

Now consider two types of sexual connection in marriage—*light-bulb sex* versus *laser-beam sex.* We engage in light-bulb sex when we spread our mental and physical energies in many different directions (such as toward the kid who needs to be disciplined, the laundry that needs to be washed, the friend we need to call, how much we wish we could get "this" over with, and so on) rather than focusing on our husbands. Such a connection may satisfy the immediate physical urge for sexual release, but its power to bond a couple together mentally, emotionally, and spiritually is greatly limited.

With laser-beam sex, however, both spouses concentrate their mental and physical energies on each other, just as rays of light are concentrated in a laser beam. They strive to meet each other's unique needs for physical and emotional intimacy. They make time for sexual intimacy a priority, even scheduling time alone together especially for this purpose, if necessary. They are physically and mentally present with each other, fully experiencing the intoxicating moments of pleasure and comfort with their mate.

Doesn't laser-beam sex sound much more appealing and ultimately satisfying to you than light-bulb sex? Sure. And which do you think would ignite more joy and passion in your husband? No doubt, he'd love to have you mentally, as well as physically, present during lovemaking. There's nothing more satisfying than knowing that you are the center of attention in your mate's mind, especially during sexual moments together.

If you are feeling inspired to connect mentally and physically with your husband, read on as we look at making a powerful spiritual and emotional connection.

the spiritual-emotional connection

One of my most surprising discoveries about sexuality came entirely by accident, and based on the number of e-mails I get each month from readers of *Every Woman's Battle,* many other women have stumbled upon the same discovery. What is that discovery? There is an incredibly fine line between spiritual and emotional connection and sexual passion. I'm just not very proud of *how* I made this discovery.

Greg and I had been married less than five years when I volunteered to be a summer camp counselor. I went to the camp expecting to get swept up in serving the needs of the teenagers. However, I got swept up in an inappropriate emotional fling with Scott, a single male counselor.

I am sure you are wondering how I could have let that happen. In my mid-twenties and incredibly naive about the dynamics of emotional affairs, I honestly thought that my actions were completely pure because Scott and I were not doing anything "sexual." We worshiped together during the evening services. We led Bible studies together with our coed small groups. We talked intimately about spiritual issues, sharing our favorite encouraging scriptures. We prayed together, holding hands only because we thought that's what people should do when they pray. As the week went on, the battle in my mind began to rage. Scott felt far more like a new boyfriend than a brother in Christ. Going home to Greg felt like a letdown.

A few days later, Scott began showing up at my house to spend his afternoons off with me while Greg was at work. It wasn't until Scott and I wound up in each other's arms that it dawned on us both that our feelings for one another had crossed the line, that confessions had to be made to my husband, and that new boundary lines had to be drawn in the relationship to avoid further inappropriate involvement. That's when I realized that there is a powerful connection between spirituality and sexuality. No wonder it's a theme in many books and movies, such as *The Grapes of Wrath, The Thorn Birds,* and *The Scarlet Letter.* Where there is a strong spiritual connection, a strong emotional bond quickly forms—and that leads to sexual passion, which is why the only man with whom you should seek a deep spiritual and emotional connection is your husband.

God designed marriage to be the place where a couple can be naked and feel no shame (see Genesis 2:25), and I believe His intention wasn't just for physical nakedness but for spiritual and emotional nakedness as well.

GETTING SPIRITUALLY AND EMOTIONALLY NAKED

Many couples mistakenly assume that sex is a *means* of closeness and intimacy, but the physical connection in marriage should be a *response* to an even deeper level of intimacy—spiritual and emotional intimacy. When a woman inspires spiritual and emotional intimacy in her relationship with her husband, she'll be a much more eager sex partner.

In the earlier years of our marriage, neither Greg nor I understood the importance of making a spiritual and emotional connection rather than just a physical one. There were many times that I thought I had married a sex addict, and Greg probably thought he had married a frigid prude.

How did we formulate these opinions? Because by the time I got my clothes and makeup off, brushed my teeth, and climbed under the covers, Greg's motor was already running. He'd look at me with a hopeful grin and say, "You want to have sex?" For him, the desire to have sex seemed to come out of nowhere, whereas the thought wouldn't have even crossed my mind. Without the opportunity to warm up to the idea, I responded coldly to the invitation. I would usually reply, "No, just hold me and let's talk." Most of those times when he tried to initiate again before going to sleep, I felt irritated or hurt that he didn't respect my earlier no.

But I noticed there were other times that the idea of giving my body to him became much more appealing as we talked, especially if we prayed together. Greg didn't have to pray either. Even if I suggested, "Can we pray?" and he responded,

"You go ahead," I found myself feeling closer to Greg as I poured my heart out to God in front of my silent husband. For me, prayer seemed an aphrodisiac of sorts, and the spiritual and emotional connection we made during this time often paved the way for incredible physical connections after the "amen" was said.

Of course, Greg wasn't always up to talking and praying at great length every time he desired sex. Maybe your husband has expressed a similar preference—that he doesn't want to *talk,* but rather *touch.* Perhaps he doesn't want to *pray,* he just wants to *play.* In those times, I've found that it helps to combine the two activities—playing and praying.

For example, as you and your husband come together, you can silently pray, *Lord, I may not feel like doing this right now, but I offer sex with my husband as an act of worship before You.* As you begin to rub his chest, visualize what's behind that rugged exterior and pray (sometimes aloud, sometimes silently), *Lord, thank You for my husband's heart. Thank You that he loves me so much, that he finds me attractive, and that he desires to be sexual with me.* As you become one in the flesh, silently pray, *Lord, thank You that You have knit us together as husband and wife. Help us remain true to our commitments to You and to each other. Strengthen us as a couple and help us to be in one accord.*

You get the idea. If the spiritual and emotional connection is what you are craving and the physical connection is what he is craving, swirl the two together and both of you can go to sleep satisfied. I think you'll find it can greatly enhance your enjoyment of the sexual experience. When two human beings make a spiritual and emotional connection, the physical sexual desires follow very naturally. God can supernaturally draw you toward each other as you draw toward Him. And as God draws you toward your husband sexually, his heart will certainly be set ablaze by your renewed interest and eagerness.

It's important to acknowledge, however, that some men don't feel safe enough (or aren't mature enough in their faith) to want to engage in spiritual acts, such as worship or prayer with their wives. When this is the case, the worst thing a wife can do is read this chapter and then badger her husband about his lack of investment in a spiritual connection. It would be even worse if she blames him for her lack of physical desire. These responses will only increase the distance between a husband and wife. Genuine intimacy can only be *inspired,* not *required.*

So what can you do if you would like to connect with your husband spiritually and emotionally, and he's not responsive to that idea just yet? Simply work on the things you have the most control over—those attitudes discussed in earlier chapters that foster mutual acceptance and appreciation. It may have taken your husband years to build up the wall that separates the two of you spiritually and emotionally, and it may take a significant amount of time and patience before the wall will be lowered. Your willingness to take emotional risks, however, may go a long way in encouraging him to do the same.

BE WILLING TO TAKE EMOTIONAL RISKS

Women are generally more emotionally stimulated than men, so we should also consider leading the way in demonstrating emotional vulnerability. Sometimes we allow unspoken insecurities to wreck our moods and put distance between us and loved ones, but when we voice those insecurities and ask our spouses for encouragement, prayer, or just a hug, we can gain the strength to keep fighting whatever battles we face in life. So don't keep what's going on inside you to yourself, even if it seems insignificant or irrational. Be willing to tell your husband things such as:

- "I'm feeling really crabby these days and I don't know why."
- "I'm struggling with feeling secure when it seems our finances are so out of control."
- "I feel like I'm not as good a mother to our children as they deserve."

When a wife is willing to take a risk and admit her feelings and even her failures, she opens the door for her husband to humbly admit his own. While it was incredibly difficult for me to confess to Greg about the emotional affair I had with Scott, God redeemed the situation and taught both Greg and me something about ourselves that we might not otherwise have recognized. Greg explains this revelation from his perspective:

> Shannon's emotional affair was definitely a wake-up call for me. Even though I was her husband, I had overlooked the importance of connecting spiritually, not just sexually, with her. We were involved in church, but I wasn't leading her and encouraging her spiritually as I should have.

The only time we prayed together was a brief blessing before a meal. We studied the Bible individually and privately. I wasn't asking about what God was teaching her, and I wasn't sharing with her what I was learning, either. We were spiritual Lone Rangers of sorts, living under the same roof and sleeping in the same bed, but oblivious to the incredible connection we were missing out on.

It took time to heal and begin to trust her again once I knew about this affair. But I knew I couldn't lose any more opportunities to make a spiritual connection with her. We began praying together that God would help me forgive her, that He would help Shannon forgive herself, and that we would learn how to worship, study Scripture, and pray

Invite Him into Your Healing Process!

For years I never told my husband I'd been sexually abused by my uncles. Why? Because I thought it didn't affect me and I didn't want to be "damaged goods" to him.

But about six years into our marriage, I finally took my counselor's advice and explained to Greg everything that had happened to me between the ages of eleven and thirteen. As I explained it to Greg, he exclaimed, "Is that why you rarely kiss me since I grew a mustache?" I had never made the connection to my memories, but I couldn't deny their sense. The next morning, Greg shaved off his mustache and scooped me in his arms to catch up on the months of kissing we'd missed. I felt so incredibly safe in his arms and discovered a new level of sexual passion for my protector.

If you've suffered any sort of sexual abuse, please know that I am so sorry you had to endure that. But don't let your abuser rob you of any more than he already has. Invite your husband into your healing process, share what you've experienced, and let his love be a healing balm to your soul.

together so that neither of us would be vulnerable to extramarital temptations like that.

Her confession also gave me the courage to admit that I'd not been 100 percent faithful, either. As vulnerable as she was being with me about her spiritual and emotional longings, I couldn't just pretend I'd been a perfect saint since our wedding day. I had to admit to Shannon, to myself, and to God that my lust for visual stimulation had led me down some roads that I wasn't proud of either. Fortunately, Shannon understood and gave me the same grace to be human that I was trying to offer her.

Not long after taking these emotional risks with each other, we went away together on a retreat, with no other agenda but to spend time with the Lord and with each other. That's when we first noticed the newfound, deeply passionate connection during our lovemaking that Shannon mentioned earlier. We intentionally invited God into our bedroom, and as a result, we discovered one of the best feelings I can imagine this side of heaven. We knew everything about each other—the good, the bad, and the ugly—yet we loved each other with every ounce of our beings. No couple should miss out on experiencing this kind of genuine intimacy. It's absolutely euphoric and incredibly healing to the human soul.

When we take emotional risks and inspire our husbands to do the same, we may find ourselves in conversations or situations where we have to turn our attentions fully toward the act of forgiveness—both the receiving and offering of such.

BE QUICK TO FORGIVE AND TO ASK FOR FORGIVENESS

Don't let past sin intimidate you into a life of shame and sexual disconnection. We all have our own unique struggles (whether they are spiritual, mental, emotional, or physical). Husbands and wives have to learn how to fight battles *together* rather than allowing them to create turmoil in the relationship. The key to fighting together instead of fighting each other is being honest with yourself and with each other, freely forgiving each other, covering each other's back, and spurring each other on toward victory. When you experience overwhelming temptations that pose threats to your marital oneness, who better to ask accountability from than the person who has a vested interest in your ability to overcome that issue?

Yes, in taking off your mask, you run the risk of losing your husband's respect if he fails to understand your struggle or if he takes it too personally. But you also stand to gain his respect and deeper levels of spiritual connection and sexual intimacy when you no longer have to pretend to be someone you are not. Knowing that Greg is aware of all the ugly stuff in my past yet is still by my side in the present and looking forward to a continued future together gives me a great sense of safety and security. It also makes me want to give him the gift of my body as an expression of my love for him.

While we are on the topic of forgiveness, I want to address an issue that frequently comes up in counseling situations. Some women admit that they hold grudges toward their husbands for luring them into sexual relationships prior to marriage, and some use this pain to justify the fact that they are less-than-eager lovers. They seem to drag a victim mentality around like a ball and chain. At the risk of sounding callous, sometimes I (very gently) ask these women, "Did your husband *rape* you prior to marriage? Did he hold a gun to your head? Could you have walked away if you truly wanted to?"

Some respond, "But I told him I was weak in this area and I needed him to be strong for me!" News flash: *We all have to take responsibility for our own weaknesses and actions.* What sexually aroused guy isn't going to feel an overwhelming temptation to pursue a woman who announces to him breathlessly, "When it comes to sex, I'm very weak! Help me!" *Yeah, right.* And who was there to help *him* resist *you?* A weak-willed woman can be a stumbling block to even the strongest of men.

I'm not saying your husband doesn't have to take responsibility for his own actions. Perhaps he does owe you an apology, but you may also owe him one. It takes two to tango, and you didn't bow out of the dance before it took a dangerous dip. Set your husband free by forgiving him for any lack of discretion during your premarital relationship. Then forgive yourself for your own lack of discretion. By doing so, you can both be set free from the painful memories of past sexual mistakes and learn to celebrate the sexual freedoms you can now enjoy as a married couple.

Before we wrap up our discussion about spiritual and emotional connections, I want to make one last point: one of the most spiritually sacred acts of worship a husband and wife can engage in is being sexual with each other.

RECOGNIZE THE SACREDNESS OF SEX

As pointed out in chapter 5, a vital part of our ministry in marriage is meeting each other's needs—including each other's sexual needs. However, a number of the husbands who responded to my questions about what wives do to make their husbands' hearts grow cold reported that their wives see sex as a secular, worldly act rather than as a sacred act of worship. To follow are two responses that reflect what many husbands said.

Victor, married eighteen years, said:

My wife spends all day catering to the needs of others and helping people in a variety of different ways, and I love that about her. She's a schoolteacher who helps kids improve their reading skills; she sings in the church choir; and she serves on the women's ministry committee and volunteers in the children's Sunday-school department. But when she comes to bed at night, I can tell by her body language that she's saying, "I don't have anything left for you, so please don't ask!" If I suggest reading the Bible, doing a devotion, or praying together, she's good with that because she sees those things as spiritual and worthy of time and energy. But she doesn't see any spiritual benefit to meeting my sexual needs. When she's so busy ministering to everyone but me, I feel like her last priority, and it makes me resent her.

Ted wrote:

Angela wants me to spend time talking with her every day. She wants me to pray with her and with the kids every night. I'm happy to do these things because it means so much to her and to our family. But when she tells me (either in so many words or by her actions) that she thinks I want sex far too often, it makes me feel like a pervert. Why can't women understand that sex is as important to a man as conversation is to a woman?

Several husbands said that their wives seemed to pick and choose which scriptures they obeyed. These wives are into the verses "love your neighbor" and "husbands, love your wives as Christ loved the church," but they often ignore the second half of the verse: "The husband should not deprive his wife of sexual intimacy, which is her right as a married woman, nor should the wife deprive her husband" (1 Corinthians 7:3) and "The wife gives authority over her body to her husband" (verse 4). These husbands expressed frustration—and understandably so. After all, sexual intimacy is God's idea. It is not dirty or worldly. Sexual intimacy, according to God's design, is the most powerful way that two humans can connect with each other. When a husband and wife come together and become one through sexual intimacy in the presence of God, they are reflecting the nature of the Trinity. When couples view sex as sacred, it can become a wonderful act of worship.

A nonbeliever once heard me say this while I was speaking on sex and marriage. He interrupted me, yelling out, "So maybe Christians should just stay home and have sex on Sunday mornings!" I think I floored him with my response when I replied, "If that's what it takes for a man and wife to have the opportunity to make a spiritual connection in the bedroom, then I believe God would be pleased." Of course, what I meant is that the worship that takes place in our bedrooms as we are naked and unashamed, in accordance with God's plan for marriage, is just as holy as the worship we offer sitting in a pew wearing our Sunday best.

Don't get me wrong. It's admirable for a woman to be actively involved in her local church. It's good for her to be hands-on in her children's lives, to fulfill various social roles and responsibilities, and to have a career if she so chooses. However, if the combination of all those things causes you to have no energy left over for sexual intimacy with your husband, then you're too busy. Consider scaling back your office hours or dropping out of a church committee or two so that you can make more time and have more energy to minister to your husband's sexual needs. Sex isn't a secular act that we squeeze in between our spiritual activities. It's one of the most important spiritual activities in existence—and you alone can rightfully fill that role. A wife is the only human on the planet whom God has ordained to satisfy her husband's sexual needs. What a unique opportunity we have been given to minister to our husbands in such a powerful way!

Of course, our husbands won't be the only ones who will benefit. Consider the following from Max Lucado's book, *It's Not About Me:*

> Sex according to God's plan nourishes the soul. Consider his plan. Two children of God make a covenant with each other. They disable the ejection seats. They burn the bridge back to Momma's house. They fall into each other's arms beneath the canopy of God's blessing, encircled by the tall fence of fidelity. Both know the other will be there in the morning. Both know the other will stay even as skin wrinkles and vigor fades. Each gives the other exclusive for-your-eyes-only privileges. Gone is the guilt. Gone the undisciplined lust. What remains is a celebration of permanence, a tender moment in which the body continues what the mind and the soul have already begun. A time in which "the man and his wife were both naked and were not ashamed" (Genesis 2:25).
>
> Such sex honors God. And such sex satisfies God's children. Several years ago *USA Today* ran an article with this lead: "Aha, call it the revenge of the church ladies." Sigmund Freud said they suffer from an "obsessional neurosis" accompanied by guilt, suppressed emotions and repressed sexuality. Former Saturday Night Live comedian Dana Carvey satirized them as uptight prudes who believe sex is downright dirty. But several major research studies show that church ladies (and the men who sleep with them) are among the most sexually satisfied people on the face of the earth. Researchers at the University of Chicago seem to think so. Several years ago when they released the results of the most "comprehensive and methodologically sound" sex survey ever conducted, they

reported that religious women experienced significantly higher levels of sexual satisfaction than non-religious women.[1]

Did you catch that? *Religious women are more sexually satisfied than nonreligious women.* I believe this is so because when the spiritual component of our sexuality is healthy, we experience the freedom to more fully experience the physical component. Obviously, Marian has become a believer in this theory as well. She shares:

I used to enjoy sex with my husband on occasion, but most of the time I was just going through the motions and usually felt guilty about

Turning Red Flags into Red Fingernails

Every once in a while I get an e-mail from a reader that I just have to share. Check out this testimony from Elizabeth:

Dear Shannon,

I had a bit of a breakthrough with my husband recently, and I know it's thanks to your books. Will has asked me several times to paint my fingernails and specifically to paint them red. I've never wanted to and always just declined without really thinking about it.

Well, after reading your book one night and asking Will what intimate stuff he'd like me to be more open to, he brought up the red fingernails thing. Immediately I felt my emotions recoiling at the idea, but for the first time I decided to figure out why I didn't want to do it rather than just decline automatically.

Get this: I realized the only woman I knew who typically had red fingernails was my maternal grandmother— a bitter, materialistic, and emotionally removed woman. Once I realized this, I was able to let it go, and I painted it afterward. I wasn't raised to be a Christian, but I was raised to be a "good girl," and my mentality was that it wasn't proper for a woman to enjoy sex like a man does. Thankfully a friend invited us to a Family Life Conference where we heard Dan Allender speak on how sex was designed by the Creator for our enjoyment and that engaging in sexual relations was actually an act of worship to God. Though I wasn't very interested at the time in having sex more often, I was very interested in worshiping God as often and as wholeheartedly as possible. So I responded more warmly to my husband's advances and even began initiating myself. This sexual paradigm shift has resulted in a much deeper

my nails red the very next day. While I'm not there yet as far as feeling sexy about them, I certainly like what they do to my husband.

I'm now looking more deliberately at why I do or don't do certain things sexually. I'm trying to look at things I'm uncomfortable with from a removed perspective, and it's helping me find where I've gotten some of my sexual beliefs. Once I put aside prior bad experiences (such as childhood molestation) and put them in the context of intimacy with my husband, some have been appealing to me for the first time.

I asked Will if he's noticed any difference in me lately, and he said I seem a lot more forward about sex, and he likes it because there is less "hinting around," which has often only led to disappointment and confusion.

Bravo, Elizabeth! What an example. Ladies, I hope you'll think about any areas where you've been sexually blocked and discover new ways to warm up your bed.

level of passion than I ever imagined possible—in my relationship with my husband, in my relationship with the Lord, and even in my own self-acceptance. Simply put, I'm a much happier, more fulfilled woman.

Marian has learned many of the secrets to becoming an eager and satisfied lover.

Would you like to feel much happier in life? experience greater fulfillment? feel a much deeper connection with your husband and with God? I hope so. But just in case there are some unaddressed issues still holding you back from becoming an eager lover, let's explore a few of the most common burning questions about sexual intimacy in marriage.

his and her
burning questions

As we were working on this book in the spring of 2005, Greg and I held an event with the help of our local church called Taking Your Marriage Over the Top: A Sex and Oneness Conference. Forty-four couples, ranging in age from early twenties to late sixties and ranging in marriage lengths from four months to over forty-two years, attended the event. The conference consisted of four sessions focusing on spiritual, emotional, mental, and physical intimacy. During the event we passed out index cards and encouraged individuals to anonymously write down any questions they had about sexual intimacy but were too fearful to ask in public, and then we answered each one at the closing session.

Several of those questions were so painfully honest and so representative of what many Christian men and women struggle with that I decided to address them in this book. But before diving into the questions and answers, let me briefly share with you the six questions I use as filters for discerning what's okay and not okay in the bedroom. The first three questions come from *Intimate Issues* by Linda Dillow and Lorraine Pintus;[1] the last three come from my partner in the Every Man series, Stephen Arterburn.

1. *Is it prohibited in Scripture?* If not, we may assume it is permitted. "Everything is permissible for me" (1 Corinthians 6:12, NIV).

Dillow and Pintus searched from Genesis to Revelation to discover everything that God has to say about sexual behaviors. They concluded that Scripture prohibits the following sexual acts:

Fornication—immoral sex, including intercourse outside of marriage

Adultery—sex with someone who is not your spouse (Jesus expanded this definition in Matthew 5:28 to include not just physical acts, but emotional and mental acts as well)

Homosexuality—sex with someone of the same sex

Impurity—defilement due to living out a secular or pagan lifestyle

Orgies—sex with more than one person at a time

Prostitution—money received in exchange for sexual acts

Lustful passions—unrestrained, indiscriminate sexual desire for men or women other than your marriage partner

Sodomy—sex between two males (in contemporary usage, the term is sometimes used to describe anal sex between a man and woman, but this is not a biblical use of the word)

Obscenity and coarse jokes—inappropriate sexual comments in a public setting

Incest—sex with family members

2. *Is it beneficial to the relationship?* Does the practice in any way harm the husband or wife or hinder the sexual relationship? If so, it should be rejected. " 'Everything is permissible for me'—but not everything is beneficial" (1 Corinthians 6:12, NIV).

3. *Does it involve anyone else?* Sexual activity is sanctioned by God for husband and wife only. If a sexual practice involves someone else or becomes public, it is wrong, based on Hebrews 13:4, which warns us to keep the marriage bed undefiled.

4. Is the act *known* by your spouse? We should refrain from sexual acts that we have to commit in secret.

5. Is the act *approved of* by your spouse? We should refrain from sexual acts that our spouses don't approve of.

6. Does it *involve* your spouse? We should refrain from sexual acts that don't involve our spouses.

In the following pages you'll likely recognize how we used these questions as a filter through which to sift out what we believe is biblical truth about sexual matters. We'll begin with some of the questions that men asked, then share the burning questions that women asked anonymously.

HIS BURNING QUESTIONS

Is it okay for a woman to stimulate herself with her hand for her to achieve an orgasm during intercourse? This seems perfectly okay to me, but my wife worries that touching herself would be sinful.

There is a big difference between touching yourself while being intimate with your husband and touching yourself privately for the purpose of independent sexual arousal without your partner. Using our six-question filter, let's consider each of these acts.

FILTER	SELF-STIMULATION WITH YOUR MARRIAGE PARTNER	SOLITARY MASTURBATION
Is it prohibited in Scripture?	Sexual stimulation within marriage is never referred to negatively in the Bible.	See 1 Thessalonians 4:3–5; Hebrews 13:4; Colossians 3:5–6; Ephesians 5:3
Is it beneficial to the relationship?	If both partners feel it is acceptable and pleasurable.	No, because it creates separation and fosters secrecy.
Does it involve anyone else?	No.	While the answer would be no if you are thinking about your husband, the answer would be yes if your sexual fantasies during masturbation involved someone other than your spouse. According to Matthew 5:28, such fantasies are sinful.
Is the act known by your spouse?	Yes.	No.
Is the act approved of by your spouse?	In this case, yes.	In most cases, no.
Does it involve your spouse?	Yes.	No.

Some individuals find it sexually arousing to watch their spouses stimulate themselves sexually as part of sexual foreplay. Again, I believe this is okay and that Scripture does not forbid it as long as it is known by your spouse, approved of by your spouse, and involves your spouse.

Are there any times when masturbation is okay, for example, if there is a time when being together isn't possible?

Some married couples must live separately for extended periods, such as in the case of military service or lengthy business trips. If this is your situation, discuss beforehand how you will handle any sexual tension either of you may experience during the absence. For example, if one partner travels for a week at a time, you may decide that saving your sexual appetites for your reunions would be the best for your relationship (after all, absence makes the heart grow fonder, right?). But if the separation could last for several weeks or even months, a husband and wife may decide that masturbation may be the best way to keep their sexual appetites from causing them to stray outside the marriage. If this arrangement is prayed over and mutually agreed upon, and if you each focus your mental fantasies on your marriage partner, then you should feel assured that there is nothing unacceptable or inappropriate about this exception to the "no solitary masturbation" rule. Obviously, this is merely *our* opinion, so we urge you to seek the counsel of the Holy Spirit if you are in this situation.

My wife is unable to have intercourse for medical reasons. Can you recommend other acceptable ways that we can be sexual? In other words, is intercourse the only proper form of sexual expression between a husband and wife?

While it's important to enjoy sex only according to God's plan and to avoid the scripturally forbidden acts mentioned earlier in the chapter, couples don't need to be legalistic about what's proper in the bedroom between husband and wife. While some Christians jokingly say that the only appropriate way for a couple to have intercourse is with the lights off and in the missionary position, they have no biblical basis for this position. (Pun intended!) Some Christians also believe that oral sex is an unholy act, but this opinion has no scriptural basis. In fact, the Song of Solomon has numerous references to oral pleasures and in no way condemns the act.

As long as a sexual position or technique is not offensive to either partner and is found to be pleasurable, then it's okay as long as it sifts successfully through the six-question grid—Is it prohibited in Scripture? beneficial to the relationship? limited to the married partners? Is it known, and approved of, by your spouse? Does it involve your spouse and bring the two of you together rather than separate you? Any sexual expression is acceptable as long as it successfully meets these criteria.

How does a husband deal with a woman who enters marriage with these myths: sex is evil, it is sin for a woman to enjoy sex, and only a whore initiates sex?

Very patiently. Unfortunately, many of us grow up hearing "good girls don't," and it's hard to put a wedding band on your finger and shift gears to "good girls do!" However, if this is an issue in your marriage, we recommend that you do a study together on Song of Solomon. Pastor Tommy Nelson at Denton Bible Church has a highly acclaimed, in-depth lecture series on the Song of Solomon, which can be ordered online at www.thesongofsolomon.com. *Intimacy Ignited,* written by Linda and Jody Dillow and Lorraine and Peter Pintus, is also a great resource that can enhance your knowledge of the Song of Solomon. A careful study of Scripture will reveal that God created sexual pleasure for married couples to enjoy without inhibition or guilt.

Keep in mind that this mentality is often adopted by women whose parents had a very dysfunctional relationship or by women who were sexually abused as children. When this is the case, a wife should see a professional counselor for help in dealing with the root causes of why healthy sex within marriage isn't an appealing proposition.

Is it wrong for a woman to offer sexual favors as bribery to get her husband to do the things she wants him to do?

As we've seen, sex can be a powerful tool, and while some husbands may enjoy being bribed in such a way, using sex to manipulate someone was never God's intention. To have a healthy relationship, a wife needs to offer sex with no strings attached, out of love and commitment rather than as a bargaining tool.

One possible reason for this dynamic is that when a woman is single and dating, she has a certain power over a man. She knows, *I've got something you want, and I'll decide when you can have it.* In withholding sex until the honeymoon, she uses her sexual power in a beneficial and godly way. However, after the vows are exchanged, this mentality needs to change. She needs to embrace the idea that *I've got something you want, and because I love you and I've committed to being your wife and your sole source of sexual satisfaction, you can have it whenever you'd like.* Of course, I'm not talking about being a sexual doormat to be walked all over without any concern for her needs or personal boundaries. I'm simply saying that sex is to be offered freely in a marriage relationship, not used as bribery.

Quantity Sex Versus Quality Sex

Recent headlines have revealed a special emphasis on married couples having frequent sex. I completely agree, but could the focus on quantity be an enemy of quality in our sexual relationships?

I'm all about quickies when necessary and squeezing in time for squeezing each other in passing. But if that's all there is—a focus strictly on the physical release with little attention to emotional connection— a woman can begin to feel like nothing more than a sexual vending machine. For women that's like a diet of candy bars. They fill you up, even satisfy for a time, but they ultimately leave a soul undernourished. A good steak dinner is important now and then too.

To set the table for a quality sexual experience, for example, when our kids were younger we had "fish stick and Tater Tot night." The kids went to grandma's for fish sticks and Tater Tots while we went back home and took advantage of two hours to lie around naked, talk about things we couldn't talk about with young children around, and indulge in leisurely sex. Now that our kids are older, we enjoy "youth group night" when our teens go to church and we go into the "upper room" (our master bedroom) for a quiet evening together.

If you don't have a game plan for a few quality sexual experiences in the coming weeks and months, develop one!

HER BURNING QUESTIONS

How much information should I share with my spouse about former relationships?
This question is best discussed prior to marriage so that there are no dark secrets or unexpected surprises for either partner after you've already walked down the aisle. However, even when we've been honest about our past prior to marriage, sometimes a guilty conscience can eat at us and cause us to wonder, *Would he really love me if he knew the whole truth of what I've done in the past?*

Just a few months into our marriage, this question haunted my thoughts. Even though Greg knew that I was not a virgin when we married and that I'd had multiple sexual partners, I wondered if he could possibly remain committed to me if he knew the reality of how many sexual relationships I'd been involved in. I listed every relationship I could remember and then approached Greg with the list, a heavy heart, and tears in my eyes. He said, "You can tell me whatever you need to in order to clear your own conscience, but there's nothing that I feel the need to know. I didn't marry you because of who you used to be, but because of who you are today and who God made you to be in the future. There's absolutely nothing on that list that could make me love you any less."

I hope your husband would have a similar response, but if he expresses a desire to know anything more than your regret over past mistakes, you don't need to give him specific names, places, positions, or acts. Such information only serves to create new trauma in his mind, especially if you run into those people, return to those places, or engage in those specific acts together. Keep in mind this guideline: the details are not what need to be confessed—only the sin. All you need to tell him is that you sinned sexually prior to meeting him. The only person who needs to know the specifics would be a counselor who is helping you process the whys of your past mistakes so that you can avoid making more of them in the future.

My husband doesn't seem to be interested in having sex very often or at all anymore. What's wrong?
Therapists report that they're seeing more cases of depressed male libido.[2] If a married man isn't interested in having sex with his wife, one or more of the following issues is behind his lack of desire:

- As a man enters into his forties, fifties, and beyond, his sexual libido often declines, but it doesn't usually diminish altogether. If he isn't old enough for Medicare just yet, this is probably not the primary issue.
- He may be receiving his sexual release outside of the marriage relationship, for example, through pornography and masturbation or through an affair. There's no way of knowing for sure unless you ask him and he gives you an honest response or unless you actually discover him in the act. If such a confession or discovery is made, we highly recommend that you seek counseling together if he's willing. If he's unwilling, seek counseling on your own to help you sort through your feelings and examine your options as to what your response needs to be to his actions. I also recommend that you read *Every Heart Restored* as you seek to heal from the pain caused by what undoubtedly feels like sexual rejection.
- Your husband could very well be experiencing a hormonal imbalance, poor testosterone production, or erectile dysfunction. Encourage him to see a doctor about his diminished sex drive and to find out about any drugs that may help remedy the problem, especially if the lack of sex is becoming an issue for either of you.
- Have you experienced major fluctuations in your weight or physical appearance since marriage? If so, he may be struggling with a lack of sexual desire due to those changes. While it's painful to hear that our excess weight may be diminishing our husbands' sexual drives, we have to remember that God created men to be visually stimulated. Therefore, your husband's sexual appetite is very much tied to the images he takes in through his eyes. That doesn't mean wives have to look like Barbie dolls or supermodels, but we can't completely let ourselves go and expect our husbands to be just as sexually attracted to us as they were when we were at a healthier weight and feeling more confident about our own bodies.

  I'm not talking about five or ten vanity pounds that you've put on since your wedding. That's just life. It's normal for a woman to gain approximately five pounds each decade of her life once she reaches adulthood. I'm referring to excess weight that would cause a doctor to be concerned about your health. So don't panic over a few extra pounds, but try not to pack them on unnecessarily, either. Such unhealthy excess weight isn't good for you or your relationship.

Women aren't the only ones who need to feel safe, secure, and emotionally connected to feel sexually aroused. So do men. As pointed out in part 3, if a wife repeatedly rejects or criticizes her husband, she will douse the flame of his passion for her. Bill's e-mail vividly illustrates this truth:

In my relationship with my wife, Lydia, our "dance" more often feels to me that she is more interested in control than oneness, which feels devastating. I feel as if I am her puppet on a string, and this wreaks havoc in our relationship. How do I continue pursuing oneness with her when oneness with me isn't in her agenda?

The second area is very confusing to me. Lydia actually has a greater appetite for sex than I do. While we have had some wonderful lovemaking, there have been many times when my lack of performance or foreplay technique has caused Lydia to become enraged. On more than one occasion she has derided me for having a short penis. All of this makes the whole idea of having sex with my wife a risky proposition that just as often deflates my confidence as boosts it and makes me feel humiliated and emasculated. In the past she has demanded that I read books about foreplay and sex (which I have) and initiate sex more…be sexier by what I wear, how I sit, and how I talk or walk.

A doctor discovered that my testosterone level is very low for my age (we don't know why—stress?). I started taking testosterone to bring it back up. While that has had the effect of elevating the need for release, it has had a limited effect on increasing my sexual desire for Lydia. We have not had sex in a few months. She's even threatened to go have sex with someone else if I don't perform better and more frequently. I've tried to relate to her the impact all this has had on me and on my motivation to pursue her sexually, but she shifts the blame and refuses to see her part in all of this.

Ray's words also confirm that there are often emotional issues that dampen a husband's sexual passion. He e-mails:

Sure, I want a passionate sexual connection with my wife just as badly as the next guy, but it takes more than a little physical stimulation to make up for the hurt that she causes me before we ever go to bed at night. My wife's "constructive criticism" is usually anything but constructive. Her expectations are so unrealistic that no man could ever live up to her standards. She uses the Bible as a weapon against what she perceives as my shortcomings. When I offer to pray with her, she feels the need to pray out loud (obviously both to God and to me) for my many weaknesses.

Women assume that our hearts and penises are made of steel and are completely disconnected from one another, but they are not. It can be just as difficult for a man to get aroused by the woman who makes his heart grow cold as it is for a woman to open herself sexually when she feels no intimate connection with her husband. There's been a lot of emphasis on how men and women are different, but we're really not that different when it comes to needing to feel somewhat appreciated and affirmed in order to feel sexually aroused.

Ray is right. There's much more to sexual intimacy than intercourse. Physical pleasure should be the dessert enjoyed after the appetizer of appreciation, the entrée of encouragement and unconditional love, and the side dish of respect. Any man who is starved of those things and only given dessert will eventually become an undernourished husband.

Is there something wrong with me if I cannot have an orgasm with intercourse but must have oral sex or the touch of my husband's hands? How do I make him feel okay with this? His expectation that I should orgasm during intercourse has often led me to fake it.
If your husband isn't aware of the intricacies of female anatomy, don't fault him. Many women don't even know their own bodies, and as a result, many have never experienced orgasm.

For years people bought into Sigmund Freud's theory that there are two types of orgasm, *vaginal* and *clitoral,* and that the center of a woman's orgasm should be transferred from the clitoris to the vagina by the time she matures into adulthood. As a result, many people believed that women were physically or psychologically inferior or abnormal if they were unable to reach orgasm through vaginal intercourse.

However, in the 1960s the research of Masters and Johnson dispelled Freud's theories. Most contemporary experts agree that female orgasm is the result of direct or indirect clitoral stimulation, either with her partner's hand, mouth, a marital aid, or indirectly during certain positions of intercourse.[3] The clitoris is the most sexually sensitive part of the female body, just as the head or tip of the penis is the most sexually sensitive part of the male body. The sole purpose of the clitoris is to provide the female with sexual pleasure, so if you feel the need for clitoral stimulation to orgasm, you should feel absolutely normal.

If you have been pretending to have orgasms, I hope that the information in this book (combined with information in any other books on healthy sexuality or with visits to a sex therapist, if necessary) will remove the need for this temptation. Even though you are faking it to protect your husband's feelings, the dishonesty and sexual frustration that result diminish the oneness and satisfaction that God desires for the two of you to enjoy.

Is it okay to use a vibrator to achieve orgasm while I'm making love with my husband?

This is a question that I've avoided in past books because it can be such a divisive topic among Christians—some feel strongly that it's perfectly acceptable, while others are vehemently opposed. However, because of the numerous e-mails I've received asking this very question, I feel it deserves a response.

First, let's make a distinction between a *marital* aid and a *masturbation* aid. I don't believe that it's okay to use a vibrator as an aid to masturbation, which is a solitary act, because God intends for our sexual pleasure to be experienced *with* our marriage partners, not separate from them. However, I believe it's acceptable for a couple to use a vibrator for the wife to reach orgasm.

Let's run this question through the filter of our six-question grid. *Is it prohibited in Scripture?* No. *Is it beneficial to the relationship?* If both partners are in wholehearted agreement about its use, yes. *Does it involve anyone else?* No. *Is the act known by your spouse, approved of by your spouse, and does it involve your spouse?* Yes, yes, and yes.

Based on the answers to this filter, I believe the use of a vibrator is a perfectly acceptable form of mutual sexual pleasure. However, if you or your partner don't feel comfortable with the idea of using a vibrator, then one shouldn't be used.

How Much Will You Let Pornography Rob from You?

If you are the wife of a recovering porn addict, I pray God will open your heart and mind to fully receive this message in the intended spirit and to encourage and inspire you to become sexually confident again.

I've had conversations with women still sorting through the layers of immense pain their husbands' addictions have caused. Cathy refuses to buy sexy lingerie, Rhonda is offended by her husband's request for a striptease or to have the lights on, and Tonya refuses any sexual position but the missionary one—all because they fear that doing these things is similar to pornography and will awaken in their husbands the urge to look at it again.

While I understand these reactions, unfortunately the philosophy behind them tries to starve a man yet encourages him to steal a steak dinner from his neighbor. If a husband can't enjoy his wife, how will he resist temptation to look elsewhere? This is no justification for pornography; you simply need to understand cause and effect. Many wives do all they can for their husbands in the bedroom and the men still porn surf. But don't increase the problem by letting porn rob you of sharing your beauty with your husband.

Remember, sexuality was God's gift to man and woman before the fall of man, and there's nothing inherently sinful about your husband's sexual desires. They are not a result of some brokenness—or pornography addiction. Yet due to your own brokenness and insecurities,

Why can't men just cuddle without the expectation that it will result in sex?
This is one of the most common complaints I hear from women. I asked Greg
how he would respond to that question, and here's what he told me:

I would tell a woman who asks this question two things. First, keep in
mind that your husband wants sex because he finds you attractive—so

you, too, might be tempted to withdraw from anything that seems to
resemble pornography. But consider this:

- There's a big difference between feeling and believing. In the
  psalms, David feels God has abandoned him to his enemies, but
  a few verses later, he reaffirms his firm belief that God will save
  him. He saw the difference between the way things looked and
  the way things were. Recognize where feelings may be overruling
  your beliefs about God's plan for your marriage.
- Pornography portrays kissing, body massage, and pleasure. Does
  that mean married couples should abandon these things? Just
  because it's been stolen by a pornographic film doesn't mean
  you have to let it remain lost. Fake love doesn't make loving
  acts dirty or bad.
- Research shows that men aren't just after bare skin and hot
  sex from pornography. Your husband needs to feel desirable
  to you to feel like a man! What an awesome power we hold
  to provide what our own minds, bodies, hearts, and souls
  long for most.

Finally, please do not withhold sex from your husband to "punish"
the lust out—because you'll only increase the damage. The emotional,
physical, and spiritual benefits of sex and intimacy are God's glue for the
two of you. Your sexual confidence can and will return when you draw
the line in the sand and refuse to let pornography rob you of anything
more than it already has.

take it as a compliment! He wants to be intimate with you. His erection is his undeniable sign of that fact.

Second, if you wave a freshly grilled steak in front of a starving man's face, he's going to want to eat it. However, if you wave the same steak in front of a well-fed man's face, he won't have any desire to take even a bite. In other words, if your husband is a relatively sexually satisfied man (meaning you don't reject his sexual advances very often), he's perfectly capable of "just cuddling." But if he's constantly wondering when he's ever going to get sex from his wife, "just cuddling" can be torture.

Greg has demonstrated the validity of this observation over the past several years. The more sexually available I am to him, the more emotionally available he is to me for things such as "just cuddling."

Keep Learning About Your Sexual Relationship

The ten "his and her" questions addressed in this chapter represent a mere fraction of the questions about human sexuality that people ask. Sexuality is such a complex topic that we could learn new things every day of our lives and still never understand all there is to know about it. So continue learning about sexuality and growing together in your sexual relationship.

Perhaps you have a few burning questions of your own. If so, seek answers to those questions, either through other Christian books, a professional Christian counselor in your area (which, again, can be located by calling 1-800-NEW-LIFE), or speaking as a couple with your pastor (yes, pastors are sexual beings too). I often think of sexual intimacy as a gift that "keeps on giving," because it's wonderful to discover new positions, new sensations, and new fantasies about how you can fulfill your partner's wildest dreams.

If a husband and wife have open attitudes, sex doesn't have to become boring or feel like just another chore. It can be an exciting and artful form of expressive communication that provides intimacy, pleasure, comfort, and affirmation.

from coasting to cruising

The first new car I purchased had a button on the dash labeled Cruise. A friend told me that if I pushed this button after the car reached a certain speed, the car would continue cruising automatically at that same speed once I took my foot off the gas pedal. (She failed to tell me that I also had to press the button labeled Set.)

I followed her instructions to the letter—and the cruise control didn't work. I tried it again and then again and still no luck. So I took the car back into the dealer, saying, "This cruise control doesn't work! I press the button, take my foot off the accelerator, then the car just slows down." I wasn't cruising at all. I was just coasting. But when I learned to press Set—voilà! I never had to coast again.

Marriage is a lot like my first new car. It holds so much promise for fulfillment, but we have to push all the right buttons to gain maximum satisfaction from it. If we fail to learn how to meet our husbands' needs (inspiring them to meet our needs as well), we'll more than likely grow complacent or self-centered. The energy we pour into and receive out of our relationships will diminish gradually over the years.

I hope that by now you know it doesn't have to be that way, and that as you've read this book, you've discovered the "buttons" that will help you begin cruising back toward the marital bliss you once had or that you've both always dreamed of. I think it's important to remind ourselves on occasion about what *not* to do, so that we don't extinguish the flame of passion, and about what we *can* do, so that we ignite our joy and passion. I've summarized them in the charts on pages 192–93.

I have one final word of wisdom I'd like to leave with you. If your desire is to have your husband's unconditional love, trust, respect, and passion, do what you can to lighten his load.

LIGHTENING HIS LOAD

Remember the big blowout I wrote about in the opening of this book? I was contemplating leaving Greg and our two young children in search of the love I felt entitled to when I tearfully exclaimed, "You just don't meet my emotional needs!" But Greg saw past my weaknesses to my genuine needs and sincerely replied, "Shannon, you have a Grand Canyon of emotional needs, and even if every man in Dallas lined up outside your doorstep to spend time with you, it wouldn't be enough! *Until you look to God to satisfy your emotional needs,* there's nothing that I, or any other man on the planet, can do to satisfy you!"

While some women may have taken this as a major insult and walked out the door, I recognized the truth in his statement. In all honesty, it was actually a relief to hear. I had given lots of men opportunities to meet my emotional needs, and the idea that God could meet them gave me a glimmer of hope. At Greg's urging, I began seeing a counselor and set out on a journey to discover a deeper level of intimacy and fulfillment in my relationship with Jesus Christ. I found that God isn't just a far-off spiritual being or father figure in the sky, but He is the passionate lover of my soul who sacrificed His son's life so that we could be together in eternity. I also learned that I can't put the burden of responsibility on my husband's shoulders to be my emotional all in all. Only God can shoulder that burden.

MENTAL AND PHYSICAL INTIMACY BUSTERS	MENTAL AND PHYSICAL INTIMACY BOOSTERS
• being a reluctant partner	• being a welcoming partner
• hitting the wall (letting your feelings dictate and rejecting his sexual advances)	• scaling the wall (responding to his advances and knowing your feelings will soon follow)
• inhibition (hiding your body out of shame)	• exhibition (visually stimulating your husband)
• obsessing over your weight or shape	• feeling good about yourself and your sex appeal
• procrastination (putting sex off indefinitely	• initiation (pursuing him sexually sooner rather than later)
• light-bulb sex (distracted sexual energies)	• laser-beam sex (focused sexual energies)

Kathleen has learned this to be true as well. She writes:

I can get so frustrated at times when I feel like my husband and I are at
an impasse, but then God graces me with a love for Brian that helps me
see past it. It comes down to whether I focus on me or on God. I have
found that when I am in daily devotions, I am much more able to focus
on God and have Him meet my needs without constantly looking for
Brian to be everything for me. This is the person I want to be. I want
Brian to be so overwhelmed with love for me, not just because of my
appearance, but because of my inner character. I want him to be proud
of his godly, strong, wise, supportive, faithful wife. I want people to see
me with Brian and think, *Wow! He is one lucky guy!*

Julie, whom we heard from in chapter 12, also tells about how she has learned
to put her hope for ultimate fulfillment in Christ rather than in her husband:

Six years into my second marriage, my life is very different than before.
Although my second husband is a much better match for me, there are
still those days when marriage could be a real letdown if I were counting
on him to make me happy or to fill up the holes—*and there will always
be holes* in this life. On those days, I now count on Jesus to be my
true, perfect husband. How do I do that? I go to Him in the Word and

EMOTIONAL AND SPIRITUAL INTIMACY BUSTERS	EMOTIONAL AND SPIRITUAL INTIMACY BOOSTERS
• sex as a means of closeness	• sex as a response to closeness
• hiding behind masks	• getting spiritually and emotionally naked
• requiring intimacy	• inspiring intimacy
• exhibiting a spirit of rejection	• exhibiting a spirit of acceptance
• inflicting or holding on to shame	• forgiveness of self and others
• considering sex a worldly act	• recognizing sex as a sacred act of worship

intimate prayer (I write my prayers out to Him), so that I can soak up His satisfying and unconditional love for me. His love fills up the holes, at times makes me giddy with joy, always soothes my anxious heart, can be counted on, and is never disappointing.

When I am loved like that, I am able to demonstrate God's amazing miraculous love to my mate, even when I think he is acting unlovable. I am able to give even when I'm not being given to. I am able to "be Jesus" to the man I'm sharing my life with. I'm able to give grace to him even when he doesn't "deserve" it. And best of all, I have taken all the pressure off the shoulders of my earthly husband to make me happy.

As my relationship with Jesus has grown, I've become aware of how He continually romances me with things like breathtaking sunsets, fields of colorful mountain wildflowers, magnificent lightning storms, and amazing creativity in animals and nature. He cares about *everything* I care about, even when my mate doesn't. He is strong and secure when my mate lets me down. He is there for me when no one else is. Now *that* is the kind of love that I can put my hope in!

When we put our hope in the unfailing love of Jesus Christ and live according to God's perfect guidelines for marriage, our whole world can change for the better.

A WHOLE NEW WORLD

While I've made great strides over the past sixteen years of marriage, I still aspire to consistently live out many of the principles in this book. I still have plenty of room for improvement in making Greg feel cherished and loved for the wonderful husband, father, and human being that he is.

Chances are, there's probably room for improvement in your marriage as well. If you agree, I don't want you to feel guilty or condemned for how you may have failed to be the wife you really want to be. None of us has been the perfect wife, nor will we ever be, even after reading a book like this. However, I hope this book has inspired you with some practical ways to avoid causing your husband's heart to grow cold, demonstrated how you can light his fire again, and shown you how you can throw fuel on his flame of love for you.

If we can learn to ignite the joy and passion that both husbands and wives desire in marriage, imagine the effect that this will have not just in our own families, but on society as a whole. There would be less stress and a much greater sense of peace in our homes. Divorce rates could decline drastically. Children would grow up in two-parent homes with the security of knowing that Mom and Dad

Wrestling the Body-Image Bear

My husband almost made me cry the other night—tears of joy. After wearing the same pair of jeans far too often because none of the rest in my closet fit right or look that great, I finally broke down and went shopping for new ones. I'd honestly rather have a root canal than shop for blue jeans or bathing suits. You feel my pain, I know.

After trying on over twenty pairs (no exaggeration), I finally purchased a couple, which still didn't excite me, but these were the lesser of the evils. I went home rather bummed about my apple-shaped body and how my muffin-top waistline got a little out of control while we were traveling the past month.

But that night, while Greg and I were making love, with the lights on, the covers off, and me in all my slightly pudgy glory, my husband scanned me up and down, rolled his eyes back in his head, and in all sincerity declared, "Oh, thank you, God, for a gorgeous wife!" I wanted to cry. But I smothered him with kisses instead.

Not even Scarlett Johansson or Angelina Jolie look like their pictures on the big screens and in magazines. Get over yourself and get naked. Even get on top so your husband can drink in your beautiful body with his eyes. Don't waste another minute moping about what you look like—enjoy your body for the incredible pleasure it provides both you and your husband!

really love each other. As a result, they would not be as tempted to turn to gangs, drugs, alcohol, cutting, or other pain-numbing activities. Young people would see that sex is worth waiting for until marriage because adults would be modeling healthy, happy, passion-filled relationships. As a result, premarital pregnancy and abortion rates would be reduced and sexually transmitted diseases could be far less of a social and economic concern.

These principles are the best way to affair-proof and divorce-proof marriages, the best way for families to live in harmony with one another, and the best way for children to grow up in homes where they learn to respect, love, and cherish others, including, some day, their own spouses.

If we can embrace and strive to apply these principles, passing these values down to future generations, we could inspire a whole new, more wonderful world in which to live—a world where marriage is once again a sacred, celebrated institution, where children can feel safe and secure, and where the lavish love of Christ is evident in our hearts and in our homes.

workbook

questions you may have about this workbook

What will the *Every Woman's Marriage Workbook* do for me?

This workbook will help you go the extra mile in applying the principles presented in *Every Woman's Marriage*, so you can change the things that only you can change for the good of your relationship. You'll discover what you may be doing to cause your husband's flame of joy and passion to die, how to reignite the flame, and how to throw fuel on it for a greatly enhanced marital connection. Through thought-provoking questions and soul-searching exercises, you'll learn how to inspire rather than require the intimacy you long to experience with your husband.

Is this workbook enough, or do I also need to read *Every Woman's Marriage?*

While this workbook contains excerpts from *Every Woman's Marriage* (each one marked at the beginning and end by this symbol: 📖), you'll need to read the book to see the big picture and get the full effect of the concepts presented.

How much time is required to complete each lesson? Do I need to work through every part of each chapter?

In addition to the time it will take you to read the accompanying chapters in *Every Woman's Marriage*, it will take thirty to forty-five minutes to answer the questions in the workbook. While it's important to work through all the questions, you may want to spend more time on areas that target your specific needs.

Each chapter contains four parts: Planting Good Seeds (Personally Seeking God's Truth), Weeding Out Deception (Recognizing the Truth), Harvesting Joy and Passion (Applying the Truth), and Growing Together (Sharing the Truth in Small-Group Discussion). The first three parts are intended for individual study. They will help you hide God's Word in your heart, help you recognize and remove things in your life that can hinder joy and passion in your marriage, and help you reap the rewards of deeper levels of marital intimacy and satisfaction. The last part of each chapter is designed especially for group discussion, although it can also be done individually.

How do I organize a group study?

You'll be amazed at how much more you'll get out of the book and workbook if you go through it with a group of like-minded women. I also recommend that husbands form a group to read and discuss the principles presented in the *Every Man's Marriage* book and workbook (by Stephen Arterburn and Fred Stoeker).

If you don't know of an existing group, start one of your own! Whether it's a Sunday-school class or a group of coworkers, neighbors, or friends, invite six to eight women to meet and discuss the book and workbook. Let them know that it will likely take a couple of hours each week to read the chapters in the book and then answer the corresponding questions in the workbook. Most women will recognize that this is a worthwhile investment of their time, and they will eagerly seek practical advice on how to ignite more joy and passion in their relationships with their husbands.

Your group will meet together eight times. Keep each meeting to a reasonable amount of time (I recommend sixty to ninety minutes) so everyone will consider it a blessing rather than a burden. If evenings are not a possibility, consider a weekly breakfast or brown-bag lunch meeting.

When women gather to discuss such an intimate topic as marriage, the temptation to go off on rabbit trails with a variety of other "safer" topics can be overwhelming, especially for those who feel uncomfortable at first. To ensure that the conversation stays on track, designate one person to be the group facilitator. This facilitator has no responsibilities to teach, lecture, or prepare anything in advance, but simply to begin and end the meeting at the designated times and to make sure the conversation is moving along in a productive manner.

Nothing heals like meeting with other women with the goal of removing your masks and talking about the struggles you each face in being the wives you long to be. You never know, perhaps your group will breathe life into someone's otherwise lifeless marriage, or prevent a woman from prematurely giving up on her husband or from falling into an extramarital affair. By learning to inspire from our husbands the intimacy we long for, we can affair-proof our relationships and divorce-proof our families like never before.

Love takes two to tango,
and as much as we want to throw stones
at our clumsy partners,
we all need to stop and ask ourselves,
What part do I play in my marriage's dance of discontentment?

—from chapter 2 of *Every Woman's Marriage*

when hearts grow cold

Read chapters 1 and 2 in *Every Woman's Marriage.*

🌱 PLANTING GOOD SEEDS
(Personally Seeking God's Truth)

As you seek to discover how to ignite the joy and passion you and your husband desire in your relationship, here is a good seed to plant in your heart:

> Consider the blameless, observe the upright;
>> there is a future for the [woman] of peace. (Psalm 37:37, NIV)

1. Prior to your wedding day, how did you envision your future with your husband? How has your reality measured up to your fantasy of marriage?
2. Have there been times when you felt desperate to change your husband, to change yourself, or to resolve a situation that was robbing you of peace in the relationship? What could God have been trying to teach you through these experiences?

> When a [woman's] ways are pleasing to the LORD,
>> he makes even [her] enemies live at peace with [her].
> Better a little with righteousness
>> than much gain with injustice.

> In [her] heart a [woman] plans [her] course,
>> but the LORD determines [her] steps. (Proverbs 16:7–9, NIV)

3. Do you believe your future together could be more joyful and passionate if you learn how to move from desperation to dependence upon the Lord? Why or why not?
4. What, specifically, can you do to make your ways of relating with your husband more pleasing to God? Give examples of what this may look like and what you hope the results of such actions will be.

⚒ WEEDING OUT DECEPTION
(Recognizing the Truth)

> 📖 I was constantly badgering Greg for not initiating romance anymore, for being too laid back. I had a long list of complaints: He never called me up for a date or offered to take me out to dinner. He didn't send cards or bring me flowers. I was weary of having to hint around for my emotional needs to be met, and I felt it didn't count if he didn't come up with the idea of how to do so himself. I was sick and tired of always picking up LEGOS and Tinkertoys, wiping children's noses and behinds, cleaning Goldfish and Cheerios out of the minivan seats, and feeling as if there had to be more to life.
>
> With each passing day, I slipped deeper into depression. In hindsight, I realize that my unhappiness wasn't about what my husband was or wasn't doing; rather, it was about how I felt about myself. I needed Greg to affirm me, to make me feel beautiful, and to convince me that I was desirable, because I didn't know how to feel any of these things on my own. But at the time, I felt sure that he was to blame. 📖

5. Have you ever felt there must be more to life and been tempted to place the blame on your husband rather than taking responsibility for your own happiness? If so, describe one such memory and how you felt at the time.

6. In hindsight, what do you think your husband should have been doing to make you feel better during this time? Would it have truly been enough to satisfy you and give you a genuine sense of peace and happiness?

7. What things could you have been doing to make yourself feel better during that season of life? If you could go back, what would you do differently?

8. The next time you experience a deep sense of disappointment and disillusionment in your life or marriage, how can you avoid placing the blame on your husband and take responsibility for your own peace and contentment? What will you do to avoid playing the blame game?

📖 After only one year of marriage, it's clear that Claire's reality isn't measuring up to her expectations. She laments: "We're usually either fighting or not talking much at all. The word *divorce* isn't in our vocabularies, but I frequently have thoughts about what my life could be like after my husband dies. I have a mental list of men I'd date. It's pretty long. They have all met different needs at different times. Then I think of how wonderful it would be to be single again. I'd be better off without his college debt and dirty socks. But I married him for a reason. What was it?"

Ironically, Claire also recalls that she was miserable as a single woman and thought that getting married would solve all her problems. As her situation illustrates, getting rid of your single status only exchanges one set of problems for another, more complex set of problems. 📖

9. Do you ever long to be single again? If so, what new problems would be created by your divorced or widowed status (socially, financially, relationally, emotionally, and so on)? Do you really prefer those problems to the ones you have experienced in your marriage?

10. Have you been tempted to buy into the lie that if you had a different man, your life would be better? Is this a realistic expectation—that a different person would solve your problems? Why or why not?

HARVESTING JOY AND PASSION
(Applying the Truth)

> 📖 Let's face it. Nothing magical happens once we put those rings on our fingers. If we were unhappy before marriage, chances are we'll go back to being unhappy shortly after the honeymoon. Marriage doesn't make us feel better about ourselves or solve our problems in the long run. No husband can be the White Knight who rescues us from all our issues and insecurities. At some point we have to put on our "big-girl panties" and go through the work of resolving our own issues, remedying our own insecurities, and becoming happy with ourselves before we can truly be happy in marriage. 📖

11. What personal issues do you struggle with that have added to the stress in your marriage relationship?

12. What work do you sense you may need to do to resolve these issues or insecurities and become truly happy with yourself? Might you need to enlist the help of others? If so, how?

> 📖 Too often we wives seem to assume that our husbands' hearts are made of steel. Perhaps the rings we wear on our fingers give us the impression that regardless of how we treat them, they'll always be by our sides.

I don't know about you, but I don't want a husband who is physically alive but emotionally dead toward me. I want Greg to be excited about our relationship and to look forward to coming home every day. I don't want him going through the motions to jump through my hoops just to keep me off his back. I want his heart to remain soft and warm toward me. However, I've come to realize that I can't have these things while taking him for granted and treating him disrespectfully, both of which I have done many times in the past. 📖

13. What about you? Do you share this desire—to have your husband look forward to coming home every day with a soft, warm heart toward you? How can you inspire this reaction in him?

14. What specific behaviors or attitudes will you strive to avoid to keep his heart from growing cold toward you?

🌿 Growing Together
(Sharing the Truth in Small-Group Discussion)

> 📖 *"You just don't meet my emotional needs!"*
> After seven years of marriage, I was actually thinking of leaving Greg and my two young children in pursuit of the "love" I felt entitled to but didn't feel I was getting in our relationship. I had no idea where I would go or how I would make it on my own, but I wasn't sure I could survive a lifeless marriage. I felt like I was nothing more than a maid, cook, nanny, and occasional outlet for sexual tension, positions for which I was sadly underpaid. 📖

15. Have you ever thought you weren't getting the "love" you felt entitled to or that your husband was taking you for granted? How did this make you feel? Why?

📖 The truth is, no marriage is exempt from disillusionment. Even the brightest relationship has dark days clouding a couple's history together, raining on their "we have the perfect marriage" parade. On the exterior, a wife may appear to have the ideal marriage, but the interior landscape of her heart often reveals deep disappointment, anger, bitterness, and regret. 📖

16. Have you believed that your marital struggles are unique? If so, how does it make you feel to know that many other women have similar experiences?

17. Why do you think most couples experience desperate times at some point (or at several points)? What can we learn from this common phenomenon? What hope can this create in us—if we allow it?

📖 It's true that many women aren't happy; it's equally true that many men aren't happy. These *are* desperate times, and perhaps this desperation is an indication that it's time for us women to take desperate measures and ask ourselves, *Am I contributing to the demise of the masculine image by how I treat my husband?* Love takes two to tango, and as much as we want to throw stones at our clumsy partners, we all need to stop and ask ourselves, *What part do I play in my marriage's dance of discontentment?*

The bottom line is this: *Even if you firmly believe that 95 percent of the issues in your marriage are your husband's fault, are you willing to focus on the 5 percent that you do have control over?* 📖

18. For a moment, ignore whatever problems you feel your husband brings into your relationship. Focus strictly on the part *you* play in the dance of discontentment. What areas do you need to work on to reignite joy and passion in your relationship?

19. What specific things can others in the group do to hold you accountable or to encourage you to make positive changes in your ways of relating to your husband?

∞

Dear Lord, we acknowledge that our society is experiencing incredibly desperate times in light of the divorce rates and all of the repercussions of so many broken homes in our world. We don't want to add to this problem. We want to be a part of the solution. We seek Your supernatural guidance in creating rock-solid marriage relationships that will withstand the test of time and be bright rays of light that drive away darkness and illuminate hope in other married couples. Help us to take the desperate measures we need to take to recognize and remedy our own problems. We seek to rediscover peace, contentment, joy, and passion in our marriages, for our own sakes and for the sakes of our husbands, children, and our grandchildren for many generations to come. Amen.

looking at
the big picture

Read chapters 3, 4, and 5 in *Every Woman's Marriage*.

PLANTING GOOD SEEDS
(Personally Seeking God's Truth)

As you reflect on God's creation of marriage, plant Paul's words deep within your heart:

> As the Scriptures say, "A man leaves his father and mother and is joined to his wife, and the two are united into one." This is a great mystery, but it is an illustration of the way Christ and the church are one. (Ephesians 5:31–32)

1. Have you ever pondered the mystery of why God calls you to be joined to your spouse as one inseparable unit? What do you think it means for two to be united into one?

2. Why do you think that an everlasting marriage commitment between two believers is so important to God? Is it as important to you? Why or why not?

3. Are there ways in which you need to focus on being more one with your spouse instead of operating separately or independently of him? If so, how?

As you consider the big-picture purpose of marriage, plant this good seed in your heart:

> You husbands must love your wives with the same love Christ showed the church. He gave up his life for her *to make her holy and clean,* washed by baptism and God's word. He did this to present her to himself as a glorious church without a spot or wrinkle or any other blemish. Instead, she will be holy and without fault. (Ephesians 5:25–27, emphasis added)

4. What difference would it make in a marriage if a husband strove to love his wife as Christ loved the church? Can you identify certain ways that your husband attempts to love you like this? If so, what are they?
5. In what ways does your marriage relationship purify you and make you more holy than when you were single? Are there particular issues in your life that have come to the surface since you've been married, forcing you to deal with them like never before?

As you consider how to love your husband, plant this seed in your heart:

> We know what real love is because Christ gave up his life for us. (1 John 3:16)

6. In what ways have you and your husband given up your lives for each other?
7. In what ways do you still need to give up your life for the sake of your husband and for unity in your marriage?

⚓ WEEDING OUT DECEPTION
(Recognizing the Truth)

📖 James seemed attentive and sounded ideal. Andrea raved about how he called several times each day just to see what she was doing, how he said the sweetest things to her, and how he continued to assure her that he (and their relationship) was truly the real deal. When Greg would call me on my cell phone, it was to talk about where each kid had to be that day or to ask what he could make for supper. He said "I love you" before we hung up, but it wasn't magical. It didn't inspire any change in my tone of voice. No sweaty palms. No butterflies in my stomach. Just a routine conversation. Our relationship hasn't always been this way. There was a time when I did backflips whenever he called.

After I hung up, I made a mental note: *Guard your heart, Shannon!* I had to be careful not to be jealous of the intensity of Andrea's new relationship. I couldn't compare my marriage of fifteen years to this fifteen-day-old relationship. Maybe Greg and I didn't have the flame of intensity anymore, but we had something far more brilliant—the glowing embers of intimacy. 📖

8. Do you ever lament because your husband no longer gives you sweaty palms or butterflies in your stomach? If so, how has this made you feel?

9. After reading part 2 of *Every Woman's Marriage,* do you agree that sweaty palms, butterflies, and fireworks aren't good indicators of relational success? Why or why not?

10. What are more accurate indicators of marital success? List as many as you can think of. As you look over your list, underline the indicators that are present in your marriage, then circle those that you'd like to strive to work on.

📖 So when Greg looked into my heart, what did he see that no one else could? He saw a hurting little girl who didn't understand who she was in Christ or that Jesus wanted to be the lover of her soul. He also saw a woman who failed to understand what high and holy callings marriage and motherhood are. Not long before this season of our lives, I had given up a challenging career in an office where I had received a lot of kudos on a regular basis, so staying at home with two kids was a hard adjustment for me. No one clapped when I scrubbed baby food off the highchair. No one cheered as I carted kids to ballet lessons and playgrounds. Greg recognized that I had looked to outside relationships for a sense of affirmation and as a remedy to the monotony of being a full-time, stay-at-home mom. 📖

11. Which, if any, of Shannon's feelings in her early years of marriage do you sympathize with? Have you also been tempted to seek affirmation outside of your roles as a mother and/or wife? Why or why not?

12. If your husband looked into your heart the way Greg was able to see into Shannon's, what would he see that probably no one else could?

13. Do you feel that things deep within your heart may be driving your current attitudes and behaviors? If so, how do those things drive you? If not, how have you safeguarded yourself from letting your innermost wounds and struggles drive you toward destructive relational patterns?

🦬 HARVESTING JOY AND PASSION
(Applying the Truth)

📖 Because Greg didn't run when I was honest with him about my struggles, I recognized what a trustworthy man I had married, and I felt safe and secure in a relationship for the first time in my life. I learned to appreciate his patience, his wisdom, and his

spiritual maturity in not blaming himself for my emotional
infidelity. Because of his help, I was able to establish my footing
upon a firmer foundation.

Discovering Greg's deep level of commitment to me has been
far more satisfying than any "intense" moment I've experienced
with him or any other guy. I have his unconditional love—in spite
of my flaws. This is what genuine intimacy is all about. And that
intimacy is far better than butterflies, sweaty palms, fireworks, or
any other form of intensity. 📖

14. Do you feel that you can be honest with your husband about your
    personal struggles? Do you feel he loves you unconditionally in spite
    of those struggles? Why or why not?

15. Do you feel that your husband can be honest with you about his per-
    sonal struggles? Can you love him unconditionally in spite of those
    struggles? Why or why not?

> 📖 Of course, intimacy doesn't just happen automatically. It takes
> a tremendous amount of time and effort. Our relationships only
> grow and blossom when we nurture them, feed them, and inten-
> tionally care for them with diligence. Greg and I have achieved
> this level of intimacy only as a result of many counseling sessions
> and many hours spent in painful, honest conversation and gut-
> wrenching prayer. I've often thought that our intimate relationship
> has required a lot of blood, sweat, and tears—Jesus's blood, Greg's
> sweat, and my tears. But the fragrant beauty of what the three of
> us have created during those tumultuous years was well worth
> every ounce of effort. 📖

16. What issues have the two of you sweated or shed tears over? How has
    God responded to your efforts and/or to the cries of your hearts to im-
    prove your relationship?

17. In what practical ways have the two of you attempted to cultivate intimacy in your marriage? Describe these attempts.

18. Is cultivating a more intimate relationship a bigger challenge than you previously imagined? Why or why not?

> 📖 Greg often serves as a full-length mirror in my life by pointing out the embarrassing spiritual "spinach in my teeth," such as impatience, pride, greed, and selfishness—things I don't always notice about myself until I recognize that *he* notices them. When my husband gently brings these issues to my attention, our marriage can feel like a refiner's fire. These issues create incredible spiritual heat and bring my impurities to the surface and into plain sight. When this happens, I can stubbornly refuse to address these issues, pretending they are not really there, or I can humbly ask God to help me skim these impurities out of my life so that I am refined and can more accurately reflect Christ's perfection.
>
> While we all hate to see the ugliness in our own lives, sanctification sessions can show us how we can grow spiritually and deepen our levels of personal holiness. When we strive toward more Christlike behavior, we are in essence saying to our spouses and to God, "You deserve better, so I'm going to try harder." Such an attitude honors both our spouses and God. 📖

19. Do you sense that your husband notices the spiritual "spinach in your teeth" more readily than the other people in your life? Why or why not?

20. Have you ever had thoughts that your husband deserves a "better" wife than you? If so, how did that thought make you feel?

21. Have you allowed feelings of insecurity or inadequacy drive you crazy, or do you allow them to drive you toward healthier choices and more mature behavior? How can you avoid the former and attempt the latter?

📖 Sure, it's disheartening when our spouses disappoint us. It can be frustrating when they don't live up to our expectations. It can be shocking when we discover that they have dark sides that we were unaware of. On the flip side, it's also humiliating to confess that we have major character flaws or that we struggle with sinful issues of our own or that we fail to live up to certain expectations that our spouses have of us. But in these times we each have a choice to make—we can choose to make things *bitter* with resentment and condemnation, or we can choose to make things *better* by displaying God's character traits of unconditional love and acceptance. 📖

22. What has been one of the most disheartening discoveries about your husband? How has he, at times, failed to live up to your expectations?

23. How can you keep a root of bitterness from developing in your heart over these issues? How can you make things better for him and for the two of you as a couple?

📖 Many people pray, "Lord, give me a ministry! Show me what I can do for you!" while the answer is right there under their noses. Yes, the world needs Jesus, but our spouses and children desperately need to be the primary recipients of our ministry efforts. If we save the world but lose our marriage or family in the process, what does that do to our witness? Can we really do more for others than we can do for those living under our same roof? As husbands and wives, fathers and mothers, we hold the power to minister to our own families in ways that no one else can. 📖

24. Have you failed to recognize the ministry opportunities that you have with the man sharing your bed every night? If so, how?

25. How have you effectively ministered to your husband in the past?

26. What do you sense he may need most from you during this season of his life? Are you willing to make him your primary ministry focus? Why or why not?

❧ GROWING TOGETHER
(Sharing the Truth in Small-Group Discussion)

📖 Because I had sought to remain in that "revved-up state of passionate love" with my husband, I failed to recognize the pleasure of our slowly developing "companionate love." Rather than beginning the hard work of stirring the embers of our relationship to renew a sense of excitement, I almost threw enough dirt on the fire to extinguish it altogether. Because I craved the euphoric happiness and intensity that are characteristic of a new relationship, I found myself gravitating toward new men—men who made me feel special, cherished, and desirable again because of the attention they gave me.

Almost everywhere I went, I would meet a man who seemed to create in me that spark of excitement that Greg didn't seem to ignite anymore. My aerobics instructor made me feel sexy again as he complimented me on how great I was looking as I lost my extra pregnancy pounds. After years of staying at home and watching too many reruns of *Sesame Street* and *Barney*, my college professor reminded me of my intelligence when he praised my research papers or class participation. A friend at church made me feel like a special confidante when he frequently called me at home during the day to complain about his marriage and to comment on how he wished his wife were more like me. I was getting lots of ego strokes, but they were all from superficial relationships—from men who only knew me from a distance. Greg, on the other hand, saw me close up. He knew the *real* me. 📖

27. Have you ever found yourself longing for those "revved-up states of passionate love"? What do you think is missing? Describe how this makes you feel and what effects it has on your contentment. If you don't long for these "revved-up states," explain how you've kept yourself grounded with more realistic expectations in your marriage.

28. How can a woman guard her heart and mind against extramarital pitfalls?

29. Rather than expecting "revved-up states of passionate love" to remain steady for decades, describe what a more mature "companionate love" might look like between you and your husband. What do you enjoy most about his companionship?

    📖 I struggled during those years of my marriage because, like many women, I had failed to understand the difference between *intensity* and *intimacy*. *Intensity* is a feeling of extreme excitement or euphoria. It is a natural by-product of a brand-spanking-new relationship. Intensity often masquerades as intimacy. When we are getting to know new things about a person, we often think we are experiencing intimacy, but discovering new things about a stranger isn't intimate—it's just new. It may be exciting. It may feel intense. But it's often superficial and temporary. At best it's incomplete. For the most part, I only got to know the sides of these men that they wanted me to see. Those relationships often *felt* intimate, but the intimacy I was feeling was a false intimacy.

    Genuine intimacy could only be found at home, where Greg and I both saw not just the good but also the bad and the ugly in each other. You see, *intimacy* can best be understood by breaking the word down into syllables: in-to-me-see. It's the ability to see into the heart, mind, and spirit of another person, which is impossible until after you've gotten to know that individual over a long period of time. It comes only after the intensity has worn off and you get to know things that most people can't possibly know unless they live with that person. 📖

30. Have you ever mistaken intensity for intimacy in a relationship? What do you recognize as the differences between the two?

31. Take what you have learned in this section of *Every Woman's Marriage* (the book) and write down a more accurate description of intimacy in marriage.

32. If a wife pursued genuine intimacy rather than intensity in her marriage, what effects might it have on her husband? herself? their relationship?

> 📖 Time is a precious commodity that few of us have to spare. In these days of dual careers and overcommitted moms, it's no surprise that busyness is one of the biggest intimacy killers. The health complaints of busy women have actually led the medical community to coin a new term called the Hurried Woman Syndrome. Someone suffering from this syndrome may experience weight gain, low sex drive, moodiness, and fatigue. Doctors believe these symptoms are caused by the stress of doing too much, spreading oneself too thin, feeling overwhelmed and underaccomplished, and growing resentful of others' expectations, all of which can ultimately lead to hostility and depression.* 📖

33. Have you ever suffered any of the symptoms of Hurried Woman Syndrome? If so, what were they and what do you believe was causing them?

34. What are the things that commonly rob you of time and energy?

35. How can you redirect some of that time and energy toward enhancing your relationship with your husband? Is this a desire you have? Why or why not?

---

* Dr. Laura Schlessinger, *The Proper Care and Feeding of Husbands* (New York: HarperCollins, 2004), 21.

📖 Imagine all the important relationships in your life and how long you get to enjoy each of them. Only one will remain consistent throughout your life—your relationship with your spouse. Decades of living under the same roof, sleeping in the same bed, eating at the same table, and sharing a rich emotional, mental, spiritual, and physical history together places this relationship in a class all by itself. Surely, the more you invest in your marriage, the greater the return on your investment. 📖

36. Based on what you currently invest in your marriage relationship, what will be the return five, ten, twenty, or even fifty years from now?

37. Are you willing you to invest more in your relationship in the present to yield a higher return in the future? If so, what would investing more look like for you?

∞

*D*ear Lord, help us to see the big picture and recognize the incredible treasure You've given us in marriage. We confess that we've perhaps not invested in our relationships as we should. Help us to embrace the companionate love we share with our husbands, to submit to the sanctification process that often accompanies marriage, and to make our husbands one of the primary recipients of our ministry efforts. Thank You for the opportunity to love them, to be loved by them, and to grow together in our love for You. Amen.

how his flame dies (part A)

Read chapters 6 and 7 in *Every Woman's Marriage*.

🪴 PLANTING GOOD SEEDS
(Personally Seeking God's Truth)

As you seek to understand how your husband's flame of joy and passion for you might die, plant these good seeds in your heart:

> So now I am giving you a new commandment: Love each other.
> Just as I have loved you, you should love each other. Your love for
> one another will prove to the world that you are my disciples.
> (John 13:34–35)

> Don't just pretend that you love others. Really love them. Hate
> what is wrong. Stand on the side of the good. Love each other
> with genuine affection, and take delight in honoring each other.
> (Romans 12:9–10)

1. According to these verses, why is loving one another so important?
   What should love look like?

2. How can we apply these verses to marriage? How can we "love each other with genuine affection, and take delight in honoring each other" in marriage?

As you seek to understand what Christian love in marriage should look like, plant this seed in your heart:

> Love is patient and kind. Love is not jealous or boastful or proud or rude. Love does not demand its own way. Love is not irritable, and it keeps no record of when it has been wronged. It is never glad about injustice but rejoices whenever the truth wins out. Love never gives up, never loses faith, is always hopeful, and endures through every circumstance. (1 Corinthians 13:4–7)

3. Is the kind of love that Paul talks of in this passage truly attainable within marriage? Why or why not?
4. What three practical things could you do this week to be more patient, loving, and kind toward your husband?

⚒ WEEDING OUT DECEPTION
(Recognizing the Truth)

> 📖 There have certainly been times when I fell into the mother role with Greg and expected him to simply obey me. I've insisted he be home from work at a certain time rather than trust that he'll come home as soon as he can. I've attempted to control what he eats and how often he exercises, as if he's clueless about living a healthy lifestyle on his own. I've created honey-do lists a mile long with the dates that I needed these things done by, as if his free time were completely mine to control.... Greg didn't appreciate it that his wife was trying to micromanage his life. 📖

5. Regardless of whether it's been your intention or not, would your husband say that you've ever tried to micromanage his life? Why or why not?

6. Have you ever felt as if someone was trying to control or manipulate you as though you were a child who had to submit to that person's authority? Describe how it made you feel or how you would imagine it to feel.

7. What are the biggest differences between the roles of a mother in a man's life and that of his wife? List as many as you can think of.

8. Describe some practical ways you can try to ensure your husband never feels as if you are trying to play the role of his mother rather than that of his wife.

📖 Although we may not have gotten *everything* we wanted when we were growing up, some girls were able to wrap their dads so tightly around their little fingers that they could bat their eyelashes and get pretty much whatever they wanted. That may be fine for a little girl, but when a woman emotionally manipulates her husband to get her way, she creates an unhealthy dynamic.

I felt sorry for one woman's husband when she told me, "I can get anything I want from Dan, within reason, of course. All I have to do is cross my legs and stop cooking, and he'll cave in after a couple of days." Translation: "I'll withhold sex and starve him until he caters to my every whim." 📖

9. Do you think it is wise for a woman to withhold sex, cooking, and so on, in an effort to manipulate her husband into doing what she wants? Why or why not?

10. Have there been times when you wanted your husband to cater to your whims or to give you what you desired most, regardless of his ability (or desire) to provide it for you? If so, describe one of these times and how it made each of you feel.

11. Describe a more effective approach that you can utilize whenever you desire your husband to do or provide something for you. What makes it more effective than manipulation?

> 📖 While I certainly don't want to minimize any woman's pain if she is living with an avowed nonbeliever, I do want to point out that legalism and self-righteousness are two things that Jesus spoke against more often than any other issue. Many of us have to admit that we often assign the bad guy role to our husbands while we wear the angelic halos. But what are we trying to accomplish when we do this? To guilt him into a more righteous lifestyle? Or to make ourselves look all the more holy by calling attention to his unholiness?
>
> Every Christian woman longs for a husband who is a strong spiritual leader in their home. But sometimes it takes years for a man to mature into such a role. Unfortunately, many women stunt that growth process with their own self-righteous indignation. 📖

12. Have there been times when you wanted your husband to be a stronger spiritual leader in your family? If so, how have you approached this situation and what's been the outcome?

13. What's a more effective approach to encouraging your husband to establish a personal relationship with Christ or to become more of a spiritual leader at home? Describe what this approach looks like

> 📖 Satan can take something as tiny as a sigh, blow it way out of proportion in a person's mind, and cause a huge downward spiral in the relationship as a result. Something is said, and the hearer takes it out of context. The speaker is maybe just having a bad day, or is tired, or is feeling stressed because of something happening in the background of life. We are tempted to take it personally, and rather than keeping a short account of offenses, we build a case in

our minds to prove that the person really doesn't love us, or respect us, or like us, or appreciate us, or want to be around us. With every negative incident that we let add up in our minds, we stack another brick between ourselves and that person, creating mental walls that only serve to separate us. But it doesn't have to be that way. 📖

14. Can you remember a time when you took a small incident and blew it way out of proportion, choosing to ride an emotional escalator rather than assuming the best about your husband? If so, what are your reflections about that experience?

15. Have you built any mental walls between you and your husband? If so, what can you do to remove the bricks and bring down that wall?

🦬 HARVESTING JOY AND PASSION
(Applying the Truth)

📖 Women frequently tell me, "I feel more like my husband's mother or boss than his partner," and that they are always harping on their husbands about helping more around the house. If this sounds familiar, remember that you can't *require* your husband's cooperation. You can, however, *inspire* it. Because you want your husband to be internally (rather than externally) motivated to help out, try encouraging him with a nice comment, such as, "Would you mind running the vacuum cleaner for me sometime today? And when you do, remember how much I appreciate how hard you work both inside and outside our home." Or when you see him doing a particular chore, you might say, "I am so thankful to have a guy who is willing to do that!" He'll feel like he's your hero rather than your rebellious child, and chances are he'll be more likely to want to play that heroic role more often in the future. 📖

16. In what ways do you make your husband feel like a hero? What compliments or appreciative comments have you given him lately?

17. What does it mean to be *internally* motivated rather than *externally* motivated? Which do you prefer? Which do you think your husband would prefer?

18. How can you *inspire* his help rather than *require* it?

> 📖 Men are problem solvers by nature. They love to be our heroes, remedy our predicaments, and rescue us from our distresses. But when our problems are incredibly complex and deeply rooted, our husbands can feel overwhelmed and frustrated by their inability to fix things. So if you need a problem solved and your husband can solve it, feel free to look to him. But if you need therapy to overcome an ongoing issue that your husband isn't trained to handle, do yourself and your husband a favor and go to a therapist.
>
> Of course, the reverse is also true. If your husband has deep-seated issues he needs to work through, it's unrealistic to expect that you are all the counselor he needs. Encourage and support him, but don't try to fix him on your own. You're his wife, not his therapist. 📖

19. What effect could it have on her marriage if a wife worked through her insecurities and hurts with a professional counselor rather than looking to her husband to "fix" her?

20. Do you have any issues that you think you (or your husband) may need to work through with the help of a counselor? If so, what keeps either of you from seeking that professional help? What good things could result in your marriage if you were to get help?

> 📖 But one particularly hectic morning of trying to get everyone up, dressed, fed, packed, and out the door for school and work,

I let Greg's poor sense of direction put me on a high-speed emotional escalator. We pulled out of our driveway and stopped at a four-way intersection. Greg, as if on automatic pilot, turned left to go toward his office, even though we were en route to the kids' school, which required a right-hand turn. My tension had already been building all morning, and this was the little push that sent me right over the edge. I slammed my foot onto the imaginary brake pedal on the passenger floorboard and yelled, "*Where* are you going? Would you get your head out of the clouds and *pay attention,* for crying out loud?" As soon as the words came out of my mouth, I was flabbergasted by my own behavior, especially since my outburst had been in front of our kids.

Another one of Greg's quirks, which I've actually come to appreciate (much more than his poor sense of direction), is his inability to get riled up. Rather than yelling right back after my outburst at that four-way intersection or sarcastically asking if I wanted to do the driving instead, Greg looked calmly at me and said, "Could you have a little more patience with me? I wasn't thinking, but that doesn't give you the right to yell at me." Of course, he wasn't calm on the inside. He admits his heart felt incredibly hardened toward me in that moment. I had already eaten breakfast, but the situation called for a big helping of humble pie for dessert....

Now, instead of yelling at Greg, I put my hand on his thigh to get his attention, give him a cute little grin and an eyebrow raise, and ask, "Where are you going?" This approach enables him to laugh at himself with me. Even if we're running short on time, I tell myself, *What difference is it going to make to anyone's salvation if we're a couple of minutes late because Greg accidentally took a wrong turn?* 📖

21. Does your husband have any quirks that drive you crazy? If so, how might you respond to them so as not to hinder his flame of joy and passion for you?

🌿 GROWING TOGETHER
(Sharing the Truth in Small-Group Discussion)

📖 Put a stop to playing games to get your needs or desires met. Granted, we all have times when we feel the need to nurture others, when we want to be nurtured by someone else, when we desire to help someone become a better person, or when we need to overcome issues to become better people ourselves, but game playing is never the answer. With God's help you can learn to recognize and verbalize those needs and desires such that your husband feels respected by you rather than manipulated.

The only way that you will ever truly experience relational fulfillment is by simply loving your husband for who God made him to be (rather than trying to make him play the role you want him to play). By recognizing and verbalizing your own needs or desires, you'll be setting the stage for *both* of you to feel like winners. 📖

22. Put a star beside the following mind games that you have played with your husband, and describe what you do when you play this game.

The Mommy-Child Game
The Spoiled Child–Sugar Daddy Game
The Holy Spirit–Wretched Sinner Game
The Patient-Psychotherapist Game
Other Mind Games

23. What unmet needs do you think you are experiencing when you play

such games? How might you inspire—rather than demand—your husband to meet those needs?

> 📖 Because I accepted his no, my husband wanted to give me a wholehearted yes whenever possible. I suspect that your husband is probably a lot like mine. When you pout, cry, or pitch a royal fit, it only makes him want all the more to dig his heels in the dirt. But if you take his no for an answer and respect his feelings, you will motivate your husband to consider seeing things from your perspective. I offer this not as a way for you to manipulate your husband more effectively but as a way to maintain unity and harmony, fueling the joy and passion you both desire and inspiring a more cooperative spirit in each of you. 📖

24. Have you ever failed to take your husband's no for an answer in order to get your way? If so, describe how he responded.
25. If you could rewind the tape and do things over again, what would you do differently to maintain unity in the relationship? Do you think it would have made a difference in your husband's response? Why or why not?

> 📖 Try to refrain from having any expectations about what his answer *should* be when you ask what he's thinking. If you expect that he should be thinking about you and this is your reason for asking, you are fishing for affirmation or a compliment. But when you ask with pure motives (simply wanting to feel a connection with him in a given moment), you'll be able to accept any answer he gives, regardless of whether it's what you hoped to hear....
>
> Don't take it personally if his words don't match up to the imaginary script you dream of in your own mind. Let him connect with you in his own words and in his own special way. 📖

26. Do you at times fish for affirmation or a compliment from your husband, then feel disappointed because you don't hear what you'd hoped to hear?

27. Do you think it would be fair for your husband to feel disappointed if he asked you a question and you didn't tell him exactly what he wanted to hear?

28. How can you guard against creating expectations in your mind that your husband can't possibly fulfill?

29. God is the only One we can always depend on for the affirmation we crave. How, practically speaking, can you turn to Him to satisfy the longings of your heart?

> 📖 Consider how it might impact your marriage for the better if you simply refused to take a small incident, blow it way out of proportion in your mind, and get overly emotional about it. What if you never sweated the small stuff and instead rolled with whatever unexpected punches life throws your way? What if you learned to laugh about your husband's poor sense of direction (or whatever little personality quirk he has that can drive you insane with frustration)? What if you could accept his no without any manipulative drama? What if you learned to give your husband the grace to have his own thoughts and you refused to take things personally? What if you held firmly to the belief that your husband loves you like crazy and desires to be intimate with you whenever possible? Wouldn't it be much easier to ignite and maintain incredible joy and passion in your relationship?
>
> You bet it would. So do yourself (and your husband) a favor and try to remain grounded whenever you sense the temptation to take another emotional escalator ride. 📖

30. Why do you think some women are prone to emotional escalation? Is this true of you? If so, in what way?

31. As you look at the things you've complained about in your marriage, ask yourself if they are important enough to warrant disrupting the harmony in your relationship. Why or why not?

32. How can you keep the main thing (joy and passion) as the main thing and not sweat the small stuff that can wreak havoc in your marriage?

∞∞

Lord Jesus, from the beginning of time, women have played manipulative mind games to get their ways or justify their bad behaviors. We deeply desire to be amazing women who exemplify Christ in our marriages and in this world, yet we often behave in ways that aren't in line with this desire. Show us what kind of mind games we fall prey to and what kind of emotional escalators we hop on, so we can avoid the dysfunctional dynamics they create in our marriages. Teach us to recognize our own needs and to communicate them to our loved ones in ways that inspire them to help meet those needs. In Your most holy and precious name, amen.

how his flame dies (part B)

Read chapters 8 and 9 of *Every Woman's Marriage.*

🌱 PLANTING GOOD SEEDS
(Personally Seeking God's Truth)

As you seek to avoid unhealthy comparisons, plant this good seed in your heart:

> We do not dare to classify or compare ourselves with some who
> commend themselves. When they measure themselves by them-
> selves and compare themselves with themselves, they are not wise.
> (2 Corinthians 10:12, NIV)

1. Why do we compare ourselves to other people? Why do we compare
   our husbands to other men?
2. How can you guard your heart against unhealthy comparisons? What
   thought can you meditate on when you catch your mind drifting in this
   direction?

As you consider how you may encourage your husband in his on- and off-
the-clock pursuits, plant these good seeds in your heart:

> But encourage one another daily, as long as it is called Today, so that
> none of you may be hardened by sin's deceitfulness. (Hebrews 3:13, NIV)

And let us consider how we may spur one another on toward love and good deeds. (Hebrews 10:24, NIV)

Therefore encourage one another and build each other up, just as in fact you are doing. Now we ask you, [sisters], to respect those who work hard among you, who are over you in the Lord and who admonish you. (1 Thessalonians 5:11–12, NIV)

3. Can you remember a specific time when someone did something that encouraged you? What did that person do? How did it make you feel?

4. How can you be more of an encouragement to your husband? How do you think he would feel if you began doing and saying things every day to encourage him?

⚒ WEEDING OUT DECEPTION
(Recognizing the Truth)

📖 What about you? Are you ever resentful of your husband's job? jealous of things he gets to do? adamant that he change or not change careers because of how it may affect you?

I realize that there are situations when a wife needs to gently speak up, especially if her husband is a workaholic or regularly ignores the needs of his family. But if you are like me, there are times when your dissatisfaction is born out of selfishness or of jealousy of the time and energy your husband pours into his career, because it takes him away from you. 📖

5. Do you ever compare your career or lifestyle to your husband's and feel envious of the time and attention he pours into his professional pursuits? Do you ever feel as if you play second fiddle to his job? Why or why not?

6. Do you think your husband would want you to feel the way you do about the time and energy he invests in his job or career? Why or why not?

7. Are you able to express appreciation for how hard your husband works outside and/or inside the home? Why or why not? What steps can you take to show him how you feel?

> 📖 I began staying home and letting Greg go to his games by himself more and more, even though he urged me to come each time. I thought I was making a point by refusing to go, but after a while, I dreaded the sound of the door closing and the car driving off while I stayed at home with two kids. I didn't like him going to games because I wanted him to stay home with me, and I made sure he knew that before he left. I felt as if softball was a much higher priority to Greg than our family was, and I felt cheated. I came to see softball as a mistress that he was more faithful to than he was to me. I couldn't recognize that softball was the outlet my husband desperately needed to recharge his physical, mental, and emotional batteries. 📖

8. Does your husband have a sport or hobby that takes a significant amount of time or takes his focus away from you? If so, how have you felt about it and why?

9. Have you ever felt you should be allowed time off to shop, do things with your girlfriends, or pursue a hobby, yet resented it when your husband expressed a similar expectation? After reading this section, have your feelings about his off-the-clock activities changed at all? If so, how? If not, why?

> 📖 One of the most shameful mistakes I've ever made was once saying to Greg early in our marriage, "You just don't seem to approach me with as much whirlwind passion as I'm used to. If

you could be a little more enthusiastic in sweeping me off my feet and into bed, I'd be more willing to go there."

He responded kindly but firmly, "Shannon, don't ever compare me to another man that you had no business being in a sexual relationship with in the first place."

It was another *Ouch!* moment in the life of Shannon Ethridge but a much needed wake-up call, pointing out that I had been unfairly comparing Greg to a past lover. If the tables had been turned and Greg had said something along the lines of, "You know, you aren't as thin or beautiful as some of the other girls I've been attracted to. If you would lose a few pounds and fix yourself up a little more, I'd be much more attentive," I would have been cut to the core. I'm sure that in that moment, he must have felt the same way. 📖

10. Have you given in to the temptation of comparing your husband to your boss? coworker? father? pastor? friend? another man? If so, who is that person and what about him do you admire or wish your husband could emulate?

11. Now list five things that your husband does well or that you love about him.

📖 Most of us have someone in our lives who drives us to unhealthy comparisons, whether it's the perky personal trainer at the fitness club, the happy little homemaker next door who has all her photos in a Creative Memories scrapbook and cuts her kids' sandwiches in the shape of stars, or the sexy glamour queens who grace the silver screen....

It's easy to compare ourselves to other women and to ruminate on all the ways that we don't measure up.... When we do this, we rob ourselves of our peace, our joy, and our confidence. We also put our husbands in an incredibly tight spot as we fish for the affirmation we need with such questions as "Am I as pretty as she is? as good a cook? as good a housekeeper?" Most men are smart enough to know that the answer to any such question should always be "Of course, dear!" so don't bother asking your husband. It only magnifies your own insecurities in both your eyes and his. It also places the burden of responsibility on his shoulders to make you feel good about yourself, but feeling good about yourself is a gift that only *you* can give *yourself*. 📖

12. To whom have you compared yourself in the past, only to feel discouraged because that individual outshines you somehow? What did you admire about this person?

13. How can you affirm that person for that particular gift, talent, or attribute without coveting it for yourself? Can you be genuinely happy for that person rather than envious? Why or why not?

14. Do you feel good about who you are—what you look like, how you interact with others, and so on? If so, list five things you like about yourself. If not, list why you don't feel good about yourself and consider seeing a counselor about those issues.

🌾 HARVESTING JOY AND PASSION
(Applying the Truth)

📖 While women often have a mind-boggling number of responsibilities to tend to, we can't forget that our husbands also face a whirlwind of challenges every day. Not only do they need to bring home the bacon, they need to make enough money to save for the future. Not only do they need to get the job done, they need to impress the boss and coworkers and meet quotas and deadlines in a way that shows they are capable, decisive, and efficient.

Your husband faces a plethora of daily pressures, and every hour

of his day can sometimes feel like an uphill battle. He needs to
know, beyond a shadow of a doubt, that someone is on his side,
regardless of how well or how poorly he feels he's doing that day.
He needs someone who is committed to rooting him on to success
both at work and at home. 📖

15. List the ways in which your husband contributes to your marriage, kids,
and household (for example, he goes to work every day to bring home
money, plays soccer with the kids, handles the bills, maintains the cars,
helps with dishes, gives me a few minutes to myself).

16. Now list some ways you can show your husband how much you appreciate his contributions (for example, make his favorite dessert, detail his
car, tuck a note in his lunch, plan a getaway date together). Once you've
made your list, circle at least one and carry it out this week.

> 📖 Greg has often felt caught between my conflicting desires.
> From one side of my mouth I'm telling him I want him to spend
> more time with our family, and from the other I'm telling him that
> I want a better standard of living....
>
> Remember, most men don't need a lot of stuff in order to be
> happy. Greg was perfectly happy in a next-to-naked apartment for
> two years before we got married. While I've learned to decorate on
> a tight budget, the most important lesson I've learned is that genu-
> ine happiness doesn't come from having nicer stuff or a bigger
> house. Happiness is found in the love we have for one another
> and the memories we make together as a family. 📖

17. Do you ever want things you can't have or afford? How does it make
you feel?

18. How do you think it makes your husband feel when he knows you want
something he can't provide?

19. Identify some of your favorite childhood memories or some special moments you've shared with your husband and kids. Why do you remember those times so fondly? Was money or stuff part of the reason?

20. What thing(s) spoke to you most in chapter 9, "Comparing Apples and Oranges"?

21. What impact would it have on your marriage and family if you learned to be content with your husband, yourself, and your possessions? How can you become more content with what you *do* have?

🍃 Growing Together
(Sharing the Truth in Small-Group Discussion)

> 📖 If your husband were unemployed and you had no salary to live on, would his current situation be a welcome change in your wondering how your family would keep a roof over its head and food in the pantry? I don't mean to be melodramatic, but let's put things into perspective. The next time you feel resentful of your husband's career, ask yourself if you have a legitimate complaint and if adjustments can be made. If so, discuss your concerns calmly and respectfully. For example, you might start off with, "Honey, can we sit down and assess how our lives are going right now and talk about what's most important to each of us and to our family?" If you realize that adjustments can't be made for whatever reason, know that your husband needs your encouraging support far more than he needs your resentment. Do what you can to let him know that you are his biggest fan and that you want him to succeed at work and to feel good about his ability to provide for his family. That's the kind of cheerleader he's going to want to come home to whenever possible. 📖

22. Tell the group about some of the things you've done or said to en-
    courage your husband in his roles as a husband, father, and employer
    or employee. How did he respond? How did his response make you
    feel?

23. Also share some of the ideas you wrote down (in question 16) for how
    you would like to express appreciation toward your husband in the
    future. Ask the group to hold you accountable for doing the thing you
    circled by the next meeting.

    📖 Over the next several years, Greg was a teetotaler, not playing
or watching any sports out of submission to my desires. But he
was also dying on the vine. Without the relief outlet he'd found in
softball, he was more stressed about his work and less excited about
life. At the time I didn't connect the change in Greg to his withdrawal from sports. But if I had been more committed to seeing
Greg's heart and to meeting his needs, I would have seen that even
though I had succeeded in getting him to spend more time with
our family, I had belittled him for his love of sports and made him
feel guilty. I may as well have literally ripped out his heart and
stomped on it....

    Perhaps your husband doesn't have a passion for sports but rather
some other activity that gives him a sense of joy and satisfaction.
Perhaps he retreats to the outdoors to hunt, fish, or dig around in
the garden, or immerses himself in a new computer software program, or hides out in the basement with his guitar or other musical
instrument. Whatever your husband's hobby, I encourage you not to
take his passion for it personally. Don't be his opponent by assuming
that he uses these hobbies as an escape from his family (which is
more than likely not true). Instead, encourage him to do the things
he loves and is energized by. When we allow our husbands this time,

we inspire them to return to us as much happier campers, with greater desires to connect emotionally with us. 📖

24. What does your husband love to do in his free time that really energizes him? How do you feel about this hobby or activity? Why?

25. What if your husband told you, "Honey, why don't you take the whole day to do whatever you love doing? I'll take care of the kids and the house. You go shopping or read a novel in front of the fireplace all day." How would you feel?

26. Now what if you told your husband, "Honey, why don't you take next Saturday to do whatever you want to do that you've not gotten to do in a while? Feel free to spend all day on the golf course or tinkering in your shop." How do you think he would feel? Can you imagine making such a gesture? Why or why not?

> 📖 Unfortunately, I'm not the only wife who has fallen into the trap of comparing her husband to other men. Consider these comments and ask yourself if you have ever alluded to such a sentiment in any way:
>
> - "Her husband still takes her out on a date each week and sends her cards and flowers often. How come you don't do that for me anymore?"
> - "Why can't you be as handy around the house as my dad? He would have had that problem fixed in no time!"
> - "It really makes me feel special when the guys at the office will take a few moments just to talk to me and ask how my day is going. Why can't you show such an interest?"
> - "He must really love his wife the way he takes such good care of their yard. How do you think the way our yard looks makes me feel?" 📖

27. Have you ever been guilty of making such comparative statements to or about your husband? If so, was the comment you made appropriate in light of what you learned in this part of the book? Why or why not?

28. How can you avoid unhealthy comparisons and become more sensitive about your choice of words?

📖 Chances are, if you are reading this book, you do have a husband—something most single women would love to have. If you are able to get up and exercise, do so with a happy heart, thanking God for your good health. If you have children of your own, be grateful that you aren't one of the multitudes of women who struggle with infertility month after month. If you have a roof over your head, food in your pantry, and gas in your car, you are actually among the wealthiest people on the planet compared to those in many other countries.

The next time you are tempted to compare apples to oranges, or to compare your own situation to a seemingly better one, remember that God has custom-tailored these blessings especially for you, especially for this season of your life. He has given you a unique size, shape, and personality, all to be used for His glory rather than your own. He has given you a marvelously unique husband and perhaps children, complete with a few character flaws that serve as great reminders that no one is perfect in every way. He has blessed you with a comfortable home where you can take refuge from the world and make memories that will warm your heart more and more with each passing birthday.

Absolutely nothing can compare to the joy of finding contentment in these remarkable gifts that the Lord lavishes upon us. And displaying that joy is the secret to fanning your husband's flame for you. Just ask any husband whose wife has learned the

art of contentment rather than the craft of comparison, and he'll
more than likely tell you that he is one happy man. 📖

29. You probably remember the hymn, "Count Your Blessings." What three
things are you most grateful for in your life?

∞

*Lord, we confess that we sometimes resent the time our husbands
spend at work and that we envy the woman next door who seems to
have her act together. Help us to be our husbands' biggest fans and
help them find confidence in the fact that their wives are their own
personal cheerleaders. Convict us when we look upon others' attributes, relationships, or possessions with jealousy rather than with genuine happiness. Remind us that in You we have everything we need,
and teach us how to be content with the multitude of blessings You
bestow on us. In Jesus's name, amen.*

from death to life again

Read chapters 10 and 11 of *Every Woman's Marriage*.

🌱 PLANTING GOOD SEEDS
(Personally Seeking God's Truth)

As you seek to understand what it means for couples to mutually submit, plant this seed in your heart:

> And further, you will submit to one another out of reverence for Christ. You wives will submit to your husbands as you do to the Lord. For a husband is the head of his wife as Christ is the head of his body, the church; he gave his life to be her Savior. As the church submits to Christ, so you wives must submit to your husbands in everything.
>
> And you husbands must love your wives with the same love Christ showed the church. (Ephesians 5:21–25)

1. Some women cringe when they hear the *s* word—*submission*. Why do women have such a negative response to this concept?
2. Why did Paul say we are to "submit to one another" in verse 21? Explain what you believe Paul meant.
3. What advice would you give a new bride who is struggling with the concept of mutual submission?

As you seek to give your husband what he really wants most (your smile!), plant these good seeds in your heart:

> Always be full of joy in the Lord. I say it again—rejoice! Let every-
> one see that you are considerate in all you do. Remember, the Lord
> is coming soon. (Philippians 4:4–5)

> We were filled with laughter,
>   and we sang for joy.
> And the other nations said,
>   "What amazing things the LORD has done
>   for them."
> Yes, the LORD has done amazing things for us!
>   What joy! (Psalm 126:2–3)

> The LORD is my strength, my shield from every danger.
>   I trust in him with all my heart.
> He helps me, and my heart is filled with joy.
>   I burst out in songs of thanksgiving. (Psalm 28:7)

4. Are you able to choose to be joyful because of what God has done for you, even if your temporary circumstances may not warrant joy at the time? Why or why not?

↘ WEEDING OUT DECEPTION
(Recognizing the Truth)

> 📖 Our husbands aren't mind readers, and they may have their own
> ideas about how they prefer to accomplish various tasks. As long as
> things get done, do they really have to get done *our* way? Only if we
> want to make our husbands resent having to help us. 📖

5. Have you ever helped someone with a particular task, only to have that person dictate exactly how you were to do the job or criticize you for not doing it "right"? If so, how did you feel? Were you inspired to continue helping?

6. Is there a specific chore or task that you insist your husband do *your* way? How do you imagine it makes him feel when you fail to appreciate *his* way of doing it?

> 📖 What might be the reason you seek to win arguments every time or to get that last word in? Is it so you can feel superior? more intelligent or articulate? Are you merely resorting to childish behavior because you've not learned to respond to strife like a mature adult? Or do you try to inflict harm on your husband so that there's some sense of justification or revenge for your own pain?
>
> When we insist on getting the last word, we don't resolve any disagreements. We only cement them in our husbands' minds as they leave the room feeling disrespected and resentful. I'm sure you'll agree with me: winning an argument isn't nearly as important as ultimately winning your husband's admiration and affection. 📖

7. Is winning your husband's admiration and affection more important to you than winning an argument? Why or why not?

8. Can you recall a time you when you sought to win an argument, even at the expense of your husband's feelings? If so, how does it make you feel in hindsight?

9. Can you recall a time when you and your husband differed on something, yet you recognized that winning the argument wasn't the most important thing? If so, how did the disagreement end? How might it have ended if you had not handled the situation the way you did?

📖 Beware of ever playing the God card.... For many women this is simply a spiritualized form of control over our husbands. If such is the case, can you imagine how God might feel about us using His name to justify our attempts at controlling our husbands? In humility, we need to remember that our believing husbands can usually hear from God as easily as we can, and there's always a possibility that God may give our husbands a word that we've not yet received. 📖

10. Are there times when you feel you are more spiritually aware than your husband of what God expects? If so, what makes you feel this way? Do you think your feelings are justified? Why or why not?

11. In your own words, explain what "playing the God card" means. What do you suspect is behind this behavior?

12. Suppose you choose *not* to play the God card but rather trust that your husband can hear from God as easily as you can. How will this make your husband feel? Why?

📖 What's usually behind a woman's quest for control? Experts agree that an overwhelming need to control is actually an outward manifestation of the inward insecurities we feel. When we're good with ourselves, we're usually good with almost everyone around us. But when we're not feeling so good about ourselves, we often seek to assign the blame to someone outside of ourselves, ruminating on such thoughts as, *If my husband were more attentive... If my kids were better behaved... If my home were more in order... If my coworkers were more appreciative... Then my world would be a better place and I'd feel and act like a better person.*

Of course, controlling women will tell you that they *must* be controlling for anything to get done because their husbands are so passive. But it's worth asking ourselves, *Am I controlling because he's so passive, or is he passive because I'm so controlling?* 📖

13. Did this particular excerpt strike a chord in you? Have you found that when you don't feel good about yourself, you need to control others? Why or why not? Or do you have another theory as to what causes you to feel out of control at times? (Remember to focus on what's going on inside of you rather than on how others around you are behaving.)

14. What things can you do to exercise the best form of control—*self-control*—rather than attempting to control those around you?

HARVESTING JOY AND PASSION
(Applying the Truth)

📖 Consider the example of a chief executive officer and a chief operations officer. (For simplicity's sake, we'll refer to the CEO as "he" and the COO as "she.") Ultimately, the CEO is the leader in charge, but he delegates the authority to lead the day-to-day operations to the COO. The COO is free to set goals, direct the staff, make decisions and suggestions, offer feedback, and so on, but she does it as an *extension* of the CEO, not because she feels the CEO is incompetent or unwilling to do it himself. She constructively controls many areas of operation, but she always respects the fact that she's under the CEO's umbrella of authority. Her position isn't a threat to the CEO at all, but rather a benefit and a blessing.

Now apply this same relational dynamic to marriage. Ultimately, God has given husbands the charge of being the spiritual head of the household, but God also created woman as a "helpmate" to man. Think of woman as a COO of sorts who is under her husband's authority, the CEO of their family. She may be the one setting certain goals, calling many shots, directing the staff (or children), making decisions, and so on. But rather than doing so begrudgingly because her husband's not around all day or because she feels he's incapable of doing it himself, she operates in this role with excellence as an extension of him. She's under his authority, but she willingly receives the delegation of certain realms of responsibility as a vital part of his team. 📖

15. Do you see yourself as a capable chief operations officer under the authority of your husband? Or are you tempted at times to think that you have to run the show because your husband's not capable? Why do you feel the way you do?

16. Would your husband agree with your assessment? If he, as your chief executive officer, were asked to give you a periodic review, how would he rate your performance? your attitude? Why?

17. Identify three things you could do to develop a more positive attitude about the roles you play within your marriage, family, and home.

18. How would it impact your life if you exhibited a positive team player attitude? How would it affect your husband? your children?

> 📖 Many women complain that their husbands don't initiate family devotions or prayer time together. So what's wrong with the wife acting as the COO and cheerfully *offering* to read a devotion or say a prayer, or respectfully *inviting* the CEO to do so? You may be amazed at how well received such an invitation, offered with the right attitude, may be. Remember, just because a wife thinks of the idea or initiates more often doesn't mean that she's the spiritual leader. It simply means she's a great help-mate. 📖

19. Have you held the opinion that for your husband to fulfill his role as the spiritual leader, he must initiate all the spiritual activity in your home? If so, what gave you this opinion?

20. How can you let go of any expectation that your husband should always be the spiritual initiator? How do you think this new perspective could affect your marriage and family?

📖 Your husband's greatest desire doesn't revolve around sex, sports, sandwiches, sitcoms, or success, but around putting a smile on your face. I've asked Greg to tell you why this is so—at least from one male's perspective: "A few years ago, Shannon asked what attracted me most to her while we were dating.... What attracted me most was that Shannon was happy whenever I was around (and relatively unhappy whenever we had to be apart). Her smile made me feel really great about myself and my ability to make a woman like her happy.... Everyone wants to be in the presence of someone who makes them feel good about *themselves*—it's just human nature.... A man's self-esteem is wrapped up in how good of a husband, father, provider, friend, and lover he is. When we're not making the grade and we see the disappointment on our wife's face as a result, it's like looking into a mirror and seeing the loser we've always feared becoming." 📖

21. How do you think your husband feels about himself when he looks at the expression you have on your face most of the time? Why?

22. If you were to make the conscious choice to smile more often, what effect might it have on your husband's self-esteem? Why?

📖 You—more than anyone else—have the power to make your husband's day. You may find it helpful to sit down and make as long a list as possible of things you can be happy about. Even when I'm in the bluest of moods, I can always rattle off a long list of blessings that God has bestowed upon me, such as my salvation, my marriage, my children, good health, a loving extended family, great friends, ministry opportunities, healing for the past, security for today, hope for tomorrow, and so on.

What about you? How long a list can you think of just off the top of your head? Enough to bless your husband with a smile and a warm look of contentment? 📖

23. Are there things in your life that you often forget to smile about? Go ahead—make a list of the blessings you can be happy about.

🍂 GROWING TOGETHER

(Sharing the Truth in Small-Group Discussion)

24. What portion of this week's readings spoke to you, convicted you, or encouraged you most? Share that passage with others and explain why it meant so much to you.

> 📖 But why do we become so controlling when company is due to arrive? Because we want our guests to feel special, but I also believe it can be a pride thing. We want others to think we are a perfect family who lives in a perfect house. But the reality is, we all have occasional dust bunnies on the floor, toothpaste in the sink, or imprints on the bedspread. Maybe we should focus more effort on developing a hospitable frame of mind before company arrives instead of obsessing over every detail of our houses and every neglectful act of our husbands. 📖

25. Do you often suffer from "precompany perfection"? If so, why? If not, how do you avoid this relational pitfall?

> 📖 We are following in Eve's footsteps when we seek control rather than submissiveness. When we seek control, we sometimes *create* the exact behavior in our husbands that we abhor. I confess I've been guilty in the past of insisting that Greg do things my way, and then resenting him for not being a stronger leader in our home. I've dragged him into counseling for his "passivity issues" when, in fact, my control issues were ultimately the real root of our problems. When this dynamic is present, it's like what Jesus said in Mark 3:25,

"If a house is divided against itself, that house cannot stand" (NIV). It creates a Catch-22 situation for both spouses. She wants him to lead, but she doesn't want to let go of the reins. He feels damned if he gives up control and damned if he doesn't. No one wins when spouses are in a power struggle. We can't complete each other as helpmates if we are competing with one another for control.

Therefore, when women ask, "How do I get my husband to take the wheel and be the leader?" I tell them, "By getting out of the driver's seat!" In most cases, as long as a wife is trying to manipulate and control, her husband will usually ride along in the backseat for the sake of unity and in an effort to keep her happy. But if a wife will trust her husband and follow him, even when she doesn't necessarily agree with how he's driving or where he's taking her, he might just develop the courage or the desire to become the leader that she wants him to be. 📖

26. If your marriage were a car, who would be in the driver's seat? Has your need for control ever been a source of tension in your relationship? Why or why not?

27. If you have a tendency to try to be in control in your marriage, how can you make a conscious effort to let go of the wheel?

28. What effect might surrendering the need for control have on your life? your marriage? your family?

📖 Indeed, happiness is a choice, and being happy can simply be a matter of smiling more often. In fact, some studies indicate that our facial expressions are not so much a reflection of our feelings, but that our feelings are largely a reflection of the facial expression we wear.* I've experimented with this theory, and it works. The

---

* Malcolm Gladwell, *Blink* (New York: Little, Brown and Company, 2005), 206.

more I smile, the happier I feel. We are free to choose both our facial expressions and our attitudes in any given situation. 📖

29. Test this theory for a moment. Look around the room and smile at several people, or if you are by yourself, smile into a mirror for a minute or two. Do you feel different? How so?

30. What difference would it make in your household if your husband and children came home each day to a woman who had a smile on her face? Why? Is this a goal you'd like to strive for?

∞

*L*ord, *You've given us so much to smile about, yet we often fail to reflect Your joy, peace, and fulfillment on our faces. Turn our frowns upside down and help us radiate Your love to others simply by choosing to be happy. Especially help us in our quest to surrender prideful forms of control when we behave like Mrs. (Always) Right. Remind us to focus our energies on controlling ourselves, our tongues, and our attitudes rather than on trying to control others. Encourage our husbands to have the confidence to fulfill their leadership roles in our homes, and give us the grace to go along with them on this wonderful ride called marriage. Amen.*

reigniting joy and passion

Read chapters 12, 13, and 14 of *Every Woman's Marriage*.

 PLANTING GOOD SEEDS
(Personally Seeking God's Truth)

As you seek to respect your husband, plant this good seed in your heart:

> So again I say, each man must love his wife as he loves himself, and
> the wife must respect her husband. (Ephesians 5:33)

1. As mentioned in chapter 12 of *Every Woman's Marriage,* the Greek word
   Paul uses for "respect" is *phobeo,* which means "to be in awe of" or "to
   revere."* Do you consider your husband worthy of high regard? Does
   he inspire awe in you? How so?
2. Do you make the choice to revere your husband? What do you do to
   express to him your reverence or respect?

---

* Shaunti Feldhahn, *For Women Only: What You Need to Know about the Inner Lives of Men*
  (Sisters, OR: Multnomah, 2004), 27.

As you seek to become a pleasant person to live with, plant these seeds in your heart:

> It is better to live alone in the corner of an attic than with a contentious wife in a lovely home. (Proverbs 21:9)

> It is better to live alone in the desert than with a crabby, complaining wife. (Proverbs 21:19)

3. Are there days when your testiness causes your husband to prefer to be in the corner of an attic or in the desert rather than be with you? If so, how can you turn your home from a place of strife to a place of sanctuary?

As you consider how you can become less irritable and more loving, plant this seed in your heart:

> If I could speak in any language in heaven or on earth but didn't love others, I would only be making meaningless noise like a loud gong or a clanging cymbal. If I had the gift of prophecy, and if I knew all the mysteries of the future and knew everything about everything, but didn't love others, what good would I be? And if I had the gift of faith so that I could speak to a mountain and make it move, without love I would be no good to anybody. If I gave everything I have to the poor and even sacrificed my body, I could boast about it; but if I didn't love others, I would be of no value whatsoever. (1 Corinthians 13:1–3)

4. Do the words "no value whatsoever" sound daunting to you? If so, what might you do to be more loving toward others so that you become more valuable to God's kingdom?

🖌 WEEDING OUT DECEPTION
(Recognizing the Truth)

📖 If you want to ignite your husband's joy and passion for you, you'll carefully consider your words to ensure that they communicate acceptance and respect. Ask him to tell you what things you say to him that cause him to feel disrespected—and then determine not to use those words again. Think about what respectful words you could use in their place, and then do so.

When you choose your words wisely and demonstrate respect for your husband, you'll reap many benefits. Not only will he feel good because he knows he pleases you, but your children will also grow to revere him all the more, and they will revere you as well…. Your marriage relationship will be enhanced, and your family will benefit from the security of a respectful atmosphere at home. Most of all, you'll please God with your attempts to show the respect that your husband, His beloved son, deserves—not because he does everything perfectly to deserve such reverence, but because he is divinely and uniquely created in his heavenly Father's image. 📖

5. If the way your husband feels about himself were contingent upon how you treat him, how do you think he feels?
6. If you have children, how do they treat their father? Are they reflecting how you treat him? How so?

📖 Of course, conflict is inevitable in any close relationship. It's not a matter of *if*, but simply a matter of *when* disagreements arise. Conflict doesn't mean we have a bad relationship or that we are unhappily married. Conflicts are simply opportunities for couples to grow in understanding of each other and to work out amiable resolutions. However, *how* we handle the conflict does have a bearing on the ongoing quality of the intimacy we share. So, in those moments when we don't see eye to eye, it's important not to let our emotions get out of control....

Most men find emotional tantrums annoying and will dig their heels in deeper rather than be manipulated by screaming or unnecessary crying.

So keep your voice at a normal level, face your husband, maintain eye contact, and even hold hands or have some part of your bodies touching. This kind of body language is much more effective than a turned back, folded arms, or rolling eyes. Remember, actions speak louder than words. 📖

7. Think of the last time you and your husband had a disagreement. What kind of body language did you use? Do you believe your actions demonstrated respect or disrespect? Why?

8. What's the difference between being upset because you are genuinely hurt versus being upset so you can punish or manipulate? Are you usually able to express your emotions calmly, or do you overdramatize so you get your way?

📖 In times of conflict, avoid taking the offensive or getting defensive and going head to head against each other. Remember that you are on the same team, fighting for victory over the opposing forces of anger, bitterness, unforgiveness, and so on.

Sadly, most of us enter conflict with one main goal—to win! And we usually assume that for us to win, the other person has to *lose.* But if you are familiar at all with Stephen Covey's *Seven Habits of Highly Effective People,* you'll more than likely recall his success strategy to develop a win-win mentality. To think win-win rather than win-lose is not only more effective in business but also in personal relationships, especially marriage. The most favorable strategy to maintain joy and passion in the midst of conflict is to figure out what kind of compromise can be had so that you both walk away feeling like a winner. 📖

9. What is the biggest recurring argument in your marriage? Who's usually on the offensive and who's on the defensive? Why?

10. What if both of you sat down and calmly discussed possible win-win solutions? Do you think you could come to an agreement? What might that agreement look like? (Remember, he needs to walk away feeling like a winner too!)

🐚 Harvesting Joy and Passion
(Applying the Truth)

📖 Intimacy is risky. As a husband and wife over time reveal to each other who they really are, they both hope that the other person will be unconditionally loving and accepting. If both spouses feel accepted and loved, then emotional, spiritual, and physical closeness usually results. But if one spouse feels unaccepted and unloved, that person will retreat, resulting in emotional, spiritual, and physical distance. To be free to open up and be ourselves in any relationship, we must first feel safe. If we feel unsafe, we will most likely withdraw into ourselves rather than risk trying to connect with the person who causes us to feel rejected in the first place. That's why acceptance is a key factor in building the kind of intimate marriage relationship we long for. 📖

11. If a stranger on the street approached your husband and asked, "Do you believe your wife accepts you for who you really are?" how do you think he would respond? Why?

12. If you long for a deeper level of intimacy with your husband, are you willing to go out of your way to demonstrate unconditional love and acceptance to inspire such intimacy? How might you do that more effectively?

> 📖 You also might want to talk with your husband about giving both of you permission to lovingly pull the other aside whenever one senses an attitude of rejection. Both of you need to feel the freedom to say, "My heart is beginning to feel closed toward you, and neither of us wants that. What's really going on here, and how can we get back on track?" or "I sense that your heart is growing cold toward me. Is there something that I've done or said that has caused you to feel this way? I really love you, and I want you to feel fully accepted, so help me treat you the way you deserve to be treated."
>
> Greg and I have given each other permission to say these kinds of things to each other, and as a result we've been better able to keep short accounts with each other and to remain spiritually connected. 📖

13. Explain what you think it means to "keep short accounts with each other." Do you believe the two of you do this successfully? Why or why not?

14. If you were feeling hurt by your husband, wouldn't you want him to ask you what he had done to hurt you and how he could make the situation right? Do you think you could demonstrate the same concern to him the next time you sense him growing distant? Why or why not?

> 📖 If couples make time (notice I said *make* time, not *find* time) to connect with each other on a regular basis, we can actually prevent conflicts from forming, or at least prevent them from becoming any more of an issue than they really need to be....

Indeed, we don't grow close or remain connected simply by coexisting in the same house and sleeping in the same bed. Lasting love takes tremendous effort. Strong relationships require work. Conflict is bound to come, but it can actually make our marriages stronger if we choose our words carefully, express our emotions calmly, respect each other's feelings, and work toward compromise. 📖

15. Because we rarely find time, how can you and your husband make time to prevent conflicts from forming? What's the best time of the day or week for you to keep an appointment to simply connect with each other?

📖 You can't blame a guy for wanting his home to reflect a little of *his* personality and hobbies, wanting to have some territory in the house that *he* can control, and wanting to have the freedom to relax and not worry about keeping everything spotless at all times. Women want the same thing. We want to reflect our tastes in our décor, to arrange rooms to suit us, and to have at least some space where we can just close the door and not worry about it being presentable all the time....

I think it's safe to say that the mood inside our homes is probably the most important part of their ambiance. We can have it decorated beautifully and immaculately clean, but as the saying goes, "If Mama ain't happy, ain't nobody happy!" 📖

16. Is there an area of your home that's strictly your husband's to control? If not, where might you make room to allow him this space?

17. Does the physical and emotional ambiance in your home reflect the mood you want to create for yourself and others? If not, what might need to be changed for your home to feel more like a safe haven for your family?

❦ GROWING TOGETHER

(Sharing the Truth in Small-Group Discussion)

📖 Our marriage was suffering because Greg was feeling the pressure to suppress his true self while I was trying to mold him into my image. I couldn't understand why he couldn't be more like me (outgoing and talkative), and I would drag him to parties and places where he could "practice" being more sociable. He would return home drained, not understanding why I thought it was necessary to try to change his more introverted personality. The problem, of course, wasn't *his*, but mine. 📖

18. Has your marriage suffered because you've tried to mold your husband into the image of who you want him to be? If so, how? If not, how have you safeguarded your relationship from this destructive dynamic?

19. What are the specific things you've tried to change about your husband in the past? In hindsight, were they really worth mentioning? Why or why not?

📖 Women often say they want their husbands to communicate more on an emotional level, but for most men to feel comfortable doing that, they must know we honor their feelings, whether we agree with their assessments or not. If your husband shares his feelings, try not to get angry with him for having them. Again, applaud his courage to confront the issue.

Greg and I were out on a date recently and saw a bumper sticker that read, "Men have feelings too! But then, who cares?" I was saddened by the expression, because I think it says what many men feel, not just because of the world we live in, but because of the women they live with....

Validating someone's feelings is simply a matter of somehow

communicating, "I'm not sure I would feel the same way in this situation, but you have a valid right to feel the way you do, and I can respect and appreciate that." Validation is our way of saying to our spouses, "I'm in your corner. I've got your back. I won't twist this knife or use this information against you or think any less of you because you feel this way. If anything, I think more highly of you for trusting me with your feelings." 📖

20. When your husband shares feelings with you that you don't necessarily agree with or appreciate hearing, do you get angry? sad? defensive? Or can you demonstrate to him that you care about his feelings?

21. Describe what it means to validate a person's feelings. How would it feel to be validated by someone you love when you are concerned about something? How would it make you feel to see others validated by your response to them?

📖 Creating a safe haven for my family isn't always easy, and I don't succeed at it on a daily basis. But because I love my husband and kids, I always *desire* to succeed at it. It takes time and energy and focus, but it's a ministry that is very worthy of all these things.

It often helps me to remember that the real me isn't the person whom others see teaching from a stage or speaking in front of a camera. That's the public side of me. The *real* me is the *private* side of me, the person with whom my husband and children have to live. If I minister to the world yet neglect my family's needs or harden their hearts toward me because of how busy I am or how difficult I am to live with, what have I gained? 📖

22. Do you ever treat your husband (or children) in ways that you would be ashamed for others to observe? If so, describe one of those times, what you did, and what you *wish* in hindsight you had done.

23. How can we avoid living a double life—acting sweet as pie when people are watching or listening, but sour as a lemon when no one besides our husband or children are around?

∞

Dear God, we confess there are times when we are difficult to live with. Marriage often brings out both the best and the worst in us. Help us in tense times or when we have major differences of opinion to always demonstrate proper respect and to fight our battles fairly so as to foster genuine intimacy, unconditional love, and acceptance in our relationships. Show us how we can create safer havens for our families to grow up in so that our husbands, children, and guests see the lavish love of God operating in our lives, and especially within the walls of our homes. For hearing these prayers, Lord, we give You thanks. Amen.

throwing fuel on his flame (part A)

Read chapters 15 and 16 of *Every Woman's Marriage*.

✦ PLANTING GOOD SEEDS
(Personally Seeking God's Truth)

As you seek to be faithful to your husband, plant these good seeds in your heart:

> You have heard that it was said, "Do not commit adultery."
> But I tell you that anyone who looks at a [man] lustfully has
> already committed adultery with [him] in [her] heart. (Matthew 5:27–28, NIV)

> But among you there must not be even a hint of sexual immorality. (Ephesians 5:3, NIV)

> God wants you to be holy, so you should keep clear of all sexual
> sin. Then each of you will control your body and live in holiness
> and honor—not in lustful passion as the pagans do, in their ignorance of God and his ways. (1 Thessalonians 4:3–5)

1. Why does God call us to control our own bodies and live in holiness and honor?

Another good seed to plant in our heart is 2 Corinthians 10:3–5 (NIV):

> For though we live in the world, we do not wage war as the world does. The weapons we fight with are not the weapons of the world…. We take captive every thought to make it obedient to Christ.

2. Explain what taking "captive every thought" and making "it obedient to Christ" means.
3. Why is learning to take thoughts captive important for a married woman? Is this something that comes naturally to you? Why or why not?

⚒ WEEDING OUT DECEPTION
(Recognizing the Truth)

📖 Just as a table has four legs that support it, we have four distinct components that comprise our sexuality: the physical, mental, emotional, and spiritual aspects. These four parts combine to form the unique sexual individual who God designed each of us to be. In other words, our sexuality isn't *what we do.* Our sexuality is *who we are,* and we were made with a body, mind, heart, and spirit, not just a body. If one of these legs is neglected, the table gets out of balance and quickly becomes a slide instead. And where might that slide lead? The pit of marital discontent, or even sexual compromise, as we may feel tempted to get one of these four needs met outside of our marriage relationship….

Genuine sexual and emotional fulfillment can only be discovered within a marriage relationship, not through an extramarital fling, solitary masturbation, lustful fantasies of other people, and so on. God designed the perfect plan of one man and one woman coming together in one unshakable union called marriage, where they can be naked and unashamed, just as Adam and Eve were before sin entered the picture and caused them to hide in shame (see Genesis 2:25 and 3:7). 📖

4. Have you ever felt that your husband wasn't meeting one of your basic needs, whether that need was physical, mental, emotional, or spiritual? If so, were you tempted to feel justified in looking outside your marriage to have that need met? Why or why not?

5. How can you safeguard yourself from giving in to this temptation in the future?

📖 Many women think that our emotional desires are by far superior to our husbands' sexual desires. We view our needs for emotional connection as legitimate and good. After all, God is exceedingly loving and wants relational intimacy with us. But we may have a hard time imagining that a man's need for sexual connection is just as legitimate and good. And that's where our theology goes awry.

Your husband, and all men, are made in the image of God, and God declared His creation "very good." Did God know Adam and all his male descendants would be visually stimulated and crave physical touch? would so deeply desire frequent and passionate sexual encounters? Yes. God designed men to be this way, and we cannot call unholy that which God has created and called good.

I can't explain this mystery, but I believe that when we get to heaven we'll say "Aha!" when we are able to understand the connection between male sexuality and God's spirituality. In the meantime, we must believe that the wife's role as the sole source of her husband's sexual satisfaction is a high and holy calling. 📖

6. Do you see your role in fulfilling your husband's sexual desires as a "high and holy calling"? Why or why not?

7. Have you ever felt as if your emotional needs were superior to your husband's physical needs? If so, how did it affect your relationship?

> 📖 When Greg gave me such a sweet compliment about how I light his fire by letting him look at me so often, I responded, "I'll bet you'll love looking at me a lot more when I lose these extra ten pounds!" He looked at my body and said, "Shannon, I can't imagine that you could ever look more beautiful to me than you do right now."
>
> There's a powerful, liberating message in Greg's words, girlfriends. We can't let a few extra vanity pounds cause such inhibition that we rob our husbands of one of the things he craves most—visual stimulation. Your husband is not as concerned with your dress size as he is with your willingness to let him look at you in (and out of) that dress. Most husbands will tell you that they don't need or even want their wives to look like anorexic celebrities. They want to gaze upon their wives' curves, regardless of their size. Your husband wants you to feel good enough about yourself that you are willing without hesitation to let him drink you in through his eyes any time he wants. 📖

8. Does the phrase "naked and unashamed" describe how you feel about yourself in your bedroom? Does it bother you that your husband longs to gaze upon your nude body? Why or why not?

9. What things can you do to foster a more uninhibited atmosphere in

your bedroom? How do you think your husband would react to your taking such measures?

10. Do you feel that being less inhibited in private with your husband is contradictory to being a "good Christian girl"? Why or why not?

HARVESTING JOY AND PASSION
(Applying the Truth)

Many women tell me that they love their husbands and even enjoy an occasional orgasm, but when their husbands try to initiate sex, these wives are often not all that interested. Some have even confessed that they wish sex wasn't a "requirement" in the relationship because they really don't feel much need for it.

If you've had similar thoughts, let me remind you that God created women, as well as men, to be sexual beings. So even if sexual stimulation and satisfaction aren't as strongly felt needs for you as they are for your husband, they *are* needs you have. Perhaps these needs are deeply buried or masked in you, but they're there nonetheless.

There have certainly been times when Greg was interested in having sex but I wasn't mentally prepared for it. I would entertain the thought in my brain for a second or two, just to see if I could muster up any desire whatsoever. If I felt as if I were hitting a wall and couldn't work up enough energy to get over that wall, my response was usually, "No, not tonight," followed by some lame excuse.

However, I have come to understand that a man can take his wife's sexual rejection very personally. It feels as if she's not just saying no to sex but no to him, and no to his love, his attention, his affection, and his desire for connection with her. I also discovered that even if I felt no desire whatsoever at the moment Greg initiated, desire would quickly blossom if I engaged in certain sexual activities out of love for him and out of my desire to receive the love he wanted to give me. In other words, I can choose to scale the wall instead of allowing it to keep me from the oneness that Greg and I can experience.

And what do I usually find on the other side of that wall? Euphoria. Some of our most intensely pleasurable moments have been experienced during times when my brain had initially told me I wasn't interested. 📖

11. Can you identify with women who say that they wish sex wasn't a requirement in the relationship? Have you buried your sexual desires somewhere so deep within that you don't know how to find them? If so, what may have been the cause?

12. What would it take for you to *scale* the wall rather than *hit* the wall the next time your husband initiates sex? Is it possible that your body could learn to enjoy that which your mind initially attempts to reject? Why or why not?

📖 When you are aware of how your lack of interest in sex can hurt your husband, it can motivate you to be more sensitive about how you respond during those times when it's really *not* a good time. So, rather than a cut-and-dried no, consider a more promising reply, such as, "This is not a good time for me right now, but can we carve out some time in the morning or tomorrow night? or this weekend?" Let your husband know that you are interested in connecting passionately with him (ideally within the next day or so), but that you prefer to wait until a more opportune time so that you can be more mentally and emotionally present or physically energized. Then make that time a priority, just as you would want him to make a date night with you a priority. Rather than perceiving this as procrastination or rejection, your husband will feel honored by your conscious effort to seize a more opportune moment in the near future for a passionate physical connection with him. Then he will melt when you make yourself ready and *you're* the one doing the initiating. 📖

13. When it's not a good time for you to engage in sexual relations, does your husband generally get a "no" response from you or a "yes, but not right now" response? How do you think your typical response makes him feel?

14. Do you believe that your husband's sexual needs are just as legitimate to him and his sense of well-being as your emotional needs are to you? Why or why not?

15. Do you appreciate that your husband finds you sexually attractive? How can you show him that you value his sexual interest in you? Think of at least three tangible ways to express your sentiments, and circle one that you intend to do within the next week.

❧ GROWING TOGETHER
(Sharing the Truth in Small-Group Discussion)

📖 [Men] want to feel special and welcomed when making love. They want their wives to sexually desire them.

When a wife loses interest, her husband feels shortchanged. It's really no different than how a woman can feel shortchanged by her husband when he seems disinterested in meeting her emotional needs. Meeting each other's needs, both sexual and emotional, is definitely a two-way street. Our husbands want us to be as excited and passionate about fulfilling their sexual needs as we want them to be about fulfilling our emotional needs.

As I've sought to become a more eager sexual partner for Greg,

I've had to learn that sexuality comprises four unique components that are intricately intertwined. I've discovered that by pursuing a physical connection with him, I'm opening the door to a more intimate emotional, mental, and spiritual connection with him as well. This revelation has helped me look forward to our lovemaking as much as I look forward to walking, talking, or worshiping with him. I've been delighted to find that my eagerness to connect with Greg physically has inspired him to connect with me on the other levels as well. 📖

16. Do you look forward to making love with your husband as much as you look forward to walking, talking, dining, or worshiping with him? Why or why not?

17. Would your husband describe you as an eager sex partner? Why or why not?

> 📖 It's been said that for a woman, sexual pleasure and orgasm are 95 percent mental and 5 percent physical, emphasizing the key role that mental preparation plays in women's lovemaking. While no one can assign an exact percentage to the importance that each component plays in creating a pleasurable sexual response, I believe it's true that preparing yourself mentally can result in more frequent and incredibly satisfying sexual encounters. 📖

18. What thoughts might a woman entertain to better prepare herself to fulfill her husband's sexual needs? (For example, what might she wear to bed, what kind of music might she play at bedtime, what could she offer to do to help him relax?)

19. What thoughts might she want to avoid as she anticipates moments alone with her husband? (For example, worrying about the cleanliness of the house or what she faces at work the next day, rehearsing how she wants to confront him about certain issues once they are alone.)

📖 Now consider two types of sexual connection in marriage—*light-bulb sex* versus *laser-beam sex*. We engage in light-bulb sex when we spread our mental and physical energies in many different directions (such as toward the kid who needs to be disciplined, the laundry that needs to be washed, the friend we need to call, how much we wish we could get "this" over with, and so on) rather than focusing on our husbands. Such a connection may satisfy the immediate physical urge for sexual release, but its power to bond a couple together mentally, emotionally, and spiritually is greatly limited.

With laser-beam sex, however, both spouses concentrate their mental and physical energies on each other.... They strive to meet each other's unique needs for physical and emotional intimacy. They make time for sexual intimacy a priority, even scheduling time alone together especially for this purpose, if necessary. They are physically and mentally present with each other, fully experiencing the intoxicating moments of pleasure and comfort with their mate.

Doesn't laser-beam sex sound much more appealing and ultimately satisfying to you than light-bulb sex? Sure. And which do you think would ignite more joy and passion in your husband? No doubt, he'd love to have you mentally, as well as physically, present during lovemaking. There's nothing more satisfying than knowing that you are the center of attention in your mate's mind, especially during sexual moments together. 📖

20. What distracting thoughts fill your mind when you are trying to focus on being intimate with your mate? What could you do to settle those issues so that they don't become distractions during times of intimacy with your mate?

21. Have you and your husband ever scheduled time alone, strictly for the purpose of making love? Does this sound like something you'd enjoy doing? Why or why not?

22. Think of at least five (ten if you are feeling inspired!) adjectives that would describe how your husband would feel if you initiated sex more often or demonstrated that you are eager to be sexually intimate with him.

23. Now think of at least five or more adjectives that would describe how it would make *you* feel to know that you've caused your husband to feel the things you've described. Would experiencing these emotions ignite the joy and passion you both desire?

∞

Heavenly Father, it's hard for us to understand the complexity of female sexuality, not to mention the complexity of male sexuality. But we know that Your perfect plan of one man and one woman being committed to each other for life enhances our abilities to be naked and unashamed with each other. Help us aspire to being the sexually eager wives that our husbands long for. Give us wisdom and discernment for how to effectively communicate our needs without ignoring or patronizing our husbands' needs. Unite us together as husbands and wives, not only as one flesh, but also one heart, one mind, and one spirit. In Jesus's name, amen.

throwing fuel on his flame (part B)

Read chapters 17, 18, and 19 of *Every Woman's Marriage*.

PLANTING GOOD SEEDS
(Personally Seeking God's Truth)

As you seek to establish a deeper level of spiritual and emotional intimacy with your husband, plant this seed in your heart:

> But what happens when we live God's way? He brings gifts into our lives, much the same way that fruit appears in an orchard— things like affection for others, exuberance about life, serenity. We develop a willingness to stick with things, a sense of compassion in the heart, and a conviction that a basic holiness permeates things and people. We find ourselves involved in loyal commitments, not needing to force our way in life, able to marshal and direct our energies wisely. (Galatians 5:22–23, MSG)

Read back through this passage on the fruits of the spirit, underlining those qualities you believe you possess in abundance, and circling those which you'd like to ask the Lord's help in developing more fully.

As you seek to lighten your husband's load by relying more on God, plant these good seeds in your heart:

> I am your shield,
> your very great reward. (Genesis 15:1, NIV)

> Your love, O LORD, reaches to the heavens,
> your faithfulness to the skies.
> Your righteousness is like the mighty mountains,
> your justice like the great deep....
> How priceless is your unfailing love!
> Both high and low...
> find refuge in the shadow of your wings.
> They feast on the abundance of your house;
> you give them drink from your river of delights.
> (Psalm 36:5–8, NIV)

1. While a husband should meet many of his wife's emotional needs, why are wives sometimes tempted to place *all* the responsibility on their husbands' shoulders rather than looking to God for the love and attention they crave? Is this sometimes a temptation for you? Why or why not?

WEEDING OUT DECEPTION
(Recognizing the Truth)

📖 Greg and I had been married less than five years when I volunteered to be a summer camp counselor. I went to the camp expecting to get swept up in serving the needs of the teenagers. However, I got swept up in an inappropriate emotional fling with Scott, a single male counselor.

I am sure you are wondering how I could have let that happen. In my midtwenties and incredibly naive about the dynamics of emotional affairs, I honestly thought that my actions were completely pure because Scott and I were not doing anything "sexual." We worshiped together during the evening services. We led Bible studies together with our coed small groups. We talked intimately about spiritual issues, sharing our favorite encouraging scriptures. We prayed together, holding hands only because we thought that's what people should do when they pray. As the week went on, the battle in my mind began to rage. Scott felt far more like a new boyfriend than a brother in Christ. Going home to Greg felt like a letdown.

A few days later, Scott began showing up at my house to spend his afternoons off with me while Greg was at work. It wasn't until Scott and I wound up in each other's arms that it dawned on us both that our feelings for one another had crossed the line, that confessions had to be made to my husband, and that new boundary lines had to be drawn in the relationship to avoid further inappropriate involvement. That's when I realized that there is a powerful connection between spirituality and sexuality. 📖

2. Have you shared (or do you currently share) a spiritual bond with another male that could pose a threat to your sexual integrity? If so, how does reading this passage from *Every Woman's Marriage* make you feel about the situation?

3. What types of spiritual activities do you think married women should avoid engaging in with men other than their husbands? Why?

📖 Don't let past sin intimidate you into a life of shame and sexual disconnection. We all have our own unique struggles (whether they are spiritual, mental, emotional, or physical). Husbands and wives have to learn how to fight battles *together* rather than allowing them to create turmoil in the relationship. The key to fighting together instead of fighting each other is being honest with yourself and with each other, freely forgiving each other, covering each other's back, and spurring each other on toward victory. When you experience overwhelming temptations that pose threats to your marital oneness, who better to ask account-ability from than the person who has a vested interest in your ability to overcome that issue?

Yes, in taking off your mask, you run the risk of losing your husband's respect if he fails to understand your struggle or if he takes it too personally. But you also stand to gain his respect and deeper levels of spiritual connection and sexual intimacy when you no longer have to pretend to be someone you are not. Knowing that Greg is aware of all the ugly stuff in my past yet is still by my side in the present and looking forward to a continued future to-gether gives me a great sense of safety and security. It also makes me want to give him the gift of my body as an expression of my love for him. 📖

4. Make a list of at least three pros and cons to living a completely open-book life with your spouse, involving him in even your deepest, darkest struggles.

5. Now take a step back and look at the big picture. Do you have more to gain or more to lose by being real in your marriage relationship? Do you believe genuine intimacy is worth the risk? Why or why not?

📖 As we've seen, sex can be a powerful tool, and while some hus-bands may enjoy being bribed in such a way, using sex to manipu-late someone was never God's intention. To have a healthy relationship, a wife needs to offer sex with no strings attached, out of love and commitment rather than as a bargaining tool.

One possible reason for this dynamic is that when a woman is single and dating, she has a certain power over a man. She knows,

I've got something you want, and I'll decide when you can have it. In
withholding sex until the honeymoon, she uses her sexual power
in a beneficial and godly way. However, after the vows are exchanged, this mentality needs to change. She needs to embrace
the idea that *I've got something you want, and because I love you
and I've committed to being your wife and your sole source of sexual
satisfaction, you can have it whenever you'd like.* Of course, I'm not
talking about being a sexual doormat to be walked all over without any con-cern for her needs or personal boundaries. I'm simply
saying that sex is to be offered freely in a marriage relationship,
not used as bribery. 📖

6. Have there been times when you offered your husband sex with strings
   attached, hoping to bribe him into giving you something you want? If
   so, how does that make you feel in hindsight?
7. If your husband spent quality time with you to bribe you into being
   willing to do something he wanted you to do, how might you respond?
   Might a husband have the right to feel the same way if his wife uses sex
   as a means of manipulating him into satisfying her own agenda? Why or
   why not?

🌾 HARVESTING JOY AND PASSION
(Applying the Truth)

📖 Of course, Greg wasn't always up to talking and praying at
great length every time he desired sex. Maybe your husband has
expressed a similar preference—that he doesn't want to *talk,* but
rather *touch.* Perhaps he doesn't want to *pray,* he just wants to *play.*
In those times, I've found that it helps to combine the two
activities—playing and praying.

For example, as you and your husband come together, you can

silently pray, *Lord, I may not feel like doing this right now, but I offer sex with my husband as an act of worship before You.* As you begin to rub his chest, visualize what's behind that rugged exterior and pray (sometimes aloud, sometimes silently), *Lord, thank You for my husband's heart. Thank You that he loves me so much, that he finds me attractive, and that he desires to be sexual with me.* As you become one in the flesh, silently pray, *Lord, thank You that You have knit us together as husband and wife. Help us remain true to our commitments to You and to each other. Strengthen us as a couple and help us to be in one accord.*

You get the idea. If the spiritual and emotional connection is what you are craving and the physical connection is what he is craving, swirl the two together and both of you can go to sleep satisfied. 📖

8. Based on what you have read in *Every Woman's Marriage,* is there a big distinction between sexual and spiritual intimacy in marriage? Is one more holy than the other? Should a wife feel offended when her husband would rather play than pray? Why or why not?

9. Do you find the idea of combining *playing* and *praying* foreign or familiar? How might this combination be beneficial in a marriage?

📖 Several husbands said that their wives seemed to pick and choose which scriptures they obeyed. These wives are into the verses "love your neighbor" and "husbands, love your wives as Christ loved the church," but they often ignore the second half of the verse: "The husband should not deprive his wife of sexual intimacy, which is her right as a married woman, nor should the wife deprive her husband" (1 Corinthians 7:3) and "The wife gives authority over her body to her husband" (verse 4). These husbands expressed frustration—and understandably so. After all, sexual intimacy is God's idea. It is not dirty or worldly. Sexual intimacy, according to God's design, is the most powerful way that two humans can connect with each other. When a husband and wife come together and become one through sexual intimacy in the presence of God, they are reflecting the nature of the Trinity. When couples view sex as sacred, it can become a wonderful act of worship. 📖

10. Explain how sexual intimacy within marriage can be an act of worship to God.

11. Do you agree with the scriptural mandate for husbands and wives not to withhold sexual pleasure from one another? Why or why not?

> 📖 It's admirable for a woman to be actively involved in her local church. It's good for her to be hands-on in her children's lives, to fulfill various social roles and responsibilities, and to have a career if she so chooses. However, if the combination of all those things causes you to have no energy left over for sexual intimacy with your husband, then you're too busy. Consider scaling back your office hours or dropping out of a church committee or two so that you can make more time and have more energy to minister to your husband's sexual needs. Sex isn't a secular act that we squeeze in between our spiritual activities. It's one of the most important spiritual activities in existence—and you alone can rightfully fill that role. A wife is the only human on the planet whom God has ordained to satisfy her husband's sexual needs. What a unique opportunity we have been given to minister to our husbands in such a powerful way! 📖

12. Do you consider your husband's sexual needs a ministry worthy of your time and attention? Why or why not?

13. What optional things in your life drain you of time and energy that you could be pouring into your sexual relationship with your husband? Are you willing to reevaluate your priorities and let some things go for the sake of your marriage? Why or why not?

> 📖 Remember the big blowout I wrote about in the opening of this book? I was contemplating leaving Greg and our two young children in search of the love I felt entitled to when I tearfully exclaimed, "You just don't meet my emotional needs!" But Greg saw past my weaknesses to my genuine needs and sincerely replied, "Shannon, you have a Grand Canyon of emotional needs, and even if every man in Dallas lined up outside your doorstep to spend time with you, it wouldn't be enough! *Until you look to God to satisfy your emotional needs,* there's nothing that I, or any other man on the planet, can do to satisfy you!"
>
> While some women may have taken this as a major insult and walked out the door, I recognized the truth in his statement. In all honesty, it was actually a relief to hear. I had given lots of men opportunities to meet my emotional needs, and the idea that God could meet them gave me a glimmer of hope. 📖

14. Does the phrase "Grand Canyon of emotional needs" strike a chord in you? Do you have emotional needs that don't ever seem to be fulfilled? Why or why not?

15. Do you agree that God is the only One who can meet *all* of your emotional needs? Why or why not? If so, write about a specific need you asked Him to meet and how He met that need in your life.

16. What effect would it have on your husband to know that you are lightening his load and looking to God to meet your emotional needs instead of demanding that your husband meet all of them? How can you give your husband this kind of gift?

🌱 GROWING TOGETHER

(Sharing the Truth in Small-Group Discussion)

📖 In the earlier years of our marriage, neither Greg nor I understood the importance of making a spiritual and emotional connection rather than just a physical one. There were many times that I thought I had married a sex addict, and Greg probably thought he had married a frigid prude.

How did we formulate these opinions? Because by the time I got my clothes and makeup off, brushed my teeth, and climbed under the covers, Greg's motor was already running. He'd look at me with a hopeful grin and say, "You want to have sex?" For him, the desire to have sex seemed to come out of nowhere, whereas the thought wouldn't have even crossed my mind. Without the opportunity to warm up to the idea, I responded coldly to the invitation. I would usually reply, "No, just hold me and let's talk." Most of those times when he tried to initiate again before going to sleep, I felt irritated or hurt that he didn't respect my earlier no. 📖

17. Do you think it is reasonable for a wife to expect that her husband should be able to "just cuddle" frequently without any hope or expectation of a sexual connection? Why or why not?
18. Should a woman be offended or flattered when her husband finds her sexually inviting? Why do you feel the way you do?

📖 While it's important to enjoy sex only according to God's plan and to avoid the scripturally forbidden acts mentioned earlier in the chapter, couples don't need to be legalistic about what's proper in the bedroom between husband and wife. While some Christians jokingly say that the only appropriate way for a couple to have intercourse is with the lights off and in the missionary position, they have no biblical basis for this position. (Pun intended!) Some Christians also believe that oral sex is an unholy act, but this opinion has no scriptural basis. In fact, the Song of Solomon has numerous references to oral pleasures and in no way condemns the act.

As long as a sexual position or technique is not offensive to either partner and is found to be pleasurable, then it's okay as long as it sifts successfully through the six-question grid—Is it prohibited in Scripture? beneficial to the relationship? limited to the married partners? Is it known, and approved of, by your spouse? Does it involve your spouse and bring the two of you together rather than separate you? Any sexual expression is acceptable as long as it successfully meets these criteria. 📖

19. Do you agree with the logic of the six-question grid discussed on pages 177–79 in chapter 18 of *Every Woman's Marriage*? Why or why not?
20. Why do you think that Christians have considered so many sexual activities taboo, even within marriage?

> 📖 There's much more to sexual intimacy than intercourse. Physical pleasure should be the dessert enjoyed after the appetizer of appreciation, the entrée of encouragement and unconditional love, and the side dish of respect. Any man who is starved of those things and only given dessert will eventually become an undernourished husband. 📖

21. Do you agree that even if a man has all the sex he wants, he'll be undernourished if he feels unappreciated, discouraged, or disrespected? Why or why not?
22. On a scale of 1 to 10 (1 being undernourished and 10 being incredibly healthy), how do you think your husband would rate the appreciation, encouragement, unconditional love, respect, and sexual pleasure he receives from you? Why?

23. What would it take on your part for your husband to increase his rating for you by at least one notch? two notches? Are you willing to try to move his rating in that direction?

> 📖 If we can learn to ignite the joy and passion that both husbands and wives desire in marriage, imagine the effect that this will have not just in our own families, but on society as a whole. There would be less stress and a much greater sense of peace in our homes. Divorce rates could decline drastically. Children would grow up in two-parent homes with the security of knowing that Mom and Dad really love each other. As a result, they would not be as tempted to turn to gangs, drugs, alcohol, cutting, or other pain-numbing activities. Young people would see that sex is worth waiting for until marriage because adults would be modeling healthy, happy, passion-filled relationships. As a result, premarital pregnancy and abortion rates would be reduced and sexually transmitted diseases could be far less of a social and economic concern.
>
> These principles are the best way to affair-proof and divorce-proof marriages, the best way for families to live in harmony with one another, and the best way for children to grow up in homes where they learn to respect, love, and cherish others, including, some day, their own spouses.
>
> If we can embrace and strive to apply these principles, passing these values down to future generations, we could inspire a whole new, more wonderful world in which to live—a world where marriage is once again a sacred, celebrated institution, where children can feel safe and secure, and where the lavish love of Christ is evident in our hearts and in our homes. 📖

24. Have you ever felt that you can't change society or that there isn't much that you alone can do to help our world become a better place? Why have you felt the way you have?

25. Does the previous excerpt give you hope that you can have a positive influence on society simply by making your own marriage stronger? Why or why not?

26. What strategies for igniting joy and passion in your marriage inspired you the most as you read *Every Woman's Marriage*? If you implemented them, what effect could it have on your life? your husband's life? your kids' lives? society as a whole?

∽

*D*ear Lord, You've given us far more power than we've ever real-ized. Not only do You allow us to control our own destinies, but You allow us to impact the destinies of many other lives as well, simply by the choices we make. If we focus on our marriage relationships as one of our top priorities, many people stand to benefit from the positive ripple effects. On the other hand, many people stand to suffer from the negative ripple effects of divorce. Strengthen us, Lord, to be the wives You desire us to be. Grant us wisdom and discernment in creat-ing marriage relationships that truly bring You glory. For it is not only our personal joy that we seek, nor that of our husbands, but we also seek Your joy as we know You take pleasure in watching us strive to become more and more like You. In Jesus's most holy and precious name we pray, amen.

don't keep it to yourself

Congratulations on finishing this workbook! I pray that in addition to learning how to avoid extinguishing your husband's flame for you, you've also gleaned many ideas on how you can rekindle and even throw fuel on the flame of joy and passion that he carries for you.

If you've benefited from completing this workbook, consider inviting a group of women together and leading them toward discovering how to ignite joy and passion in their marriage relationships as well. This can be a source of encouragement to you, but it will also enable you to encourage and help other women who may be struggling with a lack of contentment in their marriages. When we encourage one another to open up about our struggles and their effects on our marriages, we'll be able to give and receive the support we need to remain wholeheartedly committed to our husbands.

You'll find more information about starting such a group on pages 200-201 in the section "Questions You May Have About This Workbook."

Chapter 1

1. Amy Alkon, "Ask the Advice Goddess," *Dallas Morning News*, 25 October 2004.

Chapter 2

1. Diane Passno, *Feminism: Mystique or Mistake?* (Wheaton, IL: Tyndale, 2000), 7–8, 20–21.
2. Laura Schlessinger, *The Proper Care and Feeding of Husbands* (New York: HarperCollins Publishers, 2004), 53–54.
3. Federal Bureau of Investigation, "Crime in the United States, 2003," Murder by Relationship, figure 2.4, www.fbi.gov/ucr/cius_03/pdf/03sec2.pdf.
4. Schlessinger, *Husbands*, 99–100.

Chapter 3

1. T. Miracle, A. Miracle, and R. Baumeister, *Human Sexuality: Meeting Your Basic Needs* (Upper Saddle River, NJ: Prentice Hall, 2003), 465.

Chapter 4

1. Gary Thomas, *Sacred Marriage* (Grand Rapids, MI: Zondervan, 2000), 96–97.
2. C. S. Lewis, *Mere Christianity* (New York: Macmillan, 1952), 105–6.

Chapter 5

1. Schlessinger, *Husbands*, 21.

Chapter 6

1. "Nearly One in Three U.S. Adults in a Committed Relationship Has Lied to His or Her Partner About Spending Habits, New Survey Finds,"

survey commissioned by www.lawyers.com and *Redbook*, New York, New York, October 11, 2005, press release, www.lawyers.com/lawyers/ G-1029924-LDS/ REDBOOK+SURVEY.html.

Chapter 11

1. Robert Schuller, *The Be (Happy) Attitudes: 8 Positive Attitudes That Can Transform Your Life!* (Waco, TX: Word, 1985), 199–200.
2. Malcolm Gladwell, *Blink* (New York: Little, Brown and Company, 2005), 206.
3. Schlessinger, *Husbands*, 64.

Chapter 12

1. Shaunti Feldhahn, *For Women Only: What You Need to Know about the Inner Lives of Men* (Sisters, OR: Multnomah, 2004), 22–23.
2. Feldhahn, *Women*, 27.
3. Feldhahn, *Women*, 24–26.
4. Dr. John Gray, *Men, Women and Relationships* (Toronto, Canada: HarperCollins, 1993), 68–69.
5. These personality descriptions are taken from the "Servants By Design Inventory." For more information, visit www.yourunique design.com.

Chapter 13

1. Randy Fujishin, *Gifts from the Heart* (San Francisco: Acada, 1998), 87–88.
2. Tom and Nan Haygood, *Under the Umbrella: Improving Your Communication Skills* (self-published by B. Thomas Haygood, PhD, Haygood and Associates Counseling Office, 1401 WSW Loop 323, Tyler, TX 75701), 9.
3. Fujishin, *Heart*, 93.

Chapter 15

1. Feldhahn, *Women*, 93–94, 98.
2. John Eldredge, *Wild at Heart* (Nashville, TN: Thomas Nelson, 2001), 192.

Chapter 16

1. Fred and Brenda Stoeker, *Every Heart Restored* (Colorado Springs, CO: WaterBrook, 2004), 51–52, 56–57.

Chapter 17

1. Max Lucado, *It's Not About Me* (Brentwood, TN: Integrity, 2004), 114–5.

Chapter 18

1. Adapted from Linda Dillow and Lorraine Pintus, *Intimate Issues* (Colorado Springs, CO: WaterBrook, 1999), 199–201, 203–4.
2. Lorraine Ali and Lisa Miller, "The Secret Lives of Wives," *Newsweek,* 12 July 2004, 3, www.msnbc.msn.com/id/5360418/site/newsweek.
3. Miracle et al., *Sexuality,* 92–93.